IBSEN'S PROSE DRAMAS.

* * * *

IBSEN'S PROSE DRAMAS.

EDITED BY WILLIAM ARCHER.

In Five Volumes.

Uniform with the above—
PEER GYNT: A DRAMATIC POEM. By HENRIK IBSEN.

The following Dramas may also be had in separate vols.
(Pocket Edition, Royal 16mo):—

EMPEROR AND GALILEAN: A WORLD-HISTORIC DRAMA: BY HENRIK IBSEN.

AUTHORISED ENGLISH EDITION.

EDITED BY
WILLIAM ARCHER.

THE WALTER SCOTT PUBLISHING CO., LTD.,
PATERNOSTER SQUARE, LONDON, E.C.
CHARLES SCRIBNER'S SONS,
153-157 FIFTH AVENUE, NEW YORK.
1904.

CONTENTS.

———◆◆———

I.

II.

PREFATORY NOTE.

IT was during his first stay in Rome, in 1864, that Ibsen conceived and partly executed the double-drama of *Emperor and Galilean* (*Kejser og Galilæer*). In point of origin, then, it immediately follows *The Pretenders*, and precedes all the modern dramas except *Love's Comedy*. But the mood of indignation in which the poet had turned his back on his native country imperatively demanded utterance. The first plunge into Italy and antiquity had distracted his thoughts for a time ; but they soon turned northward again. Libanius and Ammian, Gibbon and Neander, were put aside ; and to the two years of intense productivity which followed, we owe the most distinctively northern of all Ibsen's works, *Brand* and *Peer Gynt*—poems of fiord and glacier, scaur and tarn. Then came *The League of Youth*, first of the social dramas, published in the autumn of 1869. There can be little doubt that Ibsen now conceived the idea, which he has carried out perhaps too resolutely, of devoting himself for the future to "actuality," realism and prose. But in the war of 1870 he saw an epoch-making event, the influence of which, upon society and upon himself, could not at once be realised. He was conscious, perhaps, of a state of fermentation within and around him which would take time to settle down. In this frame of mind he reverted to his scheme for a drama on the subject of Julian the Apostate, and determined to get it out of hand before devoting himself finally to his new line of thought and form of utterance. If this conjecture be correct, and we owe to the Franco-German war the postponement of the later social plays and the completion of *Emperor and Galilean*, I, for one, feel grateful to Prince Bismarck; though he would not, perhaps, appreciate the gratitude which regards his "world-historic drama" in the light of a mere prologue or prelude to Ibsen's. Be this as it may, we find the poet busily at work upon "a new poem of some length" in the early days of 1872; and in 1873 *Emperor and Galilean* was published, nine years after its inception.

In my introductory note to *Lady Inger* and *The Pretenders*, I gave a short sketch of the historic foundation on which these dramas were constructed. Such a sketch, in the present instance, would be superfluous if not impertinent. Norwegian history is somewhat beyond the ken of the general reader; but Julian the Apostate, unlike Inger Gyldenlöve and Earl Skule, belongs in every sense to world-history. The sources from which Ibsen has drawn his material are open to all. Much has been written, and may yet be written, as to his treatment of history; but this is a matter of opinion rather than of fact, and I have been careful, in these brief introductions, not to stray into criticism. The chief modern authorities upon Julian, apart from

the indispensable Gibbon, are Neander, *Der Kaiser
Julian und sein Zeitalter* (Leipzig, 1813), translated
by G. V. Cox (1850); D. F. Strauss, *Der Romantiker
auf dem Throne der Cäsaren*, a lecture of strong
political tendency delivered in 1847, and included
in the author's *Gesammelte Schriften*, vol. i. (Bonn,
1876); C. G. Semisch, *Julian der Abtrünnige: Ein
Charakterbild* (Breslau, 1868); Friedrich Rode, *Ges-
chichte der Reaction Kaiser Julians gegen die Christ-
liche Kirche* (Jena, 1877); H. Adrien Naville, *Julian
l'Apostat* (Paris, 1877); and Gerald Henry Rendall,
The Emperor Julian; Paganism and Christianity,
Hulsean Essay for 1876 (Cambridge, 1879). I need
scarcely remind the reader that as *Emperor and
Galilean* was published in 1873, Ibsen cannot have
consulted Rode, Naville, or Rendall. Mr. Rendall,
indeed, whose interesting work contains a full bibliography of the subject, makes several quotations from
Ibsen.

The following translation is to a large extent
founded (by arrangement) on Miss Catherine Ray's
version of *Kejser og Galilæer* (entitled *The Emperor
and the Galilean*) which appeared in 1876, and has long
been entirely out of print. To Miss Ray belongs the
credit of having been the first English translator of
Ibsen, as Mr. Gosse was his first expositor. My
principles of translation differ so widely from Miss
Ray's, that I have probably not adopted a hundred
phrases of her version in their integrity; yet her
labours have been of great assistance to me, even
where the two renderings may seem to be utterly
dissimilar.

In Ibsen's other prose plays the meaning of each particular sentence is almost always perfectly clear, however difficult it may be to render it into English. In *Emperor and Galilean*, on the other hand, there occur a few metaphysical or mystical expressions, the precise signification of which it is difficult to grasp and doubly difficult to reproduce. I have done the best I could with these. If the reader suspects my accuracy, he may turn, if not to the original, then to one of the German versions, of which there are at least two. The German vocabulary and idiom are much nearer the Norwegian than ours, so that in these versions many difficult phrases are reproduced with the utmost accuracy, by transliteration rather than translation.

One difficulty from which the German translator is free has encountered me at every turn. The Norwegians use only one word — *Riget* (German *das Reich*)—to cover the two ideas represented in English by "empire" and "kingdom." In most cases "empire" is clearly the proper rendering, since it would be absurd to speak in English of the Roman or the Byzantine Kingdom. But it would be no less impossible to say, in the Lord's Prayer, "Thine is the empire and the power and the glory." In the scene with Maximus in Ephesus, and in several other passages, I have used the word "empire" where "kingdom," in its Biblical sense, would have been preferable were it not necessary to keep the analogy or contrast between the temporal and the spiritual "empire" clearly before the reader's mind. But at the end of the fifth act of *Cæsar's Apostasy*, where

the Lord's Prayer is interwoven with the dialogue,
I have been forced to fall back on "kingdom." The
reader, then, will please remember that these two
words stand for one word—*Riget*—in the original.

The verse from Homer quoted by Julian in the
third act of the second play occurs in the twentieth
book of the *Odyssey* (line 18). Ibsen prints the
sentence which follows it as a second hexameter line ;
but either he or one of his authorities has apparently
misread the passage in the treatise "Against the
Cynic Heraclius," on which this scene is founded.
No such line occurs in Homer ; and, in the attack on
Heraclius, the phrase about the mad dog appears
as part of the author's text, not as a quotation. I
have ventured, therefore, to "render unto Cæsar the
things that are Cæsar's," and print the phrase as
Julian's own.

W. A.

CÆSAR'S APOSTASY.

DRAMA IN FIVE ACTS.

Characters.

◆◆

THE EMPEROR CONSTANTIUS.

THE EMPRESS EUSEBIA.

THE PRINCESS HELENA, *the Emperor's sister.*

PRINCE GALLUS, *the Emperor's cousin.*

PRINCE JULIAN, *Gallus's younger half-brother.*

MEMNON, *an Ethiopian, the Emperor's body-slave.*

POTAMON, *a goldsmith.*

PHOCION, *a dyer.*

EUNAPIUS, *a hair-dresser.*

A Fruit-seller.

A Captain of the Watch.

A Soldier.

A Painted Woman.

A Paralytic Man.

A Blind Beggar.

AGATHON, *the son of a Cappadocian vine-grower.*

LIBANIUS, *a Philosopher.*

GREGORY OF NAZIANZUS.

BASILIUS OF CÆSAREA.

SALLUST OF PERUSIA.

HEKEBOLIUS, *a Theologian.*

MAXIMUS THE MYSTIC.

EUTHERIUS, *Julian's chamberlain.*

LEONTES, *a Quæstor.*

MYRRHA, *a slave.*

DECENTIUS, *a Tribune.*

SINTULA, *Julian's Master of the Horse.*

FLORENTIUS, } *generals.*
SEVERUS,

ORIBASES, *a Physician.*

LAIPSO, } *subalterns.*
VARRO,

MAURUS, *a Standard-Bearer.*

Soldiers, church-goers, heathen on-lookers, courtiers, priests, students, dancing girls, servants, attendants on the Quæstor, Gallic warriors.

Visions and voices.

The first act passes in Constantinople, the second in Athens, the third in Ephesus, the fourth in Lutetia in Gaul, and the fifth in Vienna [Vienne] in the same province. The action takes place during the ten years between A.D. 351 *and* A.D. 361.

CÆSAR'S APOSTASY.

DRAMA IN FIVE ACTS.

———◆———

Act First.

*(Easter night in Constantinople. The scene is an open place,
with trees, bushes, and overthrown statues, in the vicinity
of the Imperial Palace. In the background, fully illumin-
ated, stands the Chapel Royal. To the right a marble
balustrade, from which a staircase leads down to the water.
Between the pines and cypresses appear glimpses of the
Bosphorus and the Asiatic coast.)*

*(Service in the church. Soldiers of the Imperial Guard stand
on the church steps. Great crowds of worshippers stream in.
Beggars, cripples, and blind people at the doors. Heathen
on-lookers, fruit-sellers, and water-carriers fill up the place.)*

HYMN OF PRAISE (*inside the church*).
> Never-ending adoration
> to the Cross of our salvation !
> The Serpent is hurled
> to the deepest abyss;
> the Lamb rules the world ;
> all is peace, all is bliss !

POTAMON THE GOLDSMITH (*carrying a paper lantern,
enters from the left, taps one of the soldiers on the
shoulder, and asks :*) Hist, good friend—when is the
Emperor coming ?

THE SOLDIER. I cannot tell.

PHOCION THE DYER (*in the crowd, turning his head*). The Emperor? Was not some one asking about the Emperor? The Emperor is coming a little before midnight—just before. I had it from Memnon himself.

EUNAPIUS THE BARBER (*rushes in hastily and pushes a Fruit-seller aside*). Out of the way, heathen!

THE FRUIT-SELLER. Softly, sir!

POTAMON. The swine grumbles!

EUNAPIUS. Dog, dog!

PHOCION. Grumbling at a well-dressed Christian! —at a man of the Emperor's own faith!

EUNAPIUS (*knocks the Fruit-seller down*). Into the gutter with you!

POTAMON. That's right. Wallow there along with your gods!

PHOCION (*beating him with his stick*). Take that— and that—and that!

EUNAPIUS (*kicking him*). And this—and this! I'll baste your god-detested skin for you!

(*The Fruit-seller hastens away.*)

PHOCION (*with the evident intention of being heard by the Captain of the Guard*). It is much to be desired that some one should bring this scene to our blessëd Emperor's ears. The Emperor has lately expressed his displeasure at the way in which we Christian citizens hold intercourse with the heathen, just as if no gulf divided us——

POTAMON. You refer to that placard in the market-places? I too have read it. And I hold that, as there is both true and false gold in the world——

EUNAPIUS.   ——we ought not to clip every one with the same shears; that's my way of thinking. But there are still zealous souls among us, praise be to God!

PHOCION.   We are far from being zealous enough, dear brethren! See how boldly these scoffers hold up their heads. How many of this rabble bear the sign of the cross or of the fish on their arms, think you?

POTAMON.   Not many—and yet they actually swarm in front of the Chapel Royal——

PHOCION.   ——on such a sacred night as this——

EUNAPIUS.   ——blocking the way for true sons of the Church——

A PAINTED WOMAN (*in the crowd*).   Are Donatists true sons of the Church?

PHOCION.   What? A Donatist! Are you a Donatist?

EUNAPIUS.   What then? Are not you one?

PHOCION.   I? I! May the lightning blast your tongue!

POTAMON (*making the sign of the cross*).   May plague and boils——!

PHOCION.   A Donatist! You carrion; you rotten tree!

POTAMON.   Right, right!

PHOCION.   You brand for Satan's furnace!

POTAMON.   Right! Give it him; give it him, dear brother!

PHOCION (*pushing the Goldsmith away*).   Hold your tongue; get you behind me. Now I know you; —you are Potamon the Manichæan!

EUNAPIUS. A Manichæan? A stinking heretic!
Faugh, faugh!

POTAMON (*holding up his paper lantern*). Heyday!
Why, you are Phocion the Dyer, of Antioch! The
Cainite!

EUNAPIUS. Woe is me, I have held communion
with falsehood!

PHOCION. Woe is me, I have helped a son of
Satan!

EUNAPIUS (*boxing his ear*). Take that for your
help!

PHOCION (*returning the blow*). Oh, you abandoned
hound!

POTAMON. Accursed, accursed be you both!

(*A general fight; laughter and derision among
the onlookers.*)

THE CAPTAIN OF THE GUARD (*calls to the soldiers*).
The Emperor is coming!

(*The combatants are parted and carried with the
stream of other worshippers into the church.*)

HYMN OF PRAISE (*from the high altar*)—

　　　　The Serpent is hurled
　　　　to the deepest abyss;—
　　　　the Lamb rules the world,—
　　　　all is peace, all is bliss!

(*The Court enters in a long procession from the left.
Priests with censers go before; after them men-
at-arms and torch-bearers, courtiers and body-
guards. In their midst the* EMPEROR CON-
STANTIUS, *a man of thirty-four, of distinguished
appearance, beardless, with brown curly hair;
his eyes have a dark, distrustful expression; his*

gait and whole deportment betray uneasiness and debility. Beside him, on his left, walks the EMPRESS EUSEBIA, *a pale, delicate woman, the same age as the Emperor. Behind the imperial pair follows* PRINCE JULIAN, *a yet undeveloped youth of nineteen. He has black hair, a beard beginning to grow, sparkling brown eyes with a rapid glance; his court-dress sits badly upon him; his manners are awkward, eccentric, and abrupt. The Emperor's sister, the* PRINCESS HELENA, *a voluptuous beauty of twenty-five, follows, accompanied by maidens and older women. Courtiers and men-at-arms close the procession. The Emperor's body-slave,* MEMNON, *a heavily-built, magnificently-dressed Ethiopian, is among them.*)

THE EMPEROR (*stops suddenly, turns round to* PRINCE JULIAN, *and asks sharply*). Where is Gallus?

JULIAN (*grows pale*). Gallus? What would you with Gallus?

THE EMPEROR. There, I caught you!

JULIAN. Sire——!

THE EMPRESS (*seizing the* EMPEROR'S *hand*). Come; come!

THE EMPEROR. Your conscience cried aloud. What are you two plotting?

JULIAN. We?

THE EMPEROR. You and he!

THE EMPRESS. Oh, come; come, Constantius!

THE EMPEROR. So black a deed! What did the oracle answer?

JULIAN. The oracle! By my Holy Redeemer——

THE EMPEROR. If any one maligns you, he shall pay for it at the stake. (*Draws the* PRINCE *aside.*) Oh, let us hold together, Julian! Dear kinsman, let us hold together!

JULIAN. Everything lies in your hands, my beloved lord!

THE EMPEROR. My hands——!

JULIAN. Oh, stretch them in mercy over us!

THE EMPEROR. My hands? What was in your mind as to my hands?

JULIAN (*grasps his hands and kisses them*). The Emperor's hands are white and cool.

THE EMPEROR. What else should they be? What was in your mind? There, I caught you again!

JULIAN (*kisses them again*). They are like roseleaves in this moonlight night.

THE EMPEROR. Yes yes yes, Julian!

THE EMPRESS. Forward; it is time.

THE EMPEROR. To go in before the presence of the Lord! I—I! Oh, pray for me, Julian! They will offer me the consecrated wine. I see it! It glitters in the chalice like serpents' eyes—— (*Shrieks.*) Bloody eyes——! Oh, Jesus Christ, pray for me!

THE EMPRESS. The Emperor is ill——!

THE PRINCESS HELENA. Where is Cæsarius? The surgeon, the surgeon—fetch him!

THE EMPRESS (*beckons*). Memnon, good Memnon!
  (*She speaks in a low voice to the slave.*)

JULIAN (*softly*). Sire, have pity, and send me far from here.

The Emperor.   Where would you go?

Julian.   To Egypt. I would fain go to Egypt, if you think fit. So many go thither—into the great desert.

The Emperor.   Into the great desert? Ha! In the desert one broods. I forbid you to brood.

Julian.   I will not brood, if only you will let me—— Here my anguish of soul increases day by day. Evil thoughts flock around me. For nine days I have worn a hair shirt, and it has not protected me; for nine nights I have lashed myself with thongs, but scourging does not banish them.

The Emperor.   We must be steadfast, Julian! Satan is strangely active in all of us. Consult Hekebolius——

The Slave Memnon (*to the* Emperor).   It is time now——

The Emperor.   No, no, I will not——

Memnon (*seizing him by the wrist*).   Come, gracious lord; come, I say.

The Emperor (*draws himself up, and says with dignity*).   Forward to the house of the Lord!

Memnon (*softly*).   The other matter afterwards——

The Emperor (*to* Julian).   I must see Gallus.

(Julian *folds his hands in supplication to the* Empress *behind the* Emperor's *back.*)

The Empress (*hastily and softly*).   Fear nothing!

The Emperor.   Remain outside. Do not enter the church with these evil thoughts in your mind. When you pray before the altar, it is to call down evil upon me.—Oh, lay not that sin upon your soul, my beloved kinsman!

(*The procession moves forward towards the church. On the steps, beggars, cripples, and blind men crowd round the* EMPEROR.)

A PARALYTIC. Oh, mightiest ruler on earth, let me touch the hem of thy garment, that I may become whole.

A BLIND MAN. Pray for me, anointed of the Lord, that I may receive my sight again!

THE EMPEROR. Be of good cheer, my son! Memnon, scatter silver among them. In, in!

(*The Court moves forward into the church, the doors of which are closed; the crowd gradually disperses,* PRINCE JULIAN *remaining behind in one of the avenues.*)

JULIAN (*looking towards the church*). What does he want with Gallus? On this sacred night he cannot think of——! Oh, if I only knew—— (*He turns and jostles against the blind man, who is retiring.*) Look where you go, friend!

THE BLIND MAN. I am blind, my lord!

JULIAN. Still? Can you really not see so much as yonder glittering star? Fie, man of little faith. Did not God's anointed promise to pray for your sight?

THE BLIND MAN. Who are you, that mock at a blind brother?

JULIAN. A brother in unbelief and blindness. (*He is about to go off to the left.*)

A VOICE (*softly, among the bushes behind him*). Julian, Julian!

JULIAN (*with a cry*). Ah!

THE VOICE (*nearer*). Julian!

Julian.   Stand, stand ;—I am armed !   Beware !

A Young Man (*poorly clad, and with a traveller's staff, appears among the trees*).   Hush ! It is I——

Julian.   Stay where you are !   Do not come near me, fellow !

The Young Man.   Oh, do you not remember Agathon——?

Julian.   Agathon !   What do you mean? Agathon was a boy——

Agathon.   Six years ago.   I knew you at once. (*Coming nearer.*)

Julian.   Agathon ;—ay, by the holy cross, I believe it is !

Agathon.   Look at me ; look well——

Julian (*embracing and kissing him*).   Friend of my childhood !   Playmate !   Dearest of them all ! And you are here?   How wonderful !   You have come all the long way over the mountains, and then across the sea,—the whole long way from Cappadocia ?

Agathon.   I arrived two days ago, by ship, from Ephesus.   Oh, how I have sought in vain for you these two days.   The guards would not let me pass at the palace gates, and——

Julian.   Did you mention my name to any one? or say that you were in search of me ?

Agathon.   No, I did not dare to, because——

Julian.   There you did right ; never let any one know more than is absolutely needful——

Come here, Agathon ; out into the full moonlight, that I may see you.—How you have grown, Agathon ; —how strong you look.

AGATHON. And you are paler.

JULIAN. I cannot thrive in the air of the palace. I think it is unwholesome here.—It is different from Makellon. Makellon lies high. No other town in all Cappadocia lies so high ; ah, how the fresh snow-winds from the Taurus sweep over it——! Are you weary, Agathon ?

AGATHON. Oh, in no wise.

JULIAN. Let us sit down nevertheless. It is so quiet and lonely here. Close together ; so! (*Draws him down upon a seat beside the balustrade.*)—" Can any good thing come out of Cappadocia," they say. Yes—friends can come. Can anything be better ?

(*Looks long at him.*)

How was it possible that I did not know you at once ? Oh, my beloved treasure, is it not just as when we were boys——?

AGATHON (*sinking down before him*). I at your feet, as of old.

JULIAN. No, no, no——!

AGATHON. Oh, let me kneel thus !

JULIAN. Oh, Agathon, it is a sin and a mockery to kneel to me. If you but knew how sinful I have become. Hekebolius, my beloved teacher, is deeply grieved for me, Agathon. He could tell you——

How thick and moist your hair has grown ; and how it curls.—But, Mardonius—how goes it with him ? He must be turning grey now ?

AGATHON. He is white-haired.

JULIAN. How well Mardonius could interpret Homer ! I do not believe my old Mardonius has his equal at that.—Heroes embattled against heroes—

and the gods above goading them on. I saw it, as though with my eyes.

AGATHON. Then your mind was set on becoming a great and victorious warrior.

JULIAN. They were happy times, these six years in Cappadocia. Were the years longer then than now? It seems so when I think of all they contained——

Yes, they were happy years. We at our books, and Gallus on his Persian horse. He swept over the plain like the shadow of a cloud.—Oh, but one thing you must tell me. The church——?

AGATHON. The church? Over the Holy Mamas's grave?

JULIAN (*smiling faintly*). Which Gallus and I built. Gallus got his aisle finished; but I——; mine never seemed to come right.—How has it gone on since?

AGATHON. Not at all. The builders said it was impossible as you had planned it.

JULIAN (*thoughtfully*). No doubt, no doubt. I wronged them in thinking them incapable. Now I know why it was impossible. I must tell you, Agathon;—Mamas was a false saint.

AGATHON. The Holy Mamas?

JULIAN. That Mamas was never a martyr. His whole legend was a strange delusion. Hekebolius has, with infinite research, arrived at the real truth, and I myself have lately composed a slight treatise on the subject—a treatise, my Agathon, which certain philosophers are said, strangely enough, to have spoken of in laudatory terms in the lecture-rooms——

The Lord keep my heart free from vanity! The evil tempter has countless wiles; one can never know——

That Gallus should succeed and I fail! Ah, my Agathon, when I think of that church-building, I see Cain's altar——

AGATHON. Julian!

JULIAN. God will have none of me, Agathon!

AGATHON. Ah, do not speak so! Was not God strong in you when you led me out of the darkness of heathendom, and gave me light over all my days —child though you then were!

JULIAN. Ah, all that is like a dream to me.

AGATHON. And yet so blessed a truth.

JULIAN (*sadly*). If only it were so now! Where did I find the words of fire? The air seemed full of hymns of praise—a ladder from earth to heaven—— —— (*Gazes straight before him.*) Did you see it?

AGATHON. What?

JULIAN. The star that fell; there, behind the two cypresses. (*Is silent a moment, then suddenly changes his tone.*) Have I told you what my mother dreamed the night before I was born?

AGATHON. I do not recall it.

JULIAN. No, no, I remember—I heard of it after we parted.

AGATHON. What did she dream?

JULIAN. My mother dreamed that she gave birth to Achilles.

AGATHON (*eagerly*). Is your faith in dreams as strong as ever?

JULIAN. Why do you ask?

AGATHON.   You shall hear; it concerns what has driven me to cross the sea——

JULIAN.   You have a special errand here?   I had quite forgotten to ask you——

AGATHON.   A strange errand; so strange that I am lost in doubt and indecision.   There is so much I would like to know first—about life in the city— about yourself—and the Emperor.

JULIAN (*looks hard at him*).   Tell me the truth, Agathon—with whom have you spoken before meeting me?

AGATHON.   With no one.

JULIAN.   When did you arrive?

AGATHON.   I have told you—two days ago.

JULIAN.   And already you want to know——? What do you want to know about the Emperor? Has any one set you on to——?   (*Embraces him.*) Oh, forgive me, Agathon, my friend!

AGATHON.   What?   Why?

JULIAN (*rises and listens*).   Hush!—No, it was nothing—only a bird in the bushes—— ——

I am exceedingly happy here.   Why should you doubt it?   Have I not all my family gathered here? or at least—all over whom a gracious Saviour has held his hand.

AGATHON.   And the Emperor is as a father to you?

JULIAN.   The Emperor is beyond measure wise and good.

AGATHON (*who has also risen*).   Julian, is the rumour true that you are one day to be the Emperor's successor?

JULIAN (*hastily*). Do not speak of such dangerous things. I do not know what foolish rumours are abroad.—Why do you question me so much? Not a word will I answer till you have told me what brings you to Constantinople.

AGATHON. I come at the bidding of the Lord God.

JULIAN. If you love your Saviour or your salvation, get you home again. (*Leans over the balustrade and listens.*) Speak softly; a boat is coming in——
(*Leads him over towards the other side.*)
What do you want here? To kiss the splinter of the holy cross?—Get you home again, I say! Do you know what Constantinople has become in these last fifteen months? A Babylon of blasphemy.—Have you not heard—do you not know that Libanius is here?

AGATHON. Ah, Julian, I do not know Libanius.

JULIAN. Secluded Cappadocian! Happy region, where his voice and his doctrine are unknown.

AGATHON. Ah, he is one of those heathen teachers of falsehood—— ?

JULIAN. The most dangerous of them all.

AGATHON. Surely not more dangerous than Ædesius of Pergamus?

JULIAN. Ædesius!—who now thinks of Ædesius of Pergamus? Ædesius is in his dotage——

AGATHON. Is he more dangerous than even that mysterious Maximus?

JULIAN. Maximus? Do not speak of that mountebank. Who knows anything certain of Maximus?

AGATHON.   He boasts of having slept three years in a cave beyond Jordan.

JULIAN.   Hekebolius considers him an impostor, and he is certainly not far wrong—— ——

No, no, Agathon—Libanius is the most dangerous. Our sinful earth has writhed, as it were, under this scourge.   Portents foretold his coming.   A pestilent sickness slew men by thousands in the city.   And then, when it was over, in the month of November, fire rained from heaven night by night.   Nay, do not doubt it, Agathon!   I have myself seen the stars break from their spheres, plunge down towards earth, and burn out on the way.

Since then he has lectured here, the philosopher, the orator.   All proclaim him the king of eloquence; and well they may.   I tell you he is terrible. Youths and men flock around him; he binds their souls in bonds, so that they *must* follow him; denial flows seductively from his lips, like songs about the Trojans and the Greeks——

AGATHON (*in terror*).   Oh, you too have sought him, Julian!

JULIAN (*shrinking back*).   I!—God preserve me from such a sin.   Should any rumours come to your ears, do not believe them.   It is not true that I have sought out Libanius by night, in disguise.   All contact with him would be a horror to me.   Besides, the Emperor has forbidden it, and Hekebolius still more strictly.—All believers who approach that subtle man fall away and turn to scoffers.   And not they alone. His words are borne from mouth to mouth, even into the Emperor's palace.   His scornful jests, his incon-

trovertible arguments, his lampoons, seem to blend
with my prayers;—they are to me like those monsters
in the likeness of birds who befouled all the food of a
pious wandering hero of yore. I sometimes feel with
horror that my gorge rises at the true meat of faith
and the Word—— (*With an irrepressible outburst.*)
Were the empire mine, I would send you the head of
Libanius on a charger!

AGATHON. But how can the Emperor tolerate
this? How can our pious, Christian Emperor——?

JULIAN. The Emperor? Praised be the Emperor's
faith and piety! But the Emperor has no thoughts
for anything but this luckless Persian war. All minds
are full of it. No one heeds the war that is being
waged here, against the Prince of Golgotha. Ah,
my Agathon, it is not now as it was two years ago.
Then the two brothers of the Mystic Maximus had to
pay for their heresies with their lives. You do not
know what mighty allies Libanius has. One or other
of the lesser philosophers is now and then driven
from the city; *him* no one dares to touch. I have
begged, I have implored both Hekebolius and the
Empress to procure his banishment. But no, no!—
What avails it to drive away the others? This one
man poisons the air for all of us. Oh my Saviour, if I
could but flee from all this abomination of heathendom! To live here is to live in the lion's den——

AGATHON (*eagerly*). Julian—what was that you
said?

JULIAN. Yes, yes; only a miracle can save us.

AGATHON. Oh, then listen! That miracle has
happened.

JULIAN.   What do you mean?

AGATHON.   I will tell you, Julian; for now I can
no longer doubt that it is you it concerns. What
sent me to Constantinople was a vision——

JULIAN.   A vision, you say!

AGATHON.   A heavenly revelation——

JULIAN.   Oh, for God's pity's sake, speak!—Hush,
do not speak. Wait—some one is coming. Stand
here, quite carelessly;—look unconcerned.

> (*Both remain standing beside the balustrade. A
> tall, handsome, middle-aged man, dressed, accord-
> ing to the fashion of the philosophers, in a short
> cloak, enters by the avenue on the left. A troop
> of youths accompanies him, all in girt-up gar-
> ments, with wreaths of ivy in their hair, and
> carrying books, papers, and parchments.
> Laughter and loud talk among them as they
> approach.*)

THE PHILOSOPHER.   Let nothing fall into the
water, my joyous Gregory! Remember, what you
are carrying is more precious than gold.

JULIAN (*standing close beside him*).   Your pardon,
—is any material thing more precious than
gold?

THE PHILOSOPHER.   Can you buy back the fruits
of your life for gold?

JULIAN.   True; true. But why then do you trust
to the treacherous waters?

THE PHILOSOPHER.   The favour of man is more
treacherous still.

JULIAN.   That word was wisdom. And whither
do you sail with your treasures?

THE PHILOSOPHER. To Athens. (*He is about to pass on.*)

JULIAN (*with suppressed laughter*). To Athens? Then, oh man of wealth, you do not own your own riches.

THE PHILOSOPHER (*stops*). How so?

JULIAN. Is it a wise man's business to take owls to Athens?

THE PHILOSOPHER. My owls cannot endure the church-lights here in the imperial city. (*To one of the young men.*) Give me your hand, Sallust. (*Is about to descend the steps.*)

SALLUST (*half-way down the steps, whispers*). By the gods, that is he!

THE PHILOSOPHER. He——?

SALLUST. On my life, it is! I know him;—I have seen him with Hekebolius.

THE PHILOSOPHER. Ah!

(*He looks at* JULIAN *with furtive intentness; then goes a step towards him and says :*)

You smiled just now. What did you smile at?

JULIAN. When you complained of the church-lights, I wondered whether it were not rather the imperial light of the lecture-halls that shone too bright in your eyes.

THE PHILOSOPHER. Envy cannot hide under the short cloak.

JULIAN. What cannot hide shows forth.

THE PHILOSOPHER. You have a sharp tongue, noble Galilean.

JULIAN. Why Galilean? What proclaims me a Galilean?

The Philosopher.   Your court attire.

Julian.   There is a philosopher beneath it ; for I
wear a very coarse shirt.—But tell me, what do you
seek in Athens ?

The Philosopher.   What did Pontius Pilate seek ?

Julian.   Nay, nay !   Is not truth here, where
Libanius is ?

The Philosopher (*looking hard at him*).   Hm !
—Libanius ?   Libanius will soon be silent.   Libanius
is weary of the strife, my lord !

Julian.   Weary ?   He — the invulnerable, the
ever-victorious—— ?

The Philosopher.   He is weary of waiting for
his peer.

Julian.   Now you jest, stranger !   Where can
Libanius hope to find his peer ?

The Philosopher.   His peer exists.

Julian.   Who ?   Where ?   Name him !

The Philosopher.   It might be dangerous.

Julian.   Why ?

The Philosopher.   Are you not a courtier ?

Julian.   And what then ?

The Philosopher (*in a lower voice*).   Have you
the temerity to praise the Emperor's successor ?

Julian (*deeply shaken*).   Ah !

The Philosopher (*hastily*).   If you betray me,
I shall deny all !

Julian.   I betray no man ; never fear, never fear !
—The Emperor's successor, you say ?   I cannot tell
whom you mean ;—the Emperor has chosen no
successor.—But why this jesting ?   Why did you
speak of Libanius's peer ?

THE PHILOSOPHER. Yes or no—is there at the
imperial court a youth who, by force and strict commandment, by prayers and persuasions, is held aloof
from the light of the lecture-halls?

JULIAN (*hastily*). That is done to keep his faith pure.

THE PHILOSOPHER (*smiling*). Has this young
man so scant faith in his faith? What can he know
about his faith? What does a soldier know of his
shield until he has proved it in battle?

JULIAN. True, true;—but they are loving kinsmen
and teachers, I tell you——

THE PHILOSOPHER. Phrases, my lord! Let me
tell you this: it is for the Emperor's sake that his
young kinsman is held aloof from the philosophers.
The Emperor has not the divine gift of eloquence.
Doubtless the Emperor is great; but he cannot
endure that his successor should shine forth over the
empire——

JULIAN (*in confusion*). And you dare to——!

THE PHILOSOPHER. Ay ay, you are angry on
your master's account; but——

JULIAN. Far from it; on the contrary—that is
to say——

Listen; my place is somewhat near that young
prince. I would gladly learn——

(*Turns.*)

Go apart, Agathon; I must speak alone with this
man.

(*Withdraws a few steps, along with the stranger.*)

You said "shine forth"? "Shine forth over the
empire?" What do you know, what can any of you
know, of Prince Julian?

THE PHILOSOPHER. Can Sirius be hidden by a cloud? Will not the restless wind here or there force a rift in it, so that——

JULIAN. Speak plainly, I beg you.

THE PHILOSOPHER. The palace and the church are as a double cage in which the prince is mewed up. The cage is not close enough. Now and then he lets fall a weighty word; the court vermin—forgive me, sir—the courtiers spread it abroad in scorn; its deep meaning does not exist for these worthies—pardon, sir—for most of them it does not exist.

JULIAN. For none. You may safely say for none.

THE PHILOSOPHER. Yet surely for you; and at any rate for us—— ——

Yes, he could indeed shine forth over the empire! Are there not legends of his childhood in Cappadocia, when, in disputation with his brother Gallus, he took the part of the gods, and defended them against the Galilean?

JULIAN. That was in jest, mere practice in rhetoric——

THE PHILOSOPHER. What has not Mardonius recorded of him? And Hekebolius also! What art was there not even in his boyish utterances—what beauty, what grace in the light play of his thoughts!

JULIAN. You think so?

THE PHILOSOPHER. Yes, in him we might indeed find an adversary to fear and yet to long for. What should hinder him from reaching so honourable an eminence? He lacks nothing but to pass through the same school through which Paul passed, and passed so uninjured that when he afterwards joined the

Galileans he shed more light than all the other apostles together, because he possessed knowledge and eloquence! Hekebolius fears for his pupil's faith. Oh, I know it well; the fear is his. Does he forget then, in his exceeding tenderness of conscience, that he himself, in his youth, has drunk of those very springs from which he would now have his pupil debarred? Or do you think it was not from us that he learned to use the weapons of speech which he now wields against us with such renowned dexterity?

JULIAN.   True, true; undeniably true!

THE PHILOSOPHER.   And what gifts has this Hekebolius in comparison with the gifts which declared themselves so marvellously in that princely boy, who, it is said, in Cappadocia, upon the graves of the slain Galileans, proclaimed a doctrine which I hold to be erroneous, and therefore the more difficult to enforce, but which he nevertheless proclaimed with such fervour of spirit that—if I may believe a very wide-spread rumour—a multitude of children of his own age were carried away by him, and followed him as his disciples! Ah, Hekebolius is like the rest of you—more jealous than zealous; that is why Libanius has waited in vain.

JULIAN (*seizes him by the arm*).   What has Libanius said?   Tell me, I conjure you, in the name of God!

THE PHILOSOPHER.   He has said all that you have just heard. And he has said still more. He has said: "See yon princely Galilean; he is a spiritual Achilles."

JULIAN.   Achilles!   (*Softly*) My mother's dream!

THE PHILOSOPHER.   There, in the open lecture-

halls, lies the battle-field. Light and gladness are
over the combat and the combatants. The shafts of
speech hurtle through the air; keen swords of wit
clash in the fray; the blessëd gods sit smiling in the
clouds——

JULIAN. Oh, away from me with your heathendom——

THE PHILOSOPHER. ——and the heroes go home to
their tents, their arms entwined, their hearts untouched
by rancour, their cheeks aglow, the blood coursing
swiftly through every vein, admired, applauded, and
with laurels on their brows. Ah, where is Achilles?
I cannot see him. Achilles is angry——

JULIAN. Achilles is unhappy!—But can I believe
it! Oh, tell me—my brain is dizzy—has Libanius
said all this?

THE PHILOSOPHER. What brought Libanius to
Constantinople? Had he any other object than that of
achieving the illustrious friendship of a certain youth?

JULIAN. Speak the truth! No, no; this cannot
be true. How reconcile it with all the scoffs and jibes
that——? We do not scoff at one whose friendship
we seek.

THE PHILOSOPHER. Wiles of the Galileans, to
build up a wall of wrath and hate between the two
champions.

JULIAN. Yet you will not deny that it was
Libanius——?

THE PHILOSOPHER. I will deny everything to the
uttermost.

JULIAN. The lampoons were not his?

THE PHILOSOPHER. Not one. They have one

and all been composed in the palace, and spread abroad under his name——

JULIAN. Ah, what do you tell me——?

THE PHILOSOPHER. What I will avouch before all the world. You have a sharp tongue—who knows but that you yourself——

JULIAN. I——! But can I believe this? Libanius did not write them? Not one of them?

THE PHILOSOPHER. No, no!

JULIAN. Not even those shameful lines about Atlas with the crooked shoulders?

THE PHILOSOPHER. No, no, I tell you.

JULIAN. Nor those foolish and ribald verses about the ape in court dress?

THE PHILOSOPHER. Ha-ha; that came from the church, and not from the lecture-hall. You do not believe it? I tell you it was Hekebolius——

JULIAN. Hekebolius!

THE PHILOSOPHER. Yes, Hekebolius, Hekebolius himself, to breed hatred between his enemy and his pupil——

JULIAN (*clenching his fists*). Ah, if it were so!

THE PHILOSOPHER. If that blinded and betrayed young man had known us philosophers, he would not have dealt so hardly with us.

JULIAN. What are you speaking of?

THE PHILOSOPHER. It is too late now. Farewell, my lord! (*Going.*)

JULIAN (*seizes his hand*). Friend and brother— who are you?

THE PHILOSOPHER. One who sorrows to see the God-born go to ruin.

JULIAN.   What do you call the God-born?

THE PHILOSOPHER.   The Uncreated in the Ever-changing.

JULIAN.   As dark as ever for me.

THE PHILOSOPHER.   There is a whole glorious world to which you Galileans are blind.   In it our life is one long festival, amid statues and choral songs, foaming goblets in our hands, and our locks entwined with roses.   There dizzy bridges span the gulfs between spirit and spirit, stretching away to the farthest orbs in space——

I know one who might be king of all that great and sunlit realm.

JULIAN (*in dread*).   Ay, at the cost of his salvation!

THE PHILOSOPHER.   What is salvation?   Re-union with the primal deeps?

JULIAN.   Yes, in conscious life.   Reunion for *me* as the being I am.

THE PHILOSOPHER.   Reunion like that of the raindrop with the sea, like that of the crumbling leaf with the earth that bore it.

JULIAN.   Oh, had I but learning!   Had I but the weapons to use against you!

THE PHILOSOPHER.   Take to yourself weapons, young man.   The lecture-hall is the gymnasium of intellect and talent.

JULIAN (*recoiling*).   Ah!

THE PHILOSOPHER.   Look at those joyous youths yonder.   There are Galileans among them.   Errors in things divine cause no discord among us.

Farewell!   You Galileans have sent truth into exile.   See, now, how we bear the buffets of fate

See, we hold high our wreath-crowned heads. So
we depart — shortening the night with song and
awaiting Helios.

> (*He descends the steps, where his disciples have
> waited for him; then the boat is heard rowing
> away with them.*)

JULIAN (*gazes long over the water*).   Who was he,
that mysterous man?

AGATHON (*approaching*).   Listen to me, Julian——?

JULIAN (*in lively excitement*).   *He* understood
me!   And Libanius himself, the great, incomparable
Libanius——!   Only think, Agathon, Libanius has
said—— ——   Oh, how keen that heathen eye must
be?

AGATHON.   Trust me, this meeting was a work of
the Tempter!

JULIAN (*not heeding him*).   I can no longer endure
to live among these people.   It was they, then, who
wrote those abominable lampoons!   They make a
mockery of me here; they laugh behind my back;
not one of them believes in the power that dwells in
me.   They ape my gait; they burlesque my manners
and my speech; Hekebolius himself——!   Oh, I
feel it—Christ is deserting me; I am growing evil
here.

AGATHON.   Oh, you do not know it—you, even
you, stand under special grace.

JULIAN (*walks up and down beside the balustrade*).
I am he Libanius would fain measure swords with.
How strange a wish!   Libanius accounts *me* his peer.
It is me he awaits——

AGATHON.   Hear and obey: Christ awaits you!

JULIAN.   Friend, what do you mean?

AGATHON.   The vision that sent me to Constantinople——

JULIAN.   Yes yes, the vision; I had almost forgotten it.   A revelation, you said?   Oh, speak, speak!

AGATHON.   It was at home in Cappadocia, a month ago or a little more.   There went a rumour abroad that the heathens had again begun to hold secret meetings by night in the temple of Cybele——

JULIAN.   How foolhardy!   Are they not strictly forbidden——

AGATHON.   Therefore all we believers arose in wrath.   The magistrates ordered the temple to be pulled down, and we broke in pieces the abominable idols.   The more zealous among us were impelled by the Spirit of the Lord to go still further.   With singing of psalms, and with sacred banners at our head, we marched through the town and fell upon the godless like messengers of wrath; we took away their treasures from them; many houses were set on fire, and heathens not a few perished in the flames; still more we slew in the streets as they fled.   Oh, it was a glorious time for the honour of God!

JULIAN.   And then?   The vision, my Agathon!

AGATHON.   For three whole nights and days the Lord of Vengeance was strong in us.   But at last the weak flesh could no longer keep pace with the willing spirit, and we desisted from the pursuit.—

I lay upon my bed; I could neither wake nor sleep.   I felt, as it were, an inward hollowness, as though the spirit had departed from me.   I lay in

burning heat ; I tore my hair, I wept, prayed, sang ;—
I cannot tell what came over me.—

Then, on a sudden, I saw before me by the wall a
white and shining light, and in the radiance stood a
man in a long cloak. A glory encircled his head ; he held
a reed in his hand, and fixed his eyes mildly upon me.

JULIAN. You saw that !

AGATHON. I saw it. And then he spoke and
said : " Agathon, arise ; seek him out who shall
inherit the empire ; bid him enter the lion's den
and fight with the lions."

JULIAN. Fight with the lions ! Oh, strange,
strange !—Ah, if it were——! The meeting with that
philosopher—A revelation ; a message to me—; am *I*
the chosen one ?

AGATHON. Assuredly you are.

JULIAN. Fight with the lions !—Yes, I see it ;—so
it must be, my Agathon ! It is God's will that I
should seek out Libanius——

AGATHON. No, no ; hear me out !

JULIAN. ——worm all his arts and his learning out of
him—smite the unbelievers with their own weapons—
fight, fight like Paul—conquer, like Paul, in the cause
of the Lord !

AGATHON. No, no ! that was not the intent.

JULIAN. Can you doubt it ? Libanius—is he not
strong as the mountain lion, and is not the lecture-
hall—— ?

AGATHON. I tell you it is not so ; for the vision
added : " Announce to the chosen one that he shall
shake the dust of the imperial city from his feet, and
never more enter its gates."

JULIAN. Are you sure of that, Agathon?

AGATHON. Yes, absolutely.

JULIAN. Not here, then! To fight with the lions? Where, where? Oh, where shall I find light?

(PRINCE GALLUS, *a handsome, strongly-built man of five-and-twenty, with light curly hair, and fully armed, enters by the avenue on the left.*)

JULIAN (*rushing up to him*). Gallus!

GALLUS. What now? (*Points to* AGATHON.) Who is that man?

JULIAN. Agathon.

GALLUS. What Agathon? You have so many strange companions—— Ah, by heaven, it is the Cappadocian! You have grown quite a man——

JULIAN. Do you know, Gallus—the Emperor has been asking for you.

GALLUS (*anxiously*). Just now? To-night?

JULIAN. Yes, yes; he wanted to speak with you. He seemed exceedingly angry.

GALLUS. How do you know? What did he say?

JULIAN. I did not understand it. He asked what an oracle had answered.

GALLUS. Ah!

JULIAN. Hide nothing from me. What is the matter?

GALLUS. Death or banishment is the matter.

AGATHON. Gracious Saviour!

JULIAN. I feared as much! But no, the Empress spoke hopefully. Oh, say on, say on!

GALLUS. What shall I say? If the Emperor spoke of an oracle, a certain messenger must have been intercepted, or some one must have betrayed me——

JULIAN. A messenger?—Gallus, what have you dared to do?

GALLUS. How could I live any longer this life of doubt and dread? Let him do with me as he pleases; anything is better than this——

JULIAN (*softly, leading him some paces aside*). Have a care, Gallus! What is this about a messenger?

GALLUS. I have addressed a question to the priests of Osiris in Abydus——

JULIAN. Ah, the oracle! The heathen oracle——?

GALLUS. The heathenism might be forgiven me; but—well, why should you not know it—I have inquired as to the issue of the Persian war——

JULIAN. What madness!—Gallus—I see it in your face: you have asked other questions!

GALLUS. No more; I have not asked——

JULIAN. Yes, yes; you have inquired as to a mighty man's life or death!

GALLUS. And if I had? What can be of more moment to both of us?

JULIAN (*throwing his arms round him*). Be silent, madman!

GALLUS. Away from me! Do you cringe before him like a cur! I have no mind to endure it longer. I will cry it aloud in all the market-places—— (*Calls to* AGATHON.) Have you seen him, Cappadocian? Have you seen the murderer?

JULIAN. Gallus! Brother!

AGATHON. The murderer!

GALLUS. The murderer in the purple robe; my father's murderer, my step-mother's, my eldest brother's——

JULIAN. Oh you are calling down destruction upon us!

GALLUS. Eleven heads in one single night; eleven corpses; our whole house.—Ah, but be sure conscience is torturing him; it thrills through the marrow of his bones like a swarm of serpents.

JULIAN. Do not listen to him! Away, away!

GALLUS (*seizes* JULIAN *by the shoulder*). Stay;— you look pale and disordered; is it you that have betrayed me?

JULIAN. I! Your own brother——!

GALLUS. What though you be my brother? Brotherhood protects no one in our family. Confess that you have secretly spied upon my doings! Who else should it be? Do you think I do not know what people are whispering? The Emperor intends to make you his successor.

JULIAN. Never! I swear to you, my beloved Gallus, it shall never be! I will not. One mightier than he has chosen me.—Oh, trust me, Gallus: my path is marked out for me. I will not go yonder, I tell you. Oh, God of hosts—I on the imperial throne! No, no, no!

GALLUS. Ha-ha; well acted, mummer!

JULIAN. Ay, you may scoff, since you know not what has happened. Myself, I scarcely know. Oh, Agathon—if this head were to be anointed! Would it not be an apostasy—a deadly sin? Would not the Lord's holy oil burn me like molten lead?

GALLUS. In that case our august kinsman would be balder than Julius Cæsar.

JULIAN. Beware how you speak! Render to
Cæsar the things that are Cæsar's——

GALLUS. My father's blood—your father's and
your mother's——!

JULIAN. Oh, what do we know of those horrors?
We were children then. The soldiers were chiefly to
blame; it was the rebels—evil counsellors——

GALLUS (*laughing*). The Emperor's successor is
rehearsing his part!

JULIAN (*weeping*). Oh, Gallus, would I might die
or be banished in your stead! I am wrecking my
soul here. I ought to forgive—and I cannot. Evil
grows in me; hate and revenge whisper in my
ear——

GALLUS (*rapidly, looking towards the church*).
There he comes!

JULIAN. Be prudent, my beloved brother!—Ah,
Hekebolius!

(*The church door has meanwhile been opened. The
congregation streams forth; some go away,
others remain standing to see the Court pass.
Among those who come out is* HEKEBOLIUS; *he
wears priestly dress.*)

HEKEBOLIUS (*on the point of passing out to the left*).
Is that you, my Julian? Ah! I have again passed a
heavy hour for your sake.

JULIAN. I fear you pass too many heavy hours
for my sake.

HEKEBOLIUS. Christ is wroth against you, my
son! It is your froward spirit that angers him;
it is your unloving thoughts and all the worldly
vanity——

JULIAN.   I know it, my Hekebolius! You so often tell me so.

HEKEBOLIUS.   Even now I lifted up my soul in prayer for your amendment.   Oh, it seemed as though our otherwise so gracious Saviour repulsed my prayer,—as though he would not listen to me ; he suffered my thoughts to wander upon vanities——

JULIAN.   You prayed for me? Oh, loving Hekebolius, you pray even for us dumb animals—at least when we wear court dress !

HEKEBOLIUS.   What do you mean, my son ?

JULIAN.   Hekebolius, how could you write those shameful verses ?

HEKEBOLIUS.   I ?   I swear by all that is high and holy——!

JULIAN.   I see in your eyes that you are lying ! I have full assurance that you wrote them.   How could you do it, I ask—and under Libanius's name, too ?

HEKEBOLIUS.   Well, well, my dearly beloved, since you know it, I——

JULIAN.   Ah, Hekebolius ! Deceit, and lies, and treachery——

HEKEBOLIUS.   Behold, my precious friend, how deep is my love for you !   I dare all to save the soul of that man who shall one day be the Lord's anointed. If, in my zeal for you, I have had recourse to deceit and lies, I know that a gracious God has found my course well pleasing in his sight, and has stretched forth his approving hand upon it.

JULIAN.   How blind I have been ! Let me press these perjured fingers——

HEKEBOLIUS.   The Emperor !

(*The* EMPEROR CONSTANTIUS, *with his whole
retinue, comes from the church.* AGATHON *has
already, during the foregoing, withdrawn among
the bushes on the right.*)

THE EMPEROR. Oh, how the blessed peace of
heaven has descended upon me!

THE EMPRESS. Do you feel yourself strengthened,
my Constantius?

THE EMPEROR. Yes, yes! I saw the living Dove
hovering over me. It took away the burden of all
my sin.—Now I dare venture much, Memnon!

MEMNON (*softly*). Lose not a moment, sire!

THE EMPEROR. There they both stand. (*He
goes towards the brothers.*)

GALLUS (*mechanically feels for his sword, and cries
in terror*). Do me no ill!

THE EMPEROR (*with outstretched arms*). Gallus!
Kinsman!

(*He embraces and kisses him.*)

Lo, in the light of the Easter stars, I choose the
man who lies nearest my heart.—Bow all to the earth.
Hail Gallus Cæsar![1]

(*General astonishment among the Court; a few
involuntary shouts are raised.*)

THE EMPRESS (*with a shriek*). Constantius!

GALLUS (*taken aback*). Cæsar!

JULIAN. Ah! (*He tries to seize the* EMPEROR'S
hands, as if in joy.)

THE EMPEROR (*waving him aside*). Do not come
near me! What would you have? Is not Gallus

---

[1] The name "Cæsar" was at this period used as the title of the heir
to the throne, the Emperor himself being entitled "Augustus."

the elder? What hopes have you been cherishing?
What rumours have you, in your blind presumption——? Away; away!

GALLUS. I—I Cæsar!

THE EMPEROR. My heir and my successor. In
three days you will set out for the army in Asia.
I know the Persian war is much upon your
mind——

GALLUS. Oh, my most gracious sire——!

THE EMPEROR. Thank me in deeds, my beloved
Gallus! King Sapor lies west of the Euphrates.
I know how solicitous you are for my life; be it your
task, then, to crush him.

(*He turns, takes* JULIAN'S *head between his
hands, and kisses him.*)

And you, Julian, my pious friend and brother—so
it needs must be.

JULIAN. All blessings on the Emperor's will!

THE EMPEROR. Call down no blessings! Yet
listen—I have thought of you too. Know, Julian, that
now you can breathe freely in Constantinople——

JULIAN. Yes, praise be to Christ and to the
Emperor!

THE EMPEROR. You know it already? Who has
told you?

JULIAN. What, sire?

THE EMPEROR. That Libanius is banished?

JULIAN. Libanius—banished!

THE EMPEROR. I have banished him to Athens.

JULIAN. Ah!

THE EMPEROR. Yonder lies his ship; he sails
to-night.

JULIAN (*aside*).   He himself; he himself!

THE EMPEROR.   You have long wished it.   I have not hitherto been able to fulfil your desire; but now ——; let this be a slight requital to you, my Julian.

JULIAN (*quickly seizing his hand*).   Sire, do me one grace more.

THE EMPEROR.   Ask whatever you will.

JULIAN.   Let me go to Pergamus.   You know that old Ædesius teaches there——

THE EMPEROR.   A most strange wish.   You, among the heathens——?

JULIAN.   Ædesius is not dangerous; he is a high-minded old man, drawing towards the grave——

THE EMPEROR.   And what would you with him, brother?

JULIAN.   I would learn to fight with the lions.

THE EMPEROR.   I understand your pious thought. And you are not afraid——; you think yourself strong enough——?

JULIAN.   The Lord God has called me with a loud voice.   Like Daniel, I go fearless and joyful into the lions' den.

THE EMPEROR.   Julian!

JULIAN.   To-night you have yourself been his instrument without knowing it.   Oh, let me go forth to purge the world!

GALLUS (*softly to the* EMPEROR).   Humour him, sire; it will prevent him from brooding on higher things.

THE EMPRESS.   I implore you, Constantius—do not oppose this vehement longing.

HEKEBOLIUS.   Great Emperor, let him go to

Pergamus.   I fear I am losing control of him here, and besides it is no longer so important——

The Emperor.   How could I deny you anything in such an hour?   Go with God, Julian!

Julian (*kissing his hands*).   Oh, thanks—thanks!

The Emperor.   And now to a banquet of rejoicing! My Capuan cook has invented some new fast-dishes, carp-necks in Chios wine, and—— Forward;—your place is next to me, Gallus Cæsar!

(*The procession begins to advance.*)

Gallus (*softly*).   Helena, what a marvellous change of fortune!

Helena.   Oh, Gallus, dawn is breaking over our hopes!

Gallus.   I can scarcely believe it!   Who has brought it about?

Helena.   Hush!

Gallus.   You, my beloved?   Or who—who?

Helena.   Memnon's Spartan dog.

Gallus.   What do you mean?

Helena.   Memnon's dog.   Julian kicked it; that kick is now avenged.

The Emperor.   Why so silent, Eusebia?

The Empress (*softly, in tears*).   Oh, Constantius —how could you make such a choice!

The Emperor.   Eleven ghosts demanded it.

The Empress.   Woe upon us; this will not lay the ghosts.

The Emperor (*calls loudly*).   Flute-players! Why are the rascals silent?   Play, play!

(*All, except* Prince Julian, *go out to the left.* Agathon *comes forward among the trees.*)

JULIAN.   Gallus his successor; and I—free, free, free!

AGATHON.   Marvellously are the counsels of the Lord revealed.

JULIAN.   Did you hear what passed?

AGATHON.   Yes, everything.

JULIAN.   And to-morrow, my Agathon, to-morrow to Athens!

AGATHON.   To Athens? You are going to Pergamus.

JULIAN.   Hush! You do not know——; we must be cunning as serpents.   First to Pergamus—and then to Athens!

AGATHON.   Farewell, my lord and friend!

JULIAN.   Will you go with me, Agathon?

AGATHON.   I cannot. I must go home; I have my little brother to care for.

JULIAN (*at the balustrade*).   There they are weighing anchor.—A fair wind to you, winged lion; Achilles follows in your wake.

(*Calls softly.*)

Ah!

AGATHON.   What was that?

JULIAN.   Yonder fell a star.

Act Second.

(*In Athens. An open place surrounded by colonnades. In the square, statues and a fountain. A narrow street debouches in the left-hand corner. Sunset.*)

(Basilius of Cæsarea, *a delicately-built young man, sits reading beside a pillar.* Gregory of Nazianzus *and other scholars of the University stroll in scattered groups up and down the colonnades. A larger band runs shouting across the square, and out to the right; noise in the distance.*)

Basilius (*looks up from his book*).   What is the meaning of these wild cries?

Gregory.   A ship has come in from Ephesus.

Basilius.   With new scholars?

Gregory.   Yes.

Basilius (*rising*).   Then we shall have a night of tumult. Come, Gregory; do not let us witness all this ribaldry.

Gregory (*points to the left*).   Look yonder. Is *that* a pleasanter sight?

Basilius.   Prince Julian——; with roses in his hair, his face aflame——

Gregory.   Ay, and after him the raving, glassy-eyed crew. Hear how the halting tongues babble with wine! They have sat the whole day in Lykon's tavern.

Basilius.   And many of them are from our province, Gregory; they are Christian youths——

GREGORY.   So they call themselves.   Did not
Lampon call himself a Christian—he who betrayed
the oil-seller Zeno's daughter ?   And Hilarion of
Agrigentum, and the two others who did what I
shudder to name——

PRINCE JULIAN (*is heard calling without, on the
left*).   Aha !   See, see—the Cappadocian Castor and
Pollux.

BASILIUS.   He has caught sight of us.   I will go ;
I cannot endure to see him thus.

GREGORY.   I will remain ; he needs a friend.

(BASILIUS *goes out to the right.   At the same
moment*, PRINCE JULIAN, *followed by a crowd
of young men, enters from the narrow street.
His hair is dishevelled, and he is clad in a short
cloak like the rest.   Among the scholars is*
SALLUST OF PERUSIA.)

MANY IN THE CROWD.   Long live the light of
Athens !   Long live the lover of wisdom and
eloquence !

JULIAN.   All your flattery is wasted.   Not another
verse shall you have to-day.

SALLUST.   When our leader is silent, life seems
empty, as on the morning after a night's carouse.

JULIAN.   If we must needs do something, let it be
something new.   Let us hold a mock trial.

THE WHOLE CROWD.   Yes, yes, yes ; Prince
Julian on the judgment-seat !

JULIAN.   Have done with the Prince, friends——

SALLUST.   Ascend the judgment-seat, incomparable
one !

JULIAN.   How can I presume——?   There stands

the man.   Who is so well versed in jurisprudence as
Gregory of Nazianzus?

SALLUST.   That is true!

JULIAN.   To the judgment-seat, my wise Gregory;
I am the accused.

GREGORY.   I beg you, friend, let me stand out.

JULIAN.   To the judgment-seat, I say! to the
judgment-seat.   (*To the others.*)   What is my
transgression?

SOME VOICES.   Yes, what shall it be?   Choose
yourself!

SALLUST.   Let it be something Galilean, as we
of the ungodly say.

JULIAN.   Right; something Galilean.   I have it.
I have refused to pay tribute to the Emperor——

MANY VOICES.   Ha-ha; not bad!   Excellent!

JULIAN.   Here I am dragged forward by the
nape of the neck, with my hands pinioned——

SALLUST (*to* GREGORY).   Blind judge—I mean
since Justice is blind—behold this desperate wretch;
he has refused to pay tribute to the Emperor.

JULIAN.   Let me throw one word into the scales
of judgment.   I am a Greek citizen.   How much does
a Greek citizen owe the Emperor?

GREGORY.   What the Emperor demands.

JULIAN.   Good; but how much—answer now as
though the Emperor himself were present in court—
how much has the Emperor a right to demand?

GREGORY.   Everything.

JULIAN.   Answered as though the Emperor were
present indeed!   But now comes the knotty point;
for it is written: Render unto Cæsar the things that

are Cæsar's—and unto God the things that are God's.

GREGORY. And what then?

JULIAN. Then tell me, oh sagacious judge—how much of what is mine belongs to God?

GREGORY. Everything.

JULIAN. And how much of God's property may I give to the Emperor?

GREGORY. Dear friends, no more of this sport.

THE SCHOLARS (*amid laughter and noise*). Yes, yes; answer him.

JULIAN. How much of God's property has the Emperor a right to demand?

GREGORY. I will not answer. This is unseemly both towards God and the Emperor. Let me go.

MANY VOICES. Make a ring round him!

JULIAN. Hold him fast! What, you most luckless of judges, you have bungled the Emperor's cause, and now you want to escape? You would flee? Whither, whither? To the Scythians? Bring him before me! Tell me, you servants that-are-to-be of the Emperor and of wisdom—has he not attempted to elude the Emperor's power?

THE SCHOLARS. Yes, yes.

JULIAN. And what punishment do you award to such a misdeed?

VOICES. Death! Death in a wine-jar!

JULIAN. Let us look closely into this matter. Let us answer as though the Emperor himself were present. What limit is there to the Emperor's power?

SOME OF THE CROWD. The Emperor's power has no limits.

JULIAN. So I should think. But to want to escape from the infinite, my friends, is not that madness?

THE SCHOLARS. Yes, yes; the Cappadocian is mad!

JULIAN. And what, then, is madness? How did our forefathers conceive of it? What did the Egyptian priests teach? And what says Maximus the Mystic and the other philosophers of the East? They say that the divine enigma reveals itself in the brainsick. Our Gregory—in setting himself up against the Emperor—is thus in special league with Heaven.— Make libations of wine to the Cappadocian; sing songs to our Gregory's praise;—a statue of honour for Gregory of Nazianzus!

THE SCHOLARS (*amid laughter and glee*). Praise to the Cappadocian! Praise to the Cappadocian's judge!

(*The* PHILOSOPHER LIBANIUS, *surrounded by disciples, comes across the square.*)

LIBANIUS. Ah, see—is not my brother Julian dispensing wisdom in the open market-place!

JULIAN. Say folly, dear friend; wisdom has departed the city.

LIBANIUS. Has wisdom departed the city?

JULIAN. Or is on the point of departing; for are not you also on the way to the Piræus?

LIBANIUS. I, my brother? What should I want at the Piræus?

JULIAN. Our Libanius, then, is the only teacher who does not know that a ship has just come in from Ephesus.

LIBANIUS.   Why, my friend, what have I to do
with that ship?

JULIAN.   It is loaded to the water's edge with
embryo philosophers——

LIBANIUS (*scornfully*).   They come from Ephesus!

JULIAN.   Is not gold equally weighty wherever it
comes from?

LIBANIUS.   Gold?   Ha-ha!   Maximus keeps the
golden ones to himself; he does not let them go.   What
sort of scholars is Ephesus wont to send us?   Shop-
keepers' sons, the first-born of mechanics.   Gold do
you say, my Julian?   I call it lack of gold.   But I
will turn this lack of gold to account, and out of it I
will mint for you young men a coin of true and
weighty metal.   For may not a precious lesson in life,
set forth in ingenious and attractive forms, be compared to a piece of full-weighted golden currency?——

Hear then, if you have a mind to.   Was it not said
that certain men had rushed eagerly down to the
Piræus?   Who are they, these eager ones?   Far be
it from me to mention names; they call themselves
lovers and teachers of wisdom.   Let us betake ourselves in thought to the Piræus.   What is going on
there at this moment, even as I stand here in this
circle of kindly listeners?   I will tell you what is
going on.   Those men, who give themselves out as
lovers and dispensers of wisdom, are crowding upon
the gangway, jostling, wrangling, biting, forgetting all
decorum, and throwing dignity to the winds.   And
why?   To be the first in the field,—to get hold of
the best dressed youths, to lead them home, to enter-
tain them, hoping in the end to make profit out of

them in all possible ways.   What a shamefaced, empty awakening, as after a debauch, if it should presently appear—ha-ha-ha !—that these youths have scarcely brought with them the wherewithal to pay for their supper of welcome !   Learn from this, young men, how ill it becomes a lover of wisdom, and how little it profits him, to run after good things other than the truth.

JULIAN.   Oh, my Libanius, when I listen to you with closed eyes, I seem lapped in the sweet dream that Diogenes has once more arisen in our midst.

LIBANIUS.   Your lips are princely spendthrifts of praise, beloved of my soul !

JULIAN.   Far from it.   And yet I had almost interrupted your harangue ; for in this instance, one of your colleagues will scarcely find himself disappointed.

LIBANIUS.   My friend is jesting.

JULIAN.   Your friend assures you that the two sons of the governor, Milo, are on board.

LIBANIUS (*grasping his arm*).   What do you say ?

JULIAN.   That the new Diogenes who gets them to educate will scarcely need to drink out of the hollow of his hand for poverty.

LIBANIUS.   The sons of the Governor Milo ! That noble Milo, who sent the Emperor seven Persian horses, with saddles embroidered with pearls——?

JULIAN.   Many thought that too mean a gift for Milo.

LIBANIUS.   Very true.   Milo ought to have sent a poem, or perhaps a well-polished speech, or a letter. Milo is an exceedingly able man ; all Milo's family are exceedingly able.

JULIAN.   Especially the two young men.

LIBANIUS.   No doubt, no doubt.   For the sake of their beneficent and generous father, I pray the gods that they may fall into good hands!   You were right, after all, Julian; the ship brought real gold from Ephesus.   For are not intellectual gifts the purest of gold?   But I cannot rest; these young men's welfare is, in truth, a weighty matter; so much depends on who gets hold of them first.   My young friends, if you think as I do, we will hold out a guiding hand to these two strangers, assist them to make the most advantageous choice of teacher and abode, and——

SALLUST.   I will go with you.

THE SCHOLARS.   To the Piræus!   To the Piræus!

SALLUST.   We will fight like wild boars for Milo's sons!

(*They all go out, with* LIBANIUS, *to the right; only* PRINCE JULIAN *and* GREGORY OF NAZI-ANZUS *remain behind in the colonnade.*)

JULIAN (*following them with his eyes*).   See how they go leaping like a troop of fauns.   How they lick their lips at the thought of the feast that awaits them this evening.   (*He turns to* GREGORY.)   If there is one thing they would sigh to God for at this moment, it is that he would empty their stomachs of their breakfasts.

GREGORY.   Julian——!

JULIAN.   Look at me; I am sober.

GREGORY.   I know that.   You are temperate in all things.   And yet you lead the same life as the rest.

Julian.   Why not?   Do either you or I know when the thunderbolt will fall?   Then why not make the most of the bright and sunlit day?   Do you forget that I dragged out my childhood and the first years of my youth in gilded slavery?   It had become a habit, I might almost say a necessity to me, to live under a weight of dread.   And now?   This stillness as of the grave on the Emperor's part;— this sinister silence!   I left Pergamus without the Emperor's permission; the Emperor said nothing. I went of my own will to Nicomedia; I lived there, and studied with Nikokles and others; the Emperor gave no sign.   I came to Athens, and sought out Libanius, whom the Emperor had forbidden me to see;—the Emperor has said nothing to this day. How am I to interpret this?

Gregory.   Interpret it in charity, Julian.

Julian.   Oh, you do not know——!   I hate this power without me, fearful in action—most fearful when at rest.

Gregory.   Be frank, my friend, and tell me whether it is this alone that has led you into all these strange ways?

Julian.   What do you mean by strange ways?

Gregory.   Is the rumour true which says that you pass your nights in searching out the heathen mysteries in Eleusis?

Julian.   Oh, pooh!   I assure you there is little to be learnt from these riddle-mongering dreamers. Let us talk no more about them.

Gregory.   Then it is true!   Oh, Julian, how could you seek such shameful intercourse?

JULIAN. I must live, Gregory,—and here at the
university it is not life. This Libanius! I shall never
forgive him the great love I once bore him! At my
first coming, how humbly and with what tremors of
joy did I not enter the presence of this man, bowing
myself before him, kissing him, and calling him my
great brother!

GREGORY. Yes, all we Christians thought that
you went too far.

JULIAN. And yet I came here in exaltation of
spirit. I saw, in imagination, a mighty contest between
us two,—the world's truth face to face with God's
truth.—What has it all come to? Libanius never
seriously desired that contest. He never desired any
contest whatever; he cares only for his own interest.
I tell you, Gregory—Libanius is not a great man.

GREGORY. Yet all enlightened Greece proclaims
him great.

JULIAN. A great man he is not, I tell you. Once
only have I seen Libanius great; that night in Constantinople. Then he was great, because he had
suffered a great wrong, and because he was filled with
a noble wrath. But here! Oh, what have I not seen
here? Libanius has great learning, but he is no great
man. Libanius is greedy; he is vain; he is eaten up
with envy. Do you not see how he has writhed under
the fame which I—largely, no doubt, owing to the in-
dulgence of my friends—have been so fortunate as to
acquire. Go to Libanius, and he will expound to you
the inward essence and the outward signs of all the
virtues. He has them ready to hand, just as he has
the books in his library. But does he exercise these

virtues? Is his life like his teaching? He a successor of Socrates and of Plato—ha-ha! Did he not flatter the Emperor up to the time of his banishment? Did he not flatter me at our meeting in Constantinople, that meeting which he has since attempted, most unsuccessfully, to represent in a ludicrous light! And what am I to him now? Now he writes letters to Gallus, to Gallus Cæsar, to the Emperor's heir, congratulating him on his successes against the Persians, although these successes have as yet been meagre enough, and Gallus Cæsar is not distinguished either for learning or for any particular eloquence.—And this Libanius the Greeks persist in calling the king of the philosophers! Ah, I will not deny that it stirs my indignation. I should have thought, to tell the truth, that the Greeks might have made a better choice, if they had paid a little more attention to the cultivators of wisdom and eloquence, who of late years——

BASILIUS OF CÆSAREA (*entering from the right*). Letters! Letters from Cappadocia!

GREGORY. For me too?

BASILIUS. Yes, here; from your mother.

GREGORY. My pious mother! (*He opens the paper and reads.*)

JULIAN (*to* BASILIUS). Is it your sister who writes to you?

BASILIUS (*who has entered with his own letter open*). Yes, it is Makrina. Her news is both sad and strange.

JULIAN. What? what?

BASILIUS. First of your noble brother Gallus. He rules sternly in Antioch.

JULIAN.   Yes, Gallus is hard.—Does Makrina write " sternly "?

BASILIUS (*looking at him*).   Makrina writes " bloodily "——

JULIAN.   Ah, I thought as much! Why did the Emperor marry him to that abandoned widow, that Constantina?

GREGORY (*reading*).   Oh, what unheard-of infamy!

JULIAN.   What is it, friend?

GREGORY (*to* BASILIUS).   Does Makrina say nothing of what is going on in Antioch?

BASILIUS.   She gives no particulars.   What is it? You are pale——

GREGORY.   You knew the noble Clemazius, the Alexandrian?

BASILIUS.   Yes, yes ; what of him?

GREGORY.   He is murdered, Basilius!

BASILIUS.   What do you say?   Murdered?

GREGORY.   I call it murdered ;—they have executed him without law or judgment.

JULIAN.   Who?   Who has executed him?

GREGORY.   Yes, who?   How can I say who?   My mother tells the story thus: Clemazius's mother-in-law was inflamed with an impure love for her daughter's husband ; but as she could make no impression on him, she obtained some back-stairs access to the palace——

JULIAN.   What palace?

GREGORY.   My mother only writes " the palace."

JULIAN.   Well?   And then——?

GREGORY.   It is only known that she presented a

very costly jewel to a great and powerful lady, who
was to procure a death-warrant——

JULIAN.   Ah, but they did not get it!

GREGORY.   They got it, Julian!

JULIAN.   Oh, Jesus!

BASILIUS.   Horrible!   And Clemazius——?

GREGORY.   The death-warrant was sent to the
governor, Honoratus.   That weak man dared not
disobey so high a command.   Clemazius was thrown
into prison and executed early next morning, without
being allowed, my mother writes, to open his lips in
his own defence.

JULIAN (*pale, and in a low voice*).   Burn these
dangerous letters; they might bring us all to ruin.

BASILIUS.   Such open violence; in the midst of a
great city!   Where are we; where are we?

JULIAN.   Yes, you may well ask where we are!
A Christian murderer, a Christian adulteress, a
Christian——!

GREGORY.   Denunciations will not mend the
matter.   What do you intend to do?

JULIAN.   I?   I will go no more to Eleusis; I will
break off all dealings with the heathen, and thank the
Lord my God that he spared me the temptations of
power.

GREGORY.   Good; but then?

JULIAN.   I do not understand you——

GREGORY.   Then listen.   The murder of Clemazius is not all, believe me.   This unheard-of infamy has
descended like a plague on Antioch.   All evil things
have awakened, and are swarming forth from their
lairs.   My mother writes that it seems as though

some foul abyss had opened. Wives denounce their
husbands, sons their fathers, priests the members of
their own congregations——

JULIAN. This will spread yet further. The
abomination will corrupt us all.—— Oh, Gregory,
would I could fly to the world's end——!

GREGORY. Your place is at the world's navel,
Prince Julian.

JULIAN. What would you have me do?

GREGORY. You are this bloody Cæsar's brother.
Stand forth before him—he calls himself a Christian—
and cast his crime in his teeth; smite him to the
earth in terror and remorse——

JULIAN (*shrinking*). Madman, what are you thinking of?

GREGORY. Do you love your brother? Would
you save him?

JULIAN. I once loved Gallus above all others.

GREGORY. *Once——*?

JULIAN. So long as he was only my brother. But
now——; is he not Cæsar? Gregory,—Basilius,—oh,
my beloved friends,—I tremble for my life, I draw
every breath in fear, on account of Gallus Caesar.
And you ask me to stand forth and defy him, me,
whose very existence is a danger to him?

GREGORY. Why did you come to Athens? You
gave out loudly in all quarters that Prince Julian
was setting forth from Constantinople to do battle
with philosophy, falsely so called—to champion Christian truth against heathen falsehood. What have you
done of all this?

JULIAN. Oh, it was not here that the battle was to be.

Gregory. No, it was not here;—not with phrase against phrase, not with book against book, not with mere verbal sword-play in the lecture-room! No, Julian, you must go forth into life itself, with your own life in your hands——

Julian. I see it ; I see it !

Gregory. Yes, as Libanius sees it ! You mocked at him. You said he knew the essence and the outward signs of all the virtues, but his doctrine was only a doctrine to him. How much of *you* belongs to God ? How much may the Emperor demand ?

Julian. You said yourself it was unseemly——

Gregory. Towards whom ? Towards God or the Emperor ?

Julian (*quickly*). Well then ; shall we go together?

Gregory (*evasively*). I have my little circle ; I have my family to watch over. I have neither strength nor talent for a larger task.

Julian (*is about to answer; suddenly he listens towards the right, and calls out*). To the bacchanal !

Basilius. Julian !

Julian. To the bacchanal, friends !

(Gregory of Nazianzus *looks at him a moment; then he goes off through the colonnade to the left. A large troop of scholars, with the new-comers among them, rushes into the square, amid shouts and noise.*)

Basilius (*coming nearer*). Julian, will you listen to me ?

Julian. See, see ! They have taken their new friends to the bath, and anointed their hair. See how they swing their cudgels ; how they yell and

thump the pavement! What say you, Pericles? I
think I can hear your wrathful shade——

BASILIUS. Come, come!

JULIAN. Ah, look at the man they are driving
naked among them. Now come the dancing-girls.
Ah, do you see what——!

BASILIUS. Fie! Fie!—turn away your eyes!

(*Evening has fallen. The whole troop settles down
in the square beside the fountain. Wine and
fruits are brought. Painted damsels dance by
torchlight.*)

JULIAN (*after a short silence*). Tell me, Basilius,
why was heathen sin so beautiful?

BASILIUS. You are mistaken, friend; beautiful
things have been said and sung of this heathen sin;
but it was not beautiful.

JULIAN. Oh, how can you say so? Was not
Alcibiades beautiful when, heated with wine, he
stormed at night like a young god through the
streets of Athens? Was he not beautiful in his very
audacity when he insulted Hermes and hammered
at the citizens' doors,—when he summoned their
wives and daughters forth, while within the women
trembled, and, in breathless, panting silence, wished
for nothing better than to——?

BASILIUS. Oh listen to me, I beg and entreat you.

JULIAN. Was not Socrates beautiful in the sym-
posium? And Plato, and all the joyous revellers?
And yet they did things that would make those
Christian swine out there call down the curse of God
upon themselves if but accused of them. Think of
Œdipus, Medea, Leda——

BASILIUS. Poetry, poetry ;—you mix up fancies and facts.

JULIAN. Are not the intellect and will in poetry subject to the same laws as in real life? And then look at our holy scriptures, both the old and new. Was sin beautiful in Sodom and Gomorrah? Did not Jehovah's fire avenge what Socrates did not shrink from?—Oh, as I live this life of revel and riot, I often wonder whether truth is indeed the enemy of beauty!

BASILIUS. And in such an hour can you sigh after beauty? Can you so easily forget what you have just heard——?

JULIAN (*stopping his ears*). Not a word more of those horrors! We will shake off all thoughts of Antioch——

Tell me, what does Makrina write further? There was something more; I remember, you said——, what was it you called the rest of her news?

BASILIUS. Strange.

JULIAN. Yes, yes ;—what was it?

BASILIUS. She writes about Maximus in Ephesus——

JULIAN (*eagerly*). The Mystic?

BASILIUS. Yes; that inscrutable man. He has appeared once more; this time in Ephesus. All the neighbourhood is in a ferment. Maximus is on all lips. Either he is a juggler or he has made a baleful compact with certain spirits. Even Christians are strangely affected by his impious signs and wonders.

JULIAN. More, more; I entreat you!

BASILIUS. There is no more about him. Makrina

only writes that she sees in the reappearance of
Maximus a proof that we are under the wrath of the
Lord. She believes that great afflictions are in store
for us, by reason of our sins.

JULIAN. Yes, yes, yes!—Tell me, Basilius: your
sister must surely be a remarkable woman.

BASILIUS. She is, indeed.

JULIAN. When you repeat to me passages from
her letters, they seem to fill me with a sense of
amplitude and perfection, such as I have long sighed
for. Tell me, is she still bent upon renouncing this
world, and living in the wilderness?

BASILIUS. That is her fixed intent.

JULIAN. Is it possible? She, on whom all gifts
seem to have been lavished? She, who must be both
young and beautiful; she, who has riches in prospect,
and possesses—for a woman—the rarest intellectual
acquirements? Do you know, Basilius, I long to see
her?—What has *she* to do in the wilderness?

BASILIUS. I have told you how her affianced
husband died. She regards him as her expectant
bridegroom, to whom she owes her every thought,
and whom she is pledged to meet unsullied.

JULIAN. Strange, how many feel the attraction of
solitude in these times.—When you write to Makrina
you may tell her that I too——

BASILIUS. She knows that, Julian; but she does
not believe it.

JULIAN. Why not? What does she write?

BASILIUS. I pray you, friend, spare me——

JULIAN. If you love me, do not hide from me one
word she writes.

Basilius (*giving him the letter*). Read, if you must—it begins there.

Julian (*reads*). " Whenever you write of the Emperor's young kinsman, who is your friend, my soul is filled with a great and radiant joy——" O Basilius! lend me your eyes ; read for me.

Basilius (*reading*). " Your account of the fearless confidence wherewith he came to Athens was to me as a picture from the ancient chronicles. Yes, I see in him David born again, to smite the champions of the heathen. God's spirit watch over him in the strife, now and for ever."

Julian (*grasping his arm*). Enough of that ! She too ? What is it you all, as with one mouth, demand of me ? Have I sealed you a bond to fight with the lions of power—— ?

Basilius. How comes it that all believers look towards you in breathless expectation ?

Julian (*paces once or twice up and down the colonnade, then stops and stretches out his hand for the letter*). Give it to me ; let me see. (*Reading.*) " God's spirit watch over him in the strife, now and for ever."—

Oh, Basilius, if I could——! But I feel like Dædalus, between sky and sea. An appalling height and an abysmal depth.—What sense is there in these voices calling to me, from east and west, that I must save Christendom ? Where is it to be found, this Christendom that I am to save ? With the Emperor or with Cæsar ? I think their deeds cry out, " No, no ! " Among the powerful and high-born;—among those sensual and effeminate courtiers, who fold their

hands over their full bellies, and quaver: "Was the
Son of God created out of nothing?" Or among the
men of enlightenment, those who, like you and me,
have drunk in beauty and learning from the heathen
fountains? Do not most of our fellows lean to the
Arian heresy, which the Emperor himself so greatly
favours!—And then the whole ragged rabble of the
Empire, who rage against the temples, who massacre
heathens and the children of heathens! Is it for
Christ's sake? Ha-ha! see how they fall to fighting
among themselves for the spoils of the slain.—
Ask Makrina if Christendom is to be sought in
the wilderness,—on the pillars where the stylite-
saints stand on one leg? Or is it in the cities?
Perhaps among those bakers in Constantinople who
lately took to their fists to decide the question
whether the Trinity consists of three individuals or
of three hypostases!—Which of all these would
Christ recognise if he came down to earth again?—
Out with your Diogenes-lantern, Basilius! Enlighten
this pitchy darkness.—Where is Christendom?

BASILIUS. Seek the answer where it is ever to be
found in evil days.

JULIAN. Do not stop up the well of your wisdom!
Slake my thirst, if you can. Where shall I seek and
find?

BASILIUS. In the writings of holy men.

JULIAN. The same despairing answer. Books,—
always books! When I came to Libanius, it was:
books, books! I come to you,—books, books, books!
Stones for bread! I cannot live on books;—it is life
I hunger for,—face-to-face communion with the spirit.

Was it a book that made Saul a seer ?   Was it not a
flood of light that enveloped him, a vision, a voice——?

BASILIUS.   Do you forget the vision and the voice
which that Agathon of Makellon——?

JULIAN.   An enigmatic message ; an oracle I
cannot interpret.   Was *I* the chosen one?   The
" heir to the empire," it said.   And what empire——?
That matter is involved in a thousand uncertainties.
Only this I know : Athens is not the lions' den.   But
where, where ?   Oh, I grope like Saul in the darkness.
If Christ would have aught of me he must speak
plainly.   Let me touch the nail-wound——

BASILIUS.   And yet it is written——

JULIAN (*with a gesture of impatience*).   I know
all that is written.   This " it is written " is not
living truth.   Do you not feel disgust and nausea, as
on board ship in a windless swell, heaving to and fro
between life, and written revelation, and heathen
wisdom and beauty ?   There must come a new
revelation.   Or a revelation of something new.   It
must come, I say ;—the time is ripe.—Ah, a revelation !
Oh, Basilius, if your prayers could call *that* down upon
me !   A martyr's death, if need be——!   A martyr's
death—ah, it makes me dizzy with its sweetness ; the
crown of thorns on my brows——! (*He clasps his
head with both hands, feels the wreath of roses, which
he tears off, bethinks himself long, and says softly :*)
That ! I had forgotten that ! (*Casting the wreath
away.*)   One thing alone have I learnt in Athens.

BASILIUS.   What, Julian ?

JULIAN.   The old beauty is no longer beautiful,
and the new truth is no longer true.

(LIBANIUS *enters hastily through the colonnade on
the right.*)

LIBANIUS (*still in the distance*). Now we have
him; now we have him!

JULIAN. Him? I thought you would have had
them both.

LIBANIUS. Both of whom?

JULIAN. Milo's sons.

LIBANIUS. Ah, yes, I have them too. But we
have *him*, my Julian!

JULIAN. Whom, dear brother?

LIBANIUS. He has caught himself in his own
net!

JULIAN. Aha—a philosopher?

LIBANIUS. The enemy of all wisdom.

JULIAN. Who, who, I ask?

LIBANIUS. Do you really not know? Have you
not heard the news about Maximus?

JULIAN. Maximus? Oh, pray tell me——

LIBANIUS. Who could fail to see whither that
restless visionary was tending,—step by step towards
madness——?

JULIAN. In other words, towards the highest
wisdom.

LIBANIUS. Ah, that is a figure of speech. But
now we must set to work, and seize the opportunity.
You, our dearly-prized Julian, you are the man. You
are the Emperor's near kinsman. The hopes of all
true friends of wisdom are fixed upon you, both
here and in Nikomedia——

JULIAN. Listen, oh excellent Libanius,—seeing I
am not omniscient——

LIBANIUS.   Know, then, that Maximus has lately made open avowal of what lies at the bottom of his teaching.

JULIAN.   And do you blame him for that?

LIBANIUS.   He has declared that he can command spirits and shades of the dead.

JULIAN (*grasping his cloak*).   Libanius!

LIBANIUS.   All on board the ship were full of the most marvellous stories, and here—— (*He shows a letter*), here, my colleague, Eusebius, writes in detail upon the subject.

JULIAN.   Spirits and shades——

LIBANIUS.   At Ephesus lately, in a large assembly both of his partizans and his opponents, Maximus applied forbidden arts to the statue of Hecate. It took place in the goddess's temple. Eusebius writes that he himself was present, and saw everything from first to last. It was pitch-black night all around. Maximus uttered strange incantations; then he sang a hymn, which no one understood. Then the marble torch in the statue's hand burst into flame——

BASILIUS.   Impious doings!

JULIAN (*breathlessly*).   And then——?

LIBANIUS.   In the strong bluish light, they all saw the statue's face come to life and smile at them.

JULIAN.   What more?

LIBANIUS.   Terror seized on the minds of most. All rushed towards the doors. Many have lain sick or raving ever since. But he himself—would you believe it, Julian?—in spite of the fate that befel his two brothers in Constantinople, he goes boldly forward on his reckless and scandalous way.

JULIAN. Scandalous? Do you call that way scandalous? Is not this the end of all wisdom? Communion between spirit and spirit——

BASILIUS. Oh, dear, misguided friend——!

LIBANIUS. More than scandalous, I call it! What is Hecate? What are the gods, as a whole, in the eyes of enlightened humanity? We have happily left far behind us the blind old singer's days. Maximus ought to know better than that. Has not Plato—and after him we others—shed the light of interpretation over the whole? Is it not scandalous now, in our own days, to seek to enshroud afresh in riddles and misty dreams this admirable, palpable, and, let me add, this laboriously constructed edifice of ideas and interpretations which we, as lovers of wisdom, as a school, as——

JULIAN (*wildly*). Farewell, Basilius! I see a light on my path!

BASILIUS (*flinging his arms around him*). I will not let you go; I will hold you fast!

JULIAN (*extricating himself from his grasp*). No one shall withold me;—kick not against the pricks——

LIBANIUS. What frenzy is this? Friend, brother, colleague, where are you going?

JULIAN. Thither, thither, where torches are lighted and where statues smile!

LIBANIUS. And you can do this! You, Julian, our pride, our light, our hope,—you can think of rushing to bewildered Ephesus, to give yourself into a juggler's power! Know that in the hour you so deeply debase yourself, in that same hour you throw away all the fame for learning and eloquence which, during these years in Pergamos and Nikomedia, and especially here in the great school of Athens——

JULIAN. Oh, the school, the school! Do you pore over your books ;—you have shown me the man I have been in search of. (*He goes off hastily through the colonnade to the left.*)

LIBANIUS (*looking after him awhile*). This princely youth is a menace to the cause of enlightenment.

BASILIUS (*half to himself*). Prince Julian is a menace to more than that.

Act Third.

(*In Ephesus. A brightly lighted hall in* PRINCE JULIAN'S *dwelling. The entrance from the vestibule is on the right side; further back, a smaller door, covered by a curtain. On the left, a door, which leads to the inner part of the house. The wall in the back is pierced with an archway, through which a small enclosed court is visible, decked with small statues.*)

(*Servants prepare a festal supper, and lay cushions round the table. The Chamberlain,* EUTHERIUS, *stands at the entrance, and, with much ceremony, half forces* GREGORY OF NAZIANZUS *and* BASILIUS OF CÆSAREA *to enter.*)

EUTHERIUS. Yes, yes; I assure you it is as I say.

GREGORY. Impossible! Do not make sport of us.

BASILIUS. You are jesting, friend! How can your master expect us? Not a creature knew of our leaving Athens; nothing has detained us on our way; we have kept pace with the clouds and the wild cranes.

EUTHERIUS. Look round; see yonder table. His daily fare is herbs and bread.

GREGORY. Ay, truly; all our senses bear you witness;—wine-cans, wreathed with flowers and leaves; lamps and fruits; incense filling the hall with its odour; flute-players before the door——

EUTHERIUS. Early this morning he sent for me. He seemed elated beyond his wont, for he walked up and down the room, rubbing his hands. "Prepare a rich banquet," said he, "for before evening I look for two friends from Athens——" (*He glances towards the door on the left, is suddenly silent, and draws back respectfully.*)

BASILIUS.   Is he there?

 (EUTHERIUS *nods in answer; then gives a sign to the servants to withdraw; they go out by the larger door on the right; he follows.*)

 (PRINCE JULIAN *shortly afterwards enters from the left. He is dressed in long, Oriental garb; his whole demeanour is vivacious, and betrays strong inward excitement.*)

JULIAN (*going towards them, and greeting them with great warmth*). I see you! I have you! Thanks, thanks, for sending your spirits to herald your bodies!

GREGORY.   Julian!

BASILIUS.   My friend and brother!

JULIAN.   I have been like a lover, languishing for the pressure of your hands. The court vermin, eager for certain people's applause, called me an ape;—oh, would I had an ape's four hands, to squeeze yours all at once!

GREGORY.   But explain——; your servants meet us with flutes before the door, want to lead us to the bath, to anoint our hair and deck us with roses——

JULIAN.   I saw you last night. The moon was full, you see,—and then the spirit is always strangely alert within me. I sat at the table in my library, and had fallen asleep, weary, oh! so weary, my friends, with research and writing. Suddenly it seemed as though a storm-wind filled the house; the

curtain was swept flapping aloft, and I looked out
into the night, far over the sea. I heard sweet singing; and the singers were two large birds, with
women's faces. They flew slanting towards the
shore; there they dropped gently earthwards; the
bird-forms melted away like a white mist, and in a
soft, glimmering light, I saw you two.

GREGORY. Are you sure of all this?

JULIAN. Were you thinking of me? Were you
speaking of me last night?

BASILIUS. Yes, yes—forward in the prow——

JULIAN. What time of night was it?

GREGORY. What time was your vision?

JULIAN. An hour after midnight.

GREGORY (*with a look at* BASILIUS). Strange!

JULIAN (*rubbing his hands, and walking up and
down the room*). You see! Ha-ha; you see!

BASILIUS (*following him with his eyes*). Ah, then
it is true——

JULIAN. What? What is true?

BASILIUS. The rumour of the mysterious arts you
practise here.

JULIAN. Oh, what will not rumour exaggerate?—
But tell me, what has rumour found to say? I am
told there are many reports afloat concerning me. If
I could believe some people's assurances, it would
seem that there are few men in the empire so much
talked about as I.

GREGORY. That you may safely believe.

JULIAN. And what does Libanius say to all this?
He could never endure that the multitude should be
busied with any one but himself. And what say all

my never-to-be-forgotten friends in Athens? They know I am in disgrace with the Emperor and the whole court?

GREGORY. You? I have frequent intelligence from the court; but my brother Cæsarius makes no mention of that.

JULIAN. I cannot interpret it otherwise, good Gregory! From all sides they think it necessary to watch me. The other day, Gallus Cæsar sent his chaplain Aëzius hither, to find out whether I hold fast to the orthodox faith.

BASILIUS. Well——?

JULIAN. I am seldom absent from matins in the church. Moreover, I reckon the martyrs among the noblest of men; for truly it is no light matter to endure so great torments, ay, and death itself, for the sake of one's creed. On the whole, I believe Aëzius went away quite satisfied with me.

BASILIUS (*grasping his hand*). Julian,—for the sake of our true friendship,—open your heart fully to us.

JULIAN. I am the happiest man on earth, dear friends! And Maximus—ay, he is rightly named— Maximus is the greatest man that has ever lived.

GREGORY (*preparing to depart*). We only wished to see you, my lord!

JULIAN. Can this estrange brother from brother? You shrink in affright from the inexplicable. Oh, I do not wonder. So I, too, shrank before my eyes were opened and I divined that which is the kernel of life.

BASILIUS. What do you call the kernel of life?

JULIAN.   Maximus knows it.   In him is the new revelation.

BASILIUS.   And it has been imparted to you ?

JULIAN.   Almost.   I am on the eve of learning it. This very night Maximus has promised me——

GREGORY.   Maximus is a visionary, or else he is deceiving you——!

JULIAN.   How dare you judge of these occult things ?   They are beyond *your* learning, my Gregory! Fearful is the way into the glory of glories.   Those dreamers in Eleusis were near the right track ; Maximus found it, and I after him—by his help.   I have wandered through gloomy chasms.   A black swampy pool lay on my left—I believe it was a stream that had forgotten to flow.   Piercing voices sounded through the night confusedly, suddenly, and, as it were, without cause.   Now and then I saw a bluish light ; dreadful shapes floated past me ;—I went on and on in deathly fear ; but I endured the trial to the end.—

Since then—oh, beloved ones—with this my body transformed to spirit, I have passed far into the land of paradise ; I have heard the angels chant their hymns of praise ; I have gazed at the midmost light——

GREGORY.   Woe to this ungodly Maximus !   Woe to this devil-devoted heathen juggler !

JULIAN.   Blindness, blindness !   Maximus pays homage to his precursor and brother—to both his great brothers, the law-giver of Sinai and the seer of Nazareth.——

Would you know how the spirit of realisation

filled me?—It happened on a night of prayer and fasting. I perceived that I was wafted far—far out into space, and beyond time; for there was broad sun-shimmering day around me, and I stood alone on a ship, with flapping sails, in the midst of the glassy, gleaming Grecian sea. Islands towered aloft in the distance, like dim, still banks of clouds, and the ship lay heavily, as though sleeping, upon the wine-blue plain.——

Then behold! the plain became more and more transparent, lighter, thinner; at last, it was no longer there, and my ship hung over a fearful, empty abyss. No verdure down there, no sunlight,—only the dead, black, slimy bottom of the sea, in all its ghastly nakedness.——

But above, in the boundless dome, which before had seemed to me empty,—*there* was life; there invisibility assumed form, and silence became sound.—Then I grasped the great redeeming realisation.

GREGORY. What realisation do you mean?

JULIAN. That which is, is not; and that which is not, is.

BASILIUS. Oh, you are going to wreck and ruin in this maze of mists and gleams!

JULIAN. I? Do not miracles happen? Do not both omens and certain strange phenomena among the stars declare that the divine will destines me to issues yet unrevealed?

GREGORY. Do not believe such signs; you cannot know whose work they are.

JULIAN. Am I not to believe in fortunate omens which events have already justified?

(He draws them nearer to him, and says softly)

Know, my friends, that a great revolution is at hand. Gallus Cæsar and I shall ere long share the dominion of the earth—he as Emperor, and I as— what shall I call it? the unborn cannot be called by a name, for it has none. So no more of this till the time is fulfilled. But of Cæsar I dare speak.—Have you heard of the vision on account of which Apollinaris, a citizen of Sidon, has been imprisoned and tortured?

BASILIUS. No, no; how can we know——?

JULIAN. Apollinaris declared that he heard some one knocking many times at his door by night. He arose, and went out in front of the house; and lo! there he saw an apparition—whether man or woman, he could not tell. And the apparition spoke to him, and bade him make ready a purple robe, such as newly-chosen rulers wear. But when Apollinaris, in affright, would have declined so dangerous a task, the apparition had vanished, and only a voice cried : " Go, go, Apollinaris, and speedily prepare the purple robe."

GREGORY. Was this the sign that you said events had justified?

JULIAN (*nodding slowly*). Seven days later Cæsar's wife died in Bithynia. Constantina has always been his bad angel; therefore she had to be removed in accordance with the change in the divine will. Three weeks after Constantina's death, the Emperor's emissary, the tribune Scudilo, came with a great retinue to Antioch, greeted Gallus Cæsar with imperial honours, and invited him, in the Emperor's name, to visit the imperial camp at Rome.—Cæsar's journey from province to province is now like a conquering hero's progress. In Constantinople he has held races in the hippodrome, and the multitude loudly acclaimed him when he, though as yet Cæsar only in name, stood forth after the manner of the earlier Emperors, and gave the crown to Corax, who won the race. Thus marvellously does God again exalt our house, which had sunk under sin and persecution.

GREGORY. Strange! In Athens we heard other reports.

JULIAN. I have certain information. The purple robe will soon be needed, Gregory! How, then, can I doubt as to the things which Maximus has foretold as near at hand for *me?* To-night the last veil falls. Here shall the great enigma be made manifest. Oh remain with me, my brothers—remain with me through these dark hours of anxiety and expectation! When Maximus comes you shall witness——

BASILIUS. Never!

GREGORY. It cannot be; we are on our way home to Cappadocia.

JULIAN. And what has driven you in such haste from Greece?

BASILIUS. My mother is a widow, Julian!

GREGORY. My father is feeble, both in body and mind; he needs my support.

JULIAN. Oh, but remain with me; only until to-morrow——!

GREGORY. Impossible; our travelling companions start at day-break.

JULIAN. At day-break? Before midnight the day might dawn for you.

BASILIUS. Julian, do not send me away in too great uneasiness. Tell me,—when Maximus has interpreted all riddles for you,—what then?

JULIAN. Do you remember that river Strabo writes about—that river which rises in the Lybian mountains? It grows, and grows in its course; but when it is at its greatest, it oozes into the desert sands, and buries itself in the entrails of the earth, whence it arose.

BASILIUS. You do not mean that you long for death, Julian?

JULIAN. What you slavishly hope for after death, it is the aim of the great mystery to win for all the initiated, here in our earthly life. It is regeneration that Maximus and his disciples seek,—it is our lost likeness to the godhead. Wherefore so full of doubt, my brothers? Why do you stand there, as though before something insurmountable? I know what I know. In each successive generation there has been *one* soul in whom the pure Adam has been born again; he was strong in Moses the law-giver; in the Macedonian Alexander he had power to subdue the world; he was well-nigh perfect in Jesus of Nazareth. But see, Basilius—(*He grasps him by the arm*)—all of them lacked what is promised to *me*—the pure woman!

BASILIUS (*freeing himself*). Julian, Julian!

GREGORY. Blasphemer—to this has your pride of heart brought you!

BASILIUS. Oh, Gregory, he is ill and beside himself!

JULIAN. Why all this scornful doubt? Is it my small stature that witnesses against me? Ha-ha; I tell you this gross and fleshly generation shall pass

away.   That which is to come shall be conceived
rather in the soul than in the body.   In the first
Adam, soul and body were equally balanced, as in
those statues of the god Apollo.   Since then, the
balance has not been maintained.   Was not Moses
tongue-tied?   Had not his arms to be supported
when he held them up in imprecation, there by
the Red Sea.   Did not the Macedonian need ever
to be fired by strong drinks, and other artificial
means?   And Jesus of Nazareth, too?   Was he not
feeble in body?   Did he not fall asleep in the ship
whilst the others kept awake?   Did he not faint
under the cross, that cross which the Jew Simon
carried with ease?   The two thieves did not faint.—
You call yourselves believers, and yet have so little
faith in miraculous revelation.   Wait, wait—you shall
see; the Bride shall surely be given me, and then—
hand in hand will we go forth to the east, where some
say Helios is born,—we will hide ourselves in the
wilderness, as the godhead hides itself, seek out the
grove on the banks of Euphrates, find it, and *there*
—oh glory!—thence shall a new race, perfect in beauty
and balance, go forth over the earth; there, ye book-
worshipping doubters, there shall the empire of the
spirit be founded!

BASILIUS.   Oh, well may I wring my hands in
sorrow for your sake.   Are you that same Julian who,
three years ago, came out of Constantinople?

JULIAN.   Then I was blind, as you are now; I
knew only the way that stops short at doctrine.

GREGORY.   Do you know where your present way
ends?

JULIAN. Where the path and the goal are one.—
For the last time, Gregory, Basilius—I implore you
to stay with me. The vision I had last night,—that
and many other things point to a mysterious bond
between us. To you, my Basilius, I had so much to
say. You are the head of your house; and who
knows whether all the blessings that are promised
me—— may not come through you and yours——

BASILIUS. Never! No one, with my good will,
shall have any part in your frenzies and your wild
dreams.

JULIAN. Ah, why talk of will? I see a hand
writing on the wall; soon I shall interpret the writing.

GREGORY. Come, Basilius.

JULIAN (*with outstretched arms*). Oh, my friends,
my friends!

GREGORY. Between us there is a gulf from this
day forward. (*He drags* BASILIUS *with him; both go
out to the right.*)

JULIAN (*looking after them*). Ay, go! Go, go!—
What do you two learned men know? What do you
bring from the city of wisdom? You, my strong,
masterful Gregory,—and you, Basilius, more girl than
man—you know only two streets in Athens, the
street to the schools, and the street to the church;
the third street, towards Eleusis and further, you
know nothing of, and still less——. Ah!

(*The curtain on the right is drawn aside. Two
servants in eastern costume bring in a tall, veiled
object, which they place in the corner, behind the
table. Shortly after, the* MYSTIC MAXIMUS
enters by the same door. He is a lean man, of

*middle height, with a bronzed, hawk-like face ;
his hair and beard are much grizzled, but his
thick eyebrows and moustache still retain their
pitch-black colour. He wears a pointed cap and
a long black robe ; in his hand he carries a
white staff.*)

(MAXIMUS *goes, without heeding* JULIAN, *up to
the veiled object, stops, and makes a sign to the
servants ; they retire noiselessly.*)

JULIAN (*softly*).   At last !

(MAXIMUS *draws the veil away, revealing a
bronze lamp on a high tripod ; then he takes
out a little silver pitcher, and pours oil into the
lamp-bowl. The lamp lights of itself, and burns
with a strong reddish glare.*)

JULIAN (*in eager expectancy*).   Is the time come ?

MAXIMUS (*without looking at him*).   Art thou pure
in soul and body ?

JULIAN.   I have fasted and anointed myself.

MAXIMUS.   Then may the night's solemnity
begin !

(*He gives a sign ; dancing-girls and flute-players
appear in the outer court. Music and dancing
continue during what follows.*)

JULIAN.   Maximus,—what is this ?

MAXIMUS.   Roses in the hair ! Sparkling wine !
See, see the beautiful limbs at play !

JULIAN.   And amid this whirl of the senses, you
would—— ?

MAXIMUS.   Sin lies only in thy sense of sinful-
ness.

JULIAN.   Roses in the hair ! Sparkling wine !

(*He casts himself down on one of the couches beside the table, drains a full goblet, puts it hastily from him, and asks:*) Ah! What was in the wine?

MAXIMUS. A spark from the fire Prometheus stole. (*He lies down at the opposite side of the table.*)

JULIAN. My senses exchange their functions; I hear brightness, and I see music.

MAXIMUS. Wine is the soul of the grape. The freed yet willing captive. Logos in Pan!

THE DANCING-GIRLS (*singing in the court*).

> Would'st thou know liberty?
> drain Bacchus' blood;—
> rock on the rhythm-sea,
> float with its flood!

JULIAN (*drinking*). Yes, yes; there is freedom in intoxication. Canst thou interpret this rapture?

MAXIMUS. This intoxication is thy marriage with nature's soul.

JULIAN. Sweet riddle; tempting, alluring——! What was that? Why didst thou laugh?

MAXIMUS. I?

JULIAN. There is whispering on my left hand! The silk cushions rustle——

(*Springing half up, with a pale face.*)
Maximus, we are not alone!

MAXIMUS (*loudly*). We are five at table!

JULIAN. Symposium with the spirits!

MAXIMUS. With the shades.

JULIAN. Name my guests!

MAXIMUS. Not now. Hark, hark!

JULIAN. What is that? There is a rushing, as of a storm through the house——

MAXIMUS (*shrieks*). Julian! Julian! Julian!

JULIAN. Speak, speak! What is befalling us?

MAXIMUS. The hour of annunciation is upon thee!

JULIAN (*springing up and shrinking far back from the table*). Ah!

> (*The table lamps seem on the point of extinction; over the great bronze lamp rises a bluish circle of light.*)

MAXIMUS (*casting himself wholly down*). Thine eye towards the light!

JULIAN. Yonder?

MAXIMUS. Yes, yes!

THE GIRLS' SONG (*low, from the court*).

> Night spreads her snares for thee,
> all-seeing night;
> laughing-eyed Luxury
> lures to delight.

JULIAN (*staring at the radiance*). Maximus! Maximus!

MAXIMUS (*softly*). Seest thou aught?

JULIAN. Yes.

MAXIMUS. What seest thou?

JULIAN. I see a shining countenance in the light.

MAXIMUS. Man, or woman?

JULIAN. I know not.

MAXIMUS. Speak to it.

JULIAN. Dare I?

MAXIMUS. Speak; speak!

JULIAN (*advancing*). Why was I born?

A VOICE IN THE LIGHT. To serve the spirit.

MAXIMUS. Does it answer?

JULIAN. Yes, yes.

MAXIMUS. Ask further.

JULIAN. What is my mission?

THE VOICE. To establish the empire.

JULIAN. What empire?

THE VOICE. The empire.

JULIAN. And by what way?

THE VOICE. By the way of freedom.

JULIAN. Speak clearly! What is the way of freedom?

THE VOICE. The way of necessity.

JULIAN. And by what power?

THE VOICE. By *willing*.

JULIAN. *What* shall I will?

THE VOICE. What thou must.

JULIAN. It grows pale; it vanishes——!

(*Coming closer.*)

Speak, speak! What must I will?

THE VOICE (*wailing*). Julian!

(*The circle of light passes away; the table lamps burn as before.*)

MAXIMUS (*looking up*). Gone?

JULIAN. Gone.

MAXIMUS. Dost thou *now* see clearly?

JULIAN. Now less than ever. I hang in the firmament over the yawning deep—midway between light and darkness.

(*He lies down again.*)

What is the empire?

MAXIMUS. There are three empires.

JULIAN. Three?

MAXIMUS. First that empire which was founded

on the tree of knowledge; then that which was founded on the tree of the cross——

JULIAN.   And the third?

MAXIMUS.   The third is the empire of the great mystery; that empire which shall be founded on the tree of knowledge and the tree of the cross together, because it hates and loves them both, and because it has its living Sources under Adam's grove and under Golgotha.

JULIAN.   And this empire shall come——?

MAXIMUS.   It stands on the threshold.   I have counted and counted——

JULIAN (*breaking off sharply*).   The whispering again!   Who are my guests?

MAXIMUS.   The three corner-stones under the wrath of necessity.

JULIAN.   Who, who?

MAXIMUS.   The three great helpers in denial.

JULIAN.   Name them!

MAXIMUS.   I cannot; I know them not;—but I could show them to thee——

JULIAN.   Then show me them!   At once, Maximus——!

MAXIMUS.   Beware——!

JULIAN.   At once; at once!   I will see them; I will speak with them, one by one.

MAXIMUS.   Thine be the blame.

(*He swings his staff, and calls.*)

Take shape, and come to light, thou first-elected lamb of sacrifice!

JULIAN.   Ah!

MAXIMUS (*with veiled face*).   What seest thou?

JULIAN (*in a low voice*). There he lies; just by the corner.—He is great as Hercules, and beautiful, —yet no, not——

(*Hesitatingly.*)

Speak to me, if thou canst!

A VOICE.   What wouldst thou know?

JULIAN.   What was thy task in life?

THE VOICE.   My sin.

JULIAN.   Why didst thou sin?

THE VOICE.   Why was I not my brother?

JULIAN.   Palter not with me.   Why didst thou sin?

THE VOICE.   Why was I myself?

JULIAN.   And what didst thou *will*, being thyself?

THE VOICE.   What I must.

JULIAN.   And wherefore must thou?

THE VOICE.   I was myself.

JULIAN.   Thou art sparing of words.

MAXIMUS (*without looking up*).   *In vino veritas.*

JULIAN.   Thou hast hit it, Maximus!

(*He pours forth a full goblet in front of the empty seat.*)

Bathe thee in the fumes of wine, my pallid guest! Refresh thee. Feel, feel—it mounts aloft like the smoke of sacrifice.

THE VOICE.   The smoke of sacrifice does not always *mount.*

JULIAN.   Why does that scar redden on thy brow? Nay, nay,—do not pull the hair over it.   What is it?

THE VOICE.   The mark.

JULIAN.   Hm; no more of that.   And what fruit has thy sin borne?

THE VOICE.   The most glorious.

JULIAN.   What callest thou the most glorious?

THE VOICE.   Life.

JULIAN.   And the ground of life?

THE VOICE.   Death.

JULIAN.   And of death?

THE VOICE (*losing itself as in a sigh*).   Ah, *that* is the riddle!

JULIAN.   Gone!

MAXIMUS (*looking up*).   Gone?

JULIAN.   Yes.

MAXIMUS.   Didst thou know him?

JULIAN.   Yes.

MAXIMUS.   Who was it?

JULIAN.   Cain.

MAXIMUS.   By *that* way, then!   Ask no more!

JULIAN (*with an impatient gesture*).   The second, Maximus!

MAXIMUS.   No, no, no;—I will not!

JULIAN.   The second, I say!   Thou hast sworn that I should fathom the meaning of certain things. The second, Maximus!   I will see him; I will know my guests!

MAXIMUS.   Thou hast willed it, not I.

(*He swings his staff.*)

Arise and come to light, thou willing slave, thou who didst help in the next great world-transformation!

JULIAN (*gazes for a moment into the empty space; suddenly he makes a gesture of repulsion towards the seat at his side, and says in a low voice :*) No nearer!

MAXIMUS (*who has turned his back*).   Dost thou see him?

JULIAN. Yes.

MAXIMUS. How dost thou see him?

JULIAN. I see him as a red-bearded man. His clothes are torn, and he has a rope round his neck.——

Speak to him, Maximus!

MAXIMUS. Thou must speak.

JULIAN. What wast thou in life?

A VOICE (*close beside him*). The twelfth wheel of the world-chariot.

JULIAN. The twelfth? The fifth is reckoned useless.

THE VOICE. But for me, whither had the chariot rolled?

JULIAN. Whither did it roll by means of thee?

THE VOICE. Into glorification.

JULIAN. Why didst thou help?

THE VOICE. Because I willed.

JULIAN. What didst thou will?

THE VOICE. What I must.

JULIAN. Who chose thee?

THE VOICE. The master.

JULIAN. Did the master foreknow when he chose thee?

THE VOICE. Ah, *that* is the riddle!

(*A short silence.*)

MAXIMUS. Thou art silent.

JULIAN. He is no longer here.

MAXIMUS (*looking up*). Didst thou know him?

JULIAN. Yes.

MAXIMUS. How was he called in life?

JULIAN. Judas Iscariot.

Maximus (*springing up*).   The abyss is blossoming; the night betrays itself!

Julian (*shrieks to him*).   Forth with the third!

Maximus.   He shall come!

  (*He swings the staff.*)

Come forth, thou third corner-stone!   Come forth, thou third great freed-man under necessity!

  (*He casts himself down again on the couch, and turns his face away.*)

What seest thou?

Julian.   I see nothing.

Maximus.   And yet he is here.

  (*He swings his staff again.*)

By Solomon's seal, by the eye in the triangle—I conjure thee—come to light!—— ——

What seest thou now?

Julian.   Nothing, nothing!

Maximus (*swinging his staff again*).   Come forth, thou—— !

  (*He stops suddenly, utters a shriek, and springs up from the table.*)

Ah! lightning in the night!   I see it;—all art is in vain.

Julian (*rising*).   Why?   Speak, speak!

Maximus.   The third is not yet among the shades.

Julian.   He lives?

Maximus.   Yes, he lives.

Julian.   And *here*, sayest thou——!

Maximus.   Here, or there, or among the unborn; —I know not——

Julian (*rushing at him*).   Thou liest!   Thou art deceiving me!   *Here*, here thou saidst—— !

MAXIMUS.   Let go my cloak!

JULIAN.   Then it is thou, or I!   But which of us?

MAXIMUS.   Let go my cloak, Julian!

JULIAN.   Which of us?   Which?   All hangs on that!

MAXIMUS.   Thou hast seen more clearly than I. What said the voice in the light?

JULIAN.   The voice in the light——!
   (*With a shriek.*)
The empire!   The   empire?   To found   the empire——!

MAXIMUS.   The third empire!

JULIAN.   No; a thousand times no!   Away, corrupter!   I renounce thee and all thy works——

MAXIMUS.   And necessity?

JULIAN.   I defy necessity!   I will not serve it!   I am free, free, free!
   (*A noise outside; the dancing-girls and flute-players take to flight.*)

MAXIMUS (*listening on the right*).   What is this alarm and shrieking——?

JULIAN.   Strange men are forcing their way into the house——

MAXIMUS.   They are maltreating your servants; they will murder us!

JULIAN.   Do not fear; us no one can hurt.

THE CHAMBERLAIN EUTHERIUS (*comes hastily across the court*).   My lord, my lord!

JULIAN.   Who is making that noise without?

EUTHERIUS.   Strange men have surrounded the house; they have set a watch at all the doors; they are making their way in—almost by force.   Here they come, my lord!   Here they are!

(*The* QUÆSTOR LEONTES, *with a large and richly-attired retinue, enters from the right.*)

LEONTES.   Pardon, a thousand pardons, my noble lord——

JULIAN (*falling a step backwards*).   What do I see!

LEONTES.   Your servants would have hindered me from entering ; and as my errand was of the first importance——

JULIAN.   You here, in Ephesus, my excellent Leontes !

LEONTES.   I have travelled night and day, as the Emperor's emissary.

JULIAN (*turning pale*).   To me ?   What does the Emperor want of me ?   I swear I am conscious of no crime.   I am sick, Leontes !   This man—(*Pointing to* MAXIMUS)—attends me as my physician.

LEONTES.   Permit me, my gracious lord——!

JULIAN.   Why do you force your way into my house ?   What is the Emperor's will ?

LEONTES.   His will is to gladden you, my lord, by great and weighty commands.

JULIAN.   I pray you, let me know what commands you bring.

LEONTES (*kneels*).   My most noble lord,—with praise to your good fortune and my own, I hail you Cæsar.

THE QUÆSTOR'S FOLLOWERS.   Long live Julian Cæsar !

MAXIMUS.   Cæsar !

JULIAN (*retreating, with an exclamation*).   Cæsar ! Stand up, Leontes !   What madness are you talking !

LEONTES.   I do but deliver the Emperor's commands.

JULIAN. I—I Cæsar!—Ah, where is Gallus?

LEONTES. Oh, do not ask me.

JULIAN. Where is Gallus? Tell me, I conjure you,—where is Gallus?

LEONTES (*standing up*). Gallus Cæsar is with his beloved wife.

JULIAN. Dead?

LEONTES. In bliss, with his wife.

JULIAN. Dead! dead! Gallus dead! Dead in the midst of his triumphal progress! But when,— and where?

LEONTES. Oh, my dear lord, spare me——

GREGORY OF NAZIANZUS (*struggling with the guards at the door*). I *must* go to him! Aside, I say! —Julian!

JULIAN. Gregory, brother,—you come again after all!

GREGORY. Is it true, what rumour is spreading like a storm of arrows over the city?

JULIAN. I am myself transfixed by one of its arrows. Dare I believe in this blending of good and evil fortune?

GREGORY. For Christ's sake, bid the tempter avaunt!

JULIAN. The Emperor's commands, Gregory!

GREGORY. You will trample on your brother's bloody corpse——

JULIAN. Bloody——?

GREGORY. Do you not know it? Gallus Cæsar was murdered.

JULIAN (*clasping his hands*). Murdered?

LEONTES. Ah, who is this audacious——?

Julian. Murdered? Murdered? (*To* Leontes.)
He lies, does he not?

Leontes. Gallus Cæsar has fallen by his own
misdeeds.

Julian. Murdered!—Who murdered him?

Leontes. The deed was prompted by sheer
necessity, my noble lord! Gallus Cæsar madly mis-
used his power here in the East. He was no longer
content with his rank as Cæsar. His conduct, both
in Constantinople and elsewhere on his progress,
showed clearly what was in his mind.

Julian. I do not ask about his crime; I want to
know the rest.

Leontes. Oh, let me spare a brother's ears.

Julian. A brother's ears can bear what a son's
ears have borne. Who killed him?

Leontes. The tribune Scudilo, who escorted
him, thought it advisable to have him executed.

Julian. Where? Not in Rome?

Leontes. No, my lord; it happened on the
journey thither,—in the city of Pola, in Illyria.

Julian (*bowing himself*). The Emperor is great
and righteous.—The last of the race, Gregory!—
The Emperor Constantius is great.

Leontes (*taking a purple robe from one of his
attendants*). Noble Cæsar, deign to array yourself——

Julian. Red! Away with it! Was it this he
wore at Pola——?

Leontes. This comes fresh from Sidon.

Julian (*with a look at* Maximus.) From Sidon!
The purple robe——!

Maximus. Apollinaris's vision!

GREGORY. Julian ! Julian !

LEONTES. See, this is sent you by your kinsman, the Emperor. He bids me say that, childless as he is, he looks to you to heal this the deepest wound of his life. He wishes to see you in Rome. Afterwards, it is his will that you should go, as Cæsar, to Gaul. The border tribes of the Alemanni have passed the Rhine, and made a dangerous inroad into the empire. He builds securely on the success of your campaign against the barbarians. Certain things have been revealed to him in dreams, and his last word to me at my departure was that he was assured you would succeed in establishing the empire.

JULIAN. Establish the empire! The voice in the light, Maximus !

MAXIMUS. Sign against sign.

LEONTES. How, noble Cæsar ?

JULIAN. I also have been forewarned of certain things ; but this——

GREGORY. Say no, Julian ! They are the wings of destruction you would fasten on your shoulders.

LEONTES. Who are you, that defy the Emperor ?

GREGORY. My name is Gregory ; I am the son of the Bishop of Nazianzus ;—do with me what you will.

JULIAN. He is my friend and brother ; let no one touch him !

(*A great crowd has meanwhile filled the outer court.*)

BASILIUS OF CÆSAREA (*making his way through the crowd*). Do not assume the purple, Julian !

JULIAN. You too, my faithful Basilius.

BASILIUS. Reject it ! For the Lord God's sake——

JULIAN.   What terrifies you so in this?

BASILIUS.   The horrors that will follow.

JULIAN.   Through me shall the empire be established.

BASILIUS.   Christ's empire?

JULIAN.   The Emperor's great and beautiful empire.

BASILIUS.   Was it that empire which shone before your eyes when, as a child, you preached the word beside the Cappadocian martyrs' graves? Was it that empire you set forth from Constantinople to establish on earth? Was it that empire—?

JULIAN.   Mists, mists;—all that lies behind me like a wild dream.

BASILIUS.   It were better for you that you lay at the bottom of the sea, with a mill-stone about your neck, than that that dream should lie behind you.—— Do you not see the work of the tempter? All the glory of the world is laid at your feet.

MAXIMUS.   Sign against sign, Cæsar!

JULIAN.   One word, Leontes!

(*Seizing his hand and drawing him aside.*)

Whither do you lead me?

LEONTES.   To Rome, my lord!

JULIAN.   That is not what I ask. Whither do you lead me: to fortune and power,—or to the shambles?

LEONTES.   Oh, my lord, a doubt so insulting——

JULIAN.   My brother's body has scarcely mouldered yet.

LEONTES.   I can silence all doubt. (*Taking out a paper.*) This letter from the Emperor, which I would rather have given you in private——

JULIAN. A letter? What does he write?——
(*He opens the paper and reads.*)
Ah, Helena! Oh, Leontes! Helena,—Helena to me!

LEONTES. The Emperor gives her to you, my lord! He gives you his beloved sister, for whom Gallus Cæsar begged in vain.

JULIAN. Helena to me! The unattainable attained!—But she, Leontes——?

LEONTES. At my departure he took the Princess by the hand and led her to me. A flush of maiden blood swept over her lovely cheeks, she cast down her eyes, and said: "Greet my dear kinsman, and let him know that he has ever been the man whom——"

JULIAN. Go on, Leontes!

LEONTES. There she stopped, the modest and pure woman.

JULIAN. The pure woman!—How marvellously is all fulfilled!
(*He calls loudly.*)
On with the purple!

MAXIMUS. You have chosen?

JULIAN. Chosen, Maximus!

MAXIMUS. Chosen, in spite of sign against sign?

JULIAN. Here is no sign against sign. Maximus, seer though you be, you have been blind! Robe me in the purple!

(*The* QUÆSTOR LEONTES *attires him in the mantle.*)

BASILIUS. It is done!

MAXIMUS (*murmurs to himself with upstretched hands*). Light and victory be to him who *wills!*

LEONTES.   And now to the Governor's palace ; the people would fain greet Cæsar.

JULIAN.   Cæsar, in his exaltation, remains what he was,—the poor lover of wisdom, who owes all to the Emperor's grace.—To the Governor's palace, my friends!

VOICES AMONG THE QUÆSTOR'S ATTENDANTS. Room, room for Julian Cæsar !

(All go out through the court, amid the acclamations of the crowd; only GREGORY *and* BASILIUS *remain behind.)*

BASILIUS.   Gregory!   Whatever comes of this— let us hold together.

GREGORY.   Here is my hand.

Act Fourth.

(At Lutetia, in Gaul. A hall in Cæsar's palace, "The Warm Baths," outside the city. Entrance door in the back; to the right, another smaller door; in front, on the left, is a window with curtains.)

*(*THE PRINCESS HELENA, *richly attired, with pearls in her hair, sits in an arm-chair, and looks out of the window. Her slave,* MYRRHA, *stands opposite her, and holds the curtain aside.)*

THE PRINCESS HELENA. What a multitude! The whole city is streaming out to meet them.— Hark! Myrrha,—do you not hear flutes and drums?

MYRRHA. Yes, I think I can hear——

HELENA. You lie! The noise is too great; you can hear nothing. (*Springing up.*) Oh, this torturing uncertainty! Not to know whether he comes as a conqueror or as a fugitive.

MYRRHA. Do not be afraid, my noble mistress; Cæsar has always returned a conqueror.

HELENA. Ay, hitherto; after all his lesser encounters. But this time, Myrrha! This great, fearful battle. All these conflicting rumours. If Cæsar were victorious, why should he have sent that letter to the city magistrates, forbidding them to meet him with shows of honour outside the gates?

MYRRHA. Oh, you know well, my lady, how little your noble husband cares for such things.

HELENA.   Yes yes, that is true.   And if he had been defeated—in Rome they must have known it—would the Emperor have sent us this envoy who is to arrive to-day, and whose courier has brought me all these rich ornaments and gifts?   Ah, Eutherius! Well?   Well?

THE CHAMBERLAIN EUTHERIUS (*from the back*). My Princess, it is impossible to obtain any trustworthy intelligence——

HELENA.   Impossible?   You are deceiving me! The soldiers themselves must surely know——

EUTHERIUS.   They are only barbarian auxiliaries who are coming in—Batavians and others—and they know nothing.

HELENA (*wringing her hands*).   Oh, have I deserved this torture?   Sweet, holy Christ, have I not called upon Thee day and night——

(*She listens and screams out.*)

Ah, my Julian!   I hear him!—Julian ; my beloved!

JULIAN CÆSAR (*in dusty armour, enters hastily by the back*).   Helena!

EUTHERIUS.   My noble Cæsar!

JULIAN (*vehemently embracing the Princess*). Helena!—Bar all the doors, Eutherius!

HELENA.   Defeated!   Pursued!

EUTHERIUS.   My lord!

JULIAN.   Double guards at all the doors ; let no one pass!   Tell me : has any emissary arrived from the Emperor?

EUTHERIUS.   No, my lord ; but one is expected.

JULIAN.   Go, go!   (*To the Slave.*)   Away with you.

(EUTHERIUS *and* MYRRHA *go out by the back.*)

HELENA (*sinking into the arm-chair*).   Then it is all over with us!

JULIAN (*drawing the curtains together*).   Who knows?   If we are cautious the storm may yet——

HELENA.   After such a defeat——?

JULIAN.   Defeat?   What are you talking of, my beloved?

HELENA.   Have not the Alemanni defeated you?

JULIAN.   If they had, you would not have seen me alive.

HELENA (*springing up*).   Then, Lord of Heaven, what has happened?

JULIAN (*softly*).   The worst, Helena;—a magnificent victory.

HELENA.   Victory, you say!   A magnificent victory?   You have conquered, and yet——?

JULIAN.   You cannot understand my position. You know only the gilded outside of all a Cæsar's misery.

HELENA.   Julian!

JULIAN.   Can you blame me for having hidden it from you?   Did not both duty and shame bid me——?   Ah,—what is this?   What a change——!

HELENA.   What?   What?

JULIAN.   How these months have changed you! Helena, you have been ill?

HELENA.   No, no; but tell me——

JULIAN.   Yes, you have been ill!   You must be ill now;—your fever-flushed temples, the blue rings round your eyes——

HELENA.   Oh it is nothing, my beloved!   Do

not look at me, Julian! It is only anxiety and wakeful nights on your account; ardent prayers to the blessed one on the cross——

JULIAN. Spare yourself, my precious one; it is more than doubtful whether such zeal is of any avail.

HELENA. Fie; you speak impiously.—But tell me of your own affairs, Julian! I implore you, hide nothing from me.

JULIAN. Nothing *can* now be hidden. Since the Empress's death, I have taken no single step here in Gaul that has not been evilly interpreted at court. If I went cautiously to work with the Alemanni, I was called timorous or inert. They laughed at the awkwardness of the philosopher in his coat of mail. If I gained an advantage over the barbarians, I was told that I ought to have done more.

HELENA. But all your friends in the army——

JULIAN. Who do you think are my friends in the army? I have not one, my beloved Helena! Yes, one single man—the knight Sallust, of Perusia, to whom, during our marriage festivities at Milan, I had to refuse a slight request. He magnanimously came to me in the camp, reminded me of our old friendship in Athens, and begged leave to stand at my side in all dangers. But what does Sallust count for at the imperial court? He is one of those whom they call heathens. He can be of no help to me.—And the others! Arbetio, the tribune, who left me in the lurch when I was shut up in Senones! Old Severus, burdened with the sense of his own incapacity, yet unable to reconcile himself to my new policy! Or do you think I can depend on Florentius, the captain of the Prætorians? I tell you, that turbulent man is filled with the most unbridled ambitions.

HELENA. Ah, Julian!

JULIAN (*pacing up and down*). If I could only get to the bottom of their intrigues! Every week secret letters pass between the camp and Rome. Everything I do is set down and distorted. No slave in the empire is so fettered as Cæsar. Would you believe it, Helena, even my cook has to abide by a bill of fare sent to him by the Emperor; I cannot alter or add or take away a single dish!

HELENA. And all this you have borne in silence—?

JULIAN. All know it, except you. All mock at Cæsar's powerlessness. I will bear it no longer! I will not bear it!

HELENA. But the great battle—? Tell me,— has rumour exaggerated—?

JULIAN. Rumour *could* not exaggerate.—Hush; what was that? (*Listening at the door.*) No, no; I only thought——

I may say that in these months I have done all that mortal man could do. Step by step, and in spite of all hindrances in my own camp, I drove the barbarians back towards the eastern frontier. Before Argentoratum, with the Rhine at his back, King Knodomar gathered all his forces together. Five kings and ten lesser princes supported him. But before he had collected the necessary boats for his retreat in case of need, I led my army to the attack.

HELENA. My hero, my Julian!

JULIAN. Lupicin, with the spearmen and the light-armed troops, outflanked the enemy on the north; the old legions, under Severus, drove the barbarians more and more to the eastward, towards the river; our allies, the Batavians, under the faithful Baina-baudes, stood gallantly by the legions; and when Knodomar saw that his case was desperate, he tried to make off southwards, in order to reach the islands. But before he could escape, I sent Florentius to intercept him with the Prætorian guards and the cavalry. Helena, I dare not say it aloud, but certain it is that treachery or envy had nearly robbed me of the fruits of victory. The Roman cavalry recoiled time after time before the barbarians, who threw themselves down on the ground and stabbed the horses in the belly. Defeat stared us in the face——

HELENA. But the God of Battles was with you!

JULIAN. I seized a standard, fired the Imperial Guards by my shouts, made them a hasty address, which was, perhaps, not quite unworthy of a more enlightened audience, and then, rewarded by the soldiers' acclamations, I plunged into the thickest of the fight.

HELENA. Julian! Oh, you do not love me!

JULIAN. At that moment you were not in my thoughts. I wished to die; for I despaired of victory. But it came, my love! It seemed as though lightnings of terror flashed from our lance-points. I saw Knodomar, that redoubtable warrior—ah, you have seen him too—I saw him fleeing on foot from the battle-field, and with him his brother Vestralp, and the kings Hortar and Suomar, and all who had not fallen by our swords.

HELENA.   Oh, I can see it; I can see it!   Blessed Saviour, thou didst again send forth the destroying angels of the Milvian bridge!

JULIAN.   Never have I heard such shrieks of despair; never seen such gaping wounds as those we trampled on, as we waded through the slain.   The river did the rest; the drowning men struggled among themselves until they rolled over, and went to the bottom.   Most of the princes fell living into our hands; Knodomar himself had sought refuge in a bed of reeds; one of his attendants betrayed him, and our bowmen sent a shower of arrows into his hiding-place, but without hitting him.   Then he gave himself up of his own accord.

HELENA.   And after such a victory do you not feel secure?

JULIAN (*hesitatingly*).   On the very evening of the victory an accident occurred, a trifle——

HELENA.   An accident?

JULIAN.   I prefer to call it so.   In Athens we used to speculate much upon Nemesis.—My victory was so overwhelming, Helena; my position had, as it were, lost its equipoise; I do not know——

HELENA.   Oh, speak out; you put me on the rack!

JULIAN.   It was a trifle, I tell you.   I ordered the captive Knodomar to be brought before me, in the presence of the army.   Before the battle, he had threatened that I should be flayed alive if I fell into his hands.   Now he came towards me with uncertain steps, his whole body trembling; crushed by disaster, as the barbarians are apt to be, he cast himself down before me, embraced my knees, shed tears, and begged for his life.

HELENA.   His mighty limbs quivering with dread —I can see the prostrate Knodomar.—Did you kill him, my beloved?

JULIAN.   I could not kill that man.   I granted him his life, and promised to send him as a prisoner to Rome.

HELENA.   Without torturing him?

JULIAN.   Prudence bade me deal mercifully with him.   But then—I cannot tell how it happened— with a cry of overflowing gladness, the barbarian sprang up, stretched his pinioned hands into the air, and, half-ignorant as he is of our language, shouted at the top of his voice: "Praise be to thee, Julian, thou mighty Emperor!"

HELENA.   Ah!

JULIAN.   My attendants were inclined to laugh; but the barbarian's shout flew like a lightning-flash through the surrounding soldiery, kindling as it went. "Long live the Emperor Julian," repeated the nearest; and the cry spread around in wider and ever wider circles to the furthest distance;—it was as though a Titan had hurled a mountain out into the ocean;— oh, my beloved, forgive me the heathen similitude, but——

HELENA.   Emperor Julian!   He said Emperor Julian!

JULIAN.   What did the rude Aleman know of Constantius, whom he had never seen?   I, his con- queror, was in his eyes the greatest——

HELENA.   Yes, yes; but the soldiers——?

JULIAN. I rebuked them sternly; for I saw at a glance how Florentius, Severus, and certain others stood silently by, white with fear and wrath.

HELENA. Yes, yes, *they*—but not the soldiers.

JULIAN. Before a single night had passed my secret foes had distorted the affair. "Cæsar has induced Knodomar to proclaim him Emperor," the story went, "and in return he has granted the barbarian his life." And in this inverted form the news has reached Rome.

HELENA. Are you sure of that? And through whom?

JULIAN. Ah, through whom? through whom? I myself wrote at once to the Emperor and told him everything, but——

HELENA. Well—and how did he answer?

JULIAN. As usual. You know his ominous silence when he means to strike a blow.

HELENA. I believe you misinterpret all this. It must be so. You will see his envoy will soon assure you of——

JULIAN. I *am* assured, Helena! Here, in my bosom, I have some intercepted letters, which——

HELENA. Oh, Lord my God, let me see!

JULIAN. By-and-by.

(*He walks up and down.*)

And all this after the services I have rendered him! I have put a stop to the inroads of the Alemanni for years to come, whilst he himself has suffered defeat upon defeat on the Danube, and the army in Asia seems to make no way against the Persians. Shame and disaster on all sides, except here, where he placed a reluctant philosopher at the head of affairs. Yet none the less am I the scorn of the court. Even after the last great victory, they have lampooned me, and called me Victorinus! This must come to an end.

HELENA.   So I, too, think.

JULIAN.   What is the title of Cæsar worth on such terms?

HELENA.   No; you are right, Julian; things cannot go on thus!

JULIAN (*stopping*).   Helena, could you follow me?

HELENA (*softly*).   Have no fear for me; I will not fail you.

JULIAN.   Then away from all this thankless toil; away to the solitude I have sighed for so long——!

HELENA.   What do you say?   Solitude!

JULIAN.   With you, my beloved; and with my dear books, that I have so seldom been able to open here, save only on my sleepless nights.

HELENA (*looking him down from head to foot*). Ah, that is what you mean!

JULIAN.   What else?

HELENA.   Quite so; what else?

JULIAN.   Yes,—I ask what else?

HELENA (*coming nearer*).   Julian—how did the barbarian king hail you?

JULIAN (*shrinking*).   Helena!

HELENA (*still nearer*).   What was the name that echoed through the ranks of the legions?

JULIAN.   Rash woman; there may be an eavesdropper at every door!

HELENA.   Why should you fear eavesdroppers?
Is not God's grace upon you?   Have you not been
victorious in every encounter?—I see the Saviour
calling upon you; I see the angel with the flaming
sword, who cleared the way for my father when he
drove Maxentius into the Tiber!

JULIAN.   Shall I rebel against the ruler of the
empire?

HELENA.   Only against those who stand between
you.   Oh, go, go; smite them with the lightning of
your wrath; put an end to this harassing, joyless
life!   Gaul is an outer wilderness.   I am so cold
here, Julian!   I pine for home, for the sunshine of
Rome and Greece.

JULIAN.   For home and your brother?

HELENA (*softly*).   Constantius is a wreck.

JULIAN.   Helena!

HELENA.   I can bear it no longer, I tell you.
Time is flying.   Eusebia is gone; her empty seat
invites me to honour and greatness, while I am
ageing——

JULIAN.   You are not ageing; you are young and
fair!

HELENA.   No, no, no!   Time speeds; I cannot
bear this patiently; life slips away from me!

JULIAN (*gazing at her*).   How temptingly beautiful,
how divine you are!

HELENA (*clinging to him*).   Am I, Julian?

JULIAN (*embracing her*).   You are the only woman
I have loved,—the only one who has loved me.

HELENA.   I am older than you.   I will not age
still more.   When all is over, then——

JULIAN (*tearing himself away*).   Hush!   I will hear no more.

HELENA (*following him*).   Constantius is dying by inches ; he hangs by a hair over the grave.   Oh, my beloved Julian, you have the soldiers on your side——

JULIAN.   No more, no more!

HELENA.   He can bear no excitement.   What is there, then, to recoil from ?   I mean nothing bloody. Fie, how can you think so ?   The fright will be enough ; it will fold him in its embrace and gently end his sufferings.

JULIAN.   Do you forget the invisible bodyguard around the Lord's anointed ?

HELENA.   Christ is good.   Oh, be pious, Julian, and He will forgive much.   I will help.   Prayers shall go up for you.   Praised be the saints!   Praised be the martyrs!   Trust me, we will atone for everything later.   Give me the Alemanni to convert ; I will send out priests among them ; they shall bow under the mercy of the cross.

JULIAN.   The Alemanni will not bow.

HELENA.   Then they shall die!   Like sweet incense shall their blood rise up to Him, the blessed One.   We will magnify His glory ; His praise shall be made manifest in us.   I myself will do my part. The women of the Alemanni shall be my care.   If they will not bow, they shall be offered up!   And then, my Julian—when next you see me—— ; young, young once more!   Give me the women of the Alemanni, my beloved!   Blood—it would be no murder, and the remedy is a sovereign one—a bath of young virgins' blood——

JULIAN.   Helena, the thought is crime!

HELENA.   Is it sin to commit crime for your sake?

JULIAN.   You beautiful, you peerless one!

HELENA (*bowing herself down over his hands*).   My lord, before God and men!—Do not draw back this time, Julian! My hero, my Emperor! I see heaven open. Priests shall sing praises to Christ; my women shall assemble in prayer. (*With upraised arms.*) Oh thou blessed One! Oh thou God of hosts,—thou, in whose hand lie favour and victory——

JULIAN (*with a look towards the door, exclaims*). Helena!

HELENA.   Ah!

THE CHAMBERLAIN EUTHERIUS (*from the back*). My lord, the Emperor's emissary——

JULIAN.   Is he come?

EUTHERIUS.   Yes, my lord!

JULIAN.   His name? Who is he?

EUTHERIUS.   The tribune Decentius.

HELENA.   Indeed! The pious Decentius!

JULIAN.   Has he talked with any one?

EUTHERIUS.   With no one, my lord; he has this moment arrived.

JULIAN.   I will see him at once. And listen; one thing more. Summon the captains and officers to me here.

EUTHERIUS.   It is well, most gracious Lord! (*He goes out by the back.*)

JULIAN.   Now, my Helena, now, we shall see——

HELENA (*softly*).   Whatever happens, do not forget that you can depend upon the soldiers.

JULIAN. Ah, depend, depend—— ; I am not sure that I can depend on any one.

(*The* TRIBUNE DECENTIUS *enters from the back.*)

HELENA (*meeting him*). Welcome, noble Decentius! A Roman face,—and, above all, this face,—oh! it sheds genial sunlight over our inclement Gaul.

DECENTIUS. The Emperor meets your longing and your hope half-way, noble Princess! We may hope that Gaul will not much longer hold you in its chains.

HELENA. Say you so, messenger of gladness? So the Emperor still thinks lovingly of me? How is it with his health?

JULIAN. Go, go, my beloved Helena!

DECENTIUS. The Emperor's health is certainly no worse.

HELENA. No, surely not? I thought as much. All these alarming rumours—— ; God be praised that they were but rumours! Thank him most lovingly, good Decentius! And let me thank you too. What rich presents have heralded your coming! Imperial —— no, let me say brotherly gifts indeed! Two shining black Nubians,—you should see them, my Julian!—and pearls! See, I am wearing them already. And fruits,—sweet, luscious fruits ; peaches from Damascus, peaches in chalices of gold! How they will refresh me ;—fruit, fruit; I am pining away here in Gaul.

JULIAN. A feast shall end the day ; but business first. Go, my precious wife!

HELENA. I go to the church,—to pray for my brother and for all good hopes. (*She goes out to the right.*)

JULIAN (*after an instant's pause*).   A message, or letters?

DECENTIUS.   Letters.   (*He hands him a roll of paper.*)

JULIAN (*reads, represses a smile, and holds out his hand*).   More!

DECENTIUS.   Noble Cæsar, that is well-nigh all.

JULIAN.   Indeed?   Has the Emperor sent his friend all this long way only to——?

(*He bursts into a short laugh, and then walks up and down.*)

Had Knodomar, the King of the Alemanni, arrived in Rome before you left?

DECENTIUS.   Yes, noble Cæsar!

JULIAN.   And how does he fare in the strange land, ignorant as he is of the language?   For he knows nothing of it, Decentius!   He was positively a laughing-stock to my soldiers.   Only think, he mixed up two such common words as Emperor and Cæsar.

DECENTIUS (*shrugging his shoulders*).   A barbarian. What can one expect?

JULIAN.   No, what can one expect?   But the Emperor has received him graciously?

DECENTIUS.   Knodomar is dead, my lord!

JULIAN (*stopping suddenly*).   Knodomar dead?

DECENTIUS.   Dead, in the foreigners' quarters, on the Cœlian hill.

JULIAN.   Dead?   Indeed!—Ah, the Roman air is unwholesome.

DECENTIUS.   The King of the Alemanni died of home-sickness, my lord!   The longing for kindred and freedom——

JULIAN. ——wastes a man away, Decentius; yes, yes, I know that.—I should not have sent him living to Rome. I should have had him killed here.

DECENTIUS. Cæsar's heart is merciful.

JULIAN. Hm——! Home-sickness? Indeed!
  (*To the Master of the Horse*, SINTULA, *who enters by the back.*)

Are you there, old faun? Tempt me no more. (*To* DECENTIUS.) Since the battle at Argentoratum, he is always talking to me of the triumphal chariot and the white horses. (*To* SINTULA.) It would be like Phaeton's career with the Lybian sun-horses. How did it end? Have you forgotten—have you forgotten your heathendom, I had almost said?—Pardon me, Decentius, for wounding your pious ear.

DECENTIUS. Cæsar delights his servant's ear; he does not wound it.

JULIAN. Yes, yes; bear with Cæsar's jesting. I really do not know how else to take the matter.—Here they are.

  (SEVERUS *and* FLORENTIUS, *together with other captains and gentlemen of Cæsar's court, enter from the back.*)

JULIAN (*advancing to receive them*). Greetings to you, brothers in arms and friends! Do not blame me too much for summoning you hither, straight from the dust and toil of the march; I should certainly not have grudged you some hours' rest; but——

FLORENTIUS. Has anything important happened, my lord?

JULIAN. Yes, indeed there has. Can you tell me
—what was lacking to complete Cæsar's happiness?

FLORENTIUS. What should be lacking to complete
Cæsar's happiness?

JULIAN. *Now*, nothing. (*To* DECENTIUS.) The
army has demanded that I should enter the city in
triumph. They would have had me pass through
the gates of Lutetia at the head of the legions.
Captive barbarian princes, with pinioned hands, were
to march beside my chariot-wheels ; women and
slaves from twenty conquered peoples were to follow,
crowded closely together, head against head——
(*Breaking off suddenly.*) Rejoice, my valiant fellow-
soldiers ; here you see the Tribune Decentius, the
Emperor's trusted friend and councillor. He has
arrived this morning, with gifts and greetings from
Rome.

FLORENTIUS. Ah, then indeed nothing can be
lacking to complete Cæsar's happiness.

SEVERUS (*softly to* FLORENTIUS). Incomprehensible! Then he is in the Emperor's good graces again!

FLORENTIUS (*aside*). Oh, this vacillating Emperor!

JULIAN. You seem all to be struck dumb with
astonishment.—They think the Emperor has done too
much, Decentius!

FLORENTIUS. How can Cæsar think such a
thought?

SEVERUS. Too much, noble Cæsar? By no means.
Who doubts that the Emperor knows how to set due
bounds to his favour?

FLORENTIUS. This is certainly a rare and remarkable distinction——

Severus. I should call it exceedingly rare and
remarkable——

Florentius. And especially does it afford a
striking proof that our august Emperor's mind is free
from all jealousy——

Severus. An unexampled proof, I venture to
call it.

Florentius. But then, what has not Cæsar
achieved in these few years in Gaul?

Julian. A year-long dream, dear friends! I have
accomplished nothing. Nothing, nothing.

Florentius. All this your modesty counts as
nothing? What was the army when you took
command? A disorderly rabble——

Severus. ——without coherence, without discip-
line, without direction——

Julian. You exaggerate, Severus!

Florentius. And was it not with this undiscip-
lined rabble that you took the field against the Alemanni? Did you not win battle after battle with these
levies, till your victories transformed them into an
invincible host? Did you not retake Colonia
Agrippina——?

Julian. Come come, you see with the eye of
friendship, my Florentius!—Or is it really so? Is it
a fact, that I drove the barbarians out of the islands
of the Rhine! That I placed the ruined Tres
Tabernæ in a posture of defence, making it a bulwark
of the empire? Is it really so?

Florentius. What, my lord! Can you be in
doubt as to so great deeds?

Julian. No, I cannot but think—— And the

battle of Argentoratum? Was I not there? I cannot
help fancying that I defeated Knodomar. And after
the victory——; Florentius, have I dreamt it, or did
I rebuild Trajan's fortress, when we marched into
German territory?

FLORENTIUS. Noble Cæsar, is there any man so
mad as to deny you the honour of these exploits?

SEVERUS (*to* DECENTIUS). I praise the destiny
that has vouchsafed my old age so victorious a leader.

FLORENTIUS (*also to the Tribune*). I dare scarcely
think what turn this inroad of the Alemanni might
have taken, but for Cæsar's courage and conduct.

MANY COURTIERS (*pressing forward*). Yes, yes;
Cæsar is great!

OTHERS (*clapping their hands*). Cæsar is peerless!

JULIAN (*looks for a time alternately at* DECENTIUS
*and the others; thereupon breaks out into a loud,
short laugh*). So blind is friendship, Decentius! So
blind, so blind!

    (*He turns to the rest, and taps the roll of paper in
    his hand.*)

Here I find a quite different account of things.
Listen, and drink in the refreshing dew of knowledge.
This is the Emperor's despatch to all the proconsuls of
the empire;—our excellent Decentius has brought
me a copy of it. Here we learn that I have
accomplished nothing in Gaul. It was, as I told you,
a dream. Here we have the Emperor's own words:
it was under the Emperor's fortunate auspices that
the imminent danger to the empire was averted.

FLORENTIUS. All the affairs of the empire
flourish under the Emperor's auspices.

JULIAN. More, more! It is here set forth that it was the Emperor who fought and conquered on the Rhine; it was the Emperor who raised up the King of the Alemanni, as he lay grovelling before him. My name is not fortunate enough to find any place in this document,—nor yours, Florentius, nor yours, Severus! And here, in the description of the battle of Argentoratum—where was it? Yes, here it stands! —it was the Emperor who determined the order of battle; it was the Emperor himself who, at peril of his life, fought till his sword was blunted, in the forefront of the encounter; it was the Emperor who, by the terror of his presence, put the barbarians to headlong flight——; read, read, I tell you!

SEVERUS. Noble Cæsar, your word suffices.

JULIAN. What do you mean, then, by your flattering speeches, my friends? Would you, in your excessive friendship for me, make me a parasite, to be fed with the leavings you have pilfered from my kinsman's table? What think you, Decentius? What say you to this? You see, in my own camp, I have to keep an eye on adherents who, in their blind zeal, are sometimes in danger of straying over the frontier-line of revolt.

FLORENTIUS (*hastily, to the Tribune*). I assure you, my words have been sadly misconstrued, if——

SEVERUS (*also to the Tribune*). It could never enter my head to——

JULIAN. That is right, my brothers in arms; let us all agree to swallow our vainglory. I asked what was lacking to complete Cæsar's happiness. Now you know it. It was the recognition of the truth that was lacking in Cæsar's happiness. Your silver helmet will never be dimmed with the dust of the triumph, Florentius! The Emperor has held that for us already, in Rome. He therefore declares all festivities here to be superfluous. Go, Sintula, and see that the intended procession is countermanded. The Emperor wishes to give his soldiers a much-needed rest. It is his will that they remain in the camp outside the walls.

(*The Master of the Horse*, SINTULA, *goes out by the back*.)

JULIAN. Was I not once a philosopher? They said so, at least, both in Athens and Ephesus. So weak is human nature in prosperity: I had almost been false to philosophy. The Emperor has brought me to my senses. Thank him most humbly, Decentius. Have you more to say?

DECENTIUS. One thing more. From all the Emperor has learnt, and especially from the letter you wrote him from Argentoratum, it appears that the pacification of Gaul is happily accomplished.

JULIAN. Most certainly; the Emperor, partly by his valour, partly by his magnanimous clemency——

DECENTIUS. The Rhine frontier of the empire has been placed in security.

JULIAN. By the Emperor, by the Emperor.

DECENTIUS. In the Danubian provinces, on the contrary, affairs are going ill, and still worse in Asia; King Sapor is making constant progress.

JULIAN. What audacity! Rumour has it that not even in this campaign has the Emperor been pleased to let his generals to crush him.

Decentius. The Emperor intends to do so himself in the spring. (*Taking out a roll of papers.*) Here is his will, noble Cæsar!

Julian. Let us see, let us see! (*Reading.*) Ah!
 (*He reads again for a long time, with signs of deep inward emotion; then he looks up and says :*)
Then it is the Emperor's will that——? Good, good, noble Decentius; the Emperor's will shall be done.

Decentius. It must be done, this very day.

Julian. This very day; of course. Come here, Sintula! Where is he?—Ah, I remember!—Call Sintula back!
 (*A courtier goes out by the back ;* Julian *retires to the window, and reads the papers through once more.*)

Florentius (*in a low voice, to the Tribune*). I implore you not to misinterpret what I said. When I gave Cæsar the credit, of course I did not mean to——

Severus (*in a low voice*). It could never occur to me to doubt that it was the Emperor's supreme and wise direction that——

A Courtier (*on the other side of the Tribune*). I beg you, noble sir,—put in a word for me at court, and release me from this painful position in the household of a Cæsar who——; well, he is the Emperor's exalted kinsman, but——

Another Courtier. I could tell you, alas! of things that indicate not only boundless vanity, but overweening ambition——

Julian. This very day! Let me say one word,

Decentius! It has long been my dearest wish to lay down this burden of responsibility.

DECENTIUS.   It shall be conveyed to the Emperor.

JULIAN.   I call heaven to witness that I never——; Ah, here is Sintula; now we can—— (*To the Tribune.*) You are going?

DECENTIUS.   I have affairs to transact with the generals, noble Cæsar!

JULIAN.   Without my intervention?

DECENTIUS.   The Emperor commands me to spare his beloved kinsman.

> (*He goes out by the back, followed by the others, except* SINTULA, *who remains standing at the door.*)

JULIAN (*looking at him awhile*).   Sintula!

SINTULA.   Yes, noble master!

JULIAN.   Come nearer—Yes, by my faith, you look honest. Pardon me; I never thought you could be so attached to me.

SINTULA.   How do you know that I am attached to you, my lord?

JULIAN (*pointing to the roll of paper*).   I can read it here, in this; it is written that you are to desert me.

SINTULA.   I, my lord?

JULIAN.   The Emperor disbands the army of Gaul, Sintula!

SINTULA.   Disbands——?

JULIAN.   Yes, what is it but a disbanding? The Emperor needs reinforcements, both on the Danube, and against the Persians. Our Batavian and Herulian auxiliaries are to depart with all speed, in order to reach Asia in the spring.

SINTULA. But the thing is impossible, my lord.
You have solemnly sworn to these very allies that
they shall in no case be called upon to serve beyond
the Alps.

JULIAN. Just so, Sintula! The Emperor says
that I gave that promise over hastily, and without his
consent. This is quite a new light on the matter;
but here it stands. I am to be forced to break my
word, dishonour myself in the eyes of the army,
bring down upon myself the unbridled rage of the
barbarians, perhaps their murderous weapons.

SINTULA. They cannot hurt you, my lord!
The Roman legions will make their breasts your
shield.

JULIAN. The Roman legions? Hm;—my simple-
minded friend! From every Roman legion three
hundred men are to be drafted off, and are likewise
to join the Emperor by the shortest route.

SINTULA. Ah! This is——!

JULIAN. Well planned, is it not? Every branch
of the army is to be set against me, that I may the
more easily be disarmed.

SINTULA. And I tell you, my lord, that not one
of your generals will abet such a design.

JULIAN. My generals are not to be led into
temptation. You are the man.

SINTULA. I, my Cæsar!

JULIAN. Here it is written. The Emperor com-
missions you to take all necessary measures, and then
to lead the chosen detachments to Rome.

SINTULA. This task is assigned to me? With
men here like Florentius and old Severus——

JULIAN. You have no victories on your list of misdeeds, Sintula!

SINTULA. No, that is true. They have never given me an opportunity to show——

JULIAN. I have been unjust to you. Thanks for your fidelity.

SINTULA. So great an imperial honour! My lord, may I see——

JULIAN. What would you see? You surely would not abet such a design.

SINTULA. God forbid that I should disobey the Emperor!

JULIAN. Sintula,—would you disarm your Cæsar?

SINTULA. Cæsar has ever undervalued me. Cæsar has never forgiven me the fact of his having to put up with a Master of the Horse appointed by the Emperor.

JULIAN. The Emperor is great and wise; he chooses well.

SINTULA. My lord,—I long to set about my duty; may I beg to see the Emperor's commission?

JULIAN (*handing him one of the papers*). Here is the Emperor's commission. Go and do your duty.

MYRRHA (*entering hastily from the right*). Oh merciful Redeemer!

JULIAN. Myrrha! What is the matter?

MYRRHA. Oh kind heaven, my mistress——

JULIAN. Your mistress,—what of her?

MYRRHA. Sickness or frenzy——; help, help!

JULIAN. Helena sick! The physician! Oribases must come, Sintula! Fetch him!

(SINTULA *goes out by the back*. JULIAN *is hasten-*

ing out to the right, when at the door he meets the Princess Helena, *surrounded by female slaves. Her expression is wild and distorted, her hair and clothes are in disorder.*)

Helena.   Loosen the comb! Loosen the comb, I say! It is red hot. My hair is on fire; I burn, I burn!

Julian.   Helena! For God's pity's sake——!

Helena.   Will no one help me? They are killing me with needle-pricks!

Julian.   My Helena! What has happened to you?

Helena.   Myrrha, Myrrha! Save me from the women, Myrrha!

The Physician Oribases (*entering from the back*). What horror do I hear——? Is it true? Ah!

Julian.   Helena! My love, light of my life——!

Helena.   Away from me! Oh sweet Jesus, help! (*She half swoons among the slave-girls.*)

Julian.   She is raving. What can it be, Oribases? —See—see her eyes, how large——!

Oribases (*to* Myrrha). What has the Princess taken? What has she been eating or drinking?

Julian.   Ah, you think——?

Oribases.   Answer, women; what have you given the Princess?

Myrrha.   We? Oh nothing, I swear; she herself——

Oribases.   Well? Well?

Myrrha.   Some fruits; they were peaches, I think;—oh, I do not know——

JULIAN. Fruits! Peaches? Some of those which—— ?

MYRRHA. Yes—no—yes; I do not know, my lord;—it was two Nubians——

JULIAN. Help, help, Oribases!

ORIBASES. Alas, I fear——

JULIAN. No, no, no!

ORIBASES. Hush, gracious lord; she is coming to herself.

HELENA (*whispering*). Why did the sun go down? Oh holy mysterious darkness!

JULIAN. Helena! Listen; collect your thoughts——

ORIBASES. My noble Princess——

JULIAN. It is the physician, Helena! (*He takes her hand.*) No, here, where I stand.

HELENA (*tearing her hand away*). Faugh! there he was again!

JULIAN. She does not see me. Here, here, Helena!

HELENA. The loathsome creature;—he is always with me.

JULIAN. What does she mean?

ORIBASES. Stand apart, gracious lord——!

HELENA. Sweet stillness! He does not dream——; oh my Gallus!

JULIAN. Gallus?

ORIBASES. Go, noble Cæsar; it is not meet——

HELENA. How boldly your close wavy hair curves over your neck! Oh that short, thick neck——

JULIAN. Abyss of abysses——!

ORIBASES. The delirium is increasing——

JULIAN.   I see, I see.   We must take note,
Oribases!

HELENA (*laughing softly*).   Now he would be
taking notes again.   Ink on his fingers; book-dust in
his hair—unwashed; faugh, faugh, how he stinks.

MYRRHA.   My lord, shall I not——?

JULIAN.   Away with you, woman!

HELENA.   How could you let yourself be conquered by him, you great-limbed, bronzed barbarian?
He cannot conquer women.   How I loathe this
impotent virtue.

JULIAN.   Away, all of you!   Not so near, Oribases!
I myself will watch the Princess.

HELENA.   Art thou wroth with me, thou glorious
one?   Gallus is dead.   Beheaded.   What a blow that
must have been!   Be not jealous, oh my first and
last?   Burn Gallus in hell fire;—it was none but
thou, thou, thou——!

JULIAN.   No nearer, Oribases!

HELENA.   Kill the priest, too!   I will not see him
after this.   Thou knowest our sweet secret.   Oh thou,
my day's desire, my night's delight!   It was thou
thyself—in the form of thy servant—in the oratory;
yes, yes, thou wert there; it was thou—in the darkness, in the heavy air, in the shrouding incense-clouds,
that night, when the Cæsar growing beneath my
heart——

JULIAN (*shrinking back with a cry*).   Ah!

HELENA (*stretching out her arms*).   My lover and
my lord!   Mine, mine——!

> (*She falls swooning on the floor; the slave-girls
> hasten forward and crowd round her.*)

JULIAN (*stands a moment immovable; then shakes his clenched fist in the air, and cries:*) Galilean!

> (*The slave-girls carry the Princess out on the right; at the same moment the Knight* SALLUST *comes hastily in by the door in the back.*)

SALLUST. The Princess in a swoon! Oh, then it is true!

JULIAN (*grasps the physician by the arm, and leads him aside*). Tell me the truth! Did you know before to-day that——; you understand me; have you known anything of—— the Princess's condition?

ORIBASES. I, like every one else, my lord!

JULIAN. And you said nothing to me, Oribases!

ORIBASES. Of what, my Cæsar?

JULIAN. How dared you conceal it from me?

ORIBASES. My lord, there was one thing we none of us knew.

JULIAN. And that was?

ORIBASES. That Cæsar knew nothing. (*He is going.*)

JULIAN. Where are you going?

ORIBASES. To try the remedies my art prescribes——

JULIAN. I believe your art will prove powerless.

ORIBASES. My lord, it is possible that——

JULIAN. Powerless, I tell you!

ORIBASES (*retiring a step*). Noble Cæsar, it is my duty to disobey you in this.

JULIAN. What do you think I mean? Go, go; try what your art——; save the Emperor's sister; the Emperor will be inconsolable if his thoughtful

affection should bring any disaster in its train. Of
course you know that those fruits were a present from
the Emperor?

ORIBASES.   Ah!

JULIAN.   Go, go,—try what your art——

ORIBASES (*bowing reverently*).   I believe my art
will prove powerless, my lord! (*He goes out to the
right*).

JULIAN.   Ah, is it you, Sallust?   What do you
think?   The waves of fate are once more beginning
to sweep over my race.

SALLUST.   Oh, but rescue is at hand.   Oribases
will——

JULIAN (*shortly and decisively*).   The Princess will
die.

SALLUST.   Oh, if I dared speak!   If I dared trace
out the secret threads in this web of destruction!

JULIAN.   Be of good cheer, friend; all the threads
shall be brought to light, and then——

DECENTIUS (*entering from the back*).   How shall I
look Cæsar in the face!   How inscrutable are the
ways of God!   Crushed to earth—— ; oh that you
could but read my heart!   That I should be the
harbinger of sorrow and disaster——!

JULIAN.   Yes, that you may say twice over, noble
Decentius!   And how shall I find soft and specious
enough terms to bring this in any endurable guise to
the ears of her imperial brother!

DECENTIUS.   Alas that such a thing should happen
at the very moment of my mission!   And just at this
juncture of affairs!   Oh, what a thunderbolt from
a cloudless sky of hope!

JULIAN. Oh, this towering and devouring tempest, just as the ship seemed running into the long-desired haven! Oh, this—this——! Sorrow makes us eloquent, Decentius,—you as well as me. But business first. The two Nubians must be seized and examined.

DECENTIUS. The Nubians, my lord? Could you dream that my indignant zeal would suffer the two negligent servants for another instant to——?

JULIAN. What! Surely you have not already——?

DECENTIUS. Call me hasty, if you will, noble Cæsar; but my love to the Emperor and to his sorrow-stricken house would in truth be less than it is if, in such an hour, I were capable of calm reflection.

JULIAN. Have you killed both the slaves?

DECENTIUS. Had not their negligence deserved a sevenfold death? They were two heathen savages, my lord! Their testimony would have been of no value; it was impossible to extract anything from them, but that they had left their precious charge standing for some time unprotected in the antechamber, accessible to every one——

JULIAN. Aha! Had they indeed, Decentius?

DECENTIUS. I accuse no one. But oh, beloved Cæsar, I warn you; for you are surrounded by faithless servants. Your court—by an unhappy misunderstanding!—fancies that some sort of disfavour—or what should I call it?—is implied in the measures which the Emperor has found it necessary to adopt; in short——

SINTULA (*entering from the back*). My lord, you have imposed on me a charge I can in no way fulfil.

JULIAN.   The Emperor imposed it, good Sintula!

SINTULA.   Relieve me from it, my lord; it is utterly beyond me.

DECENTIUS.   What has happened?

SINTULA.   The camp is in a wild uproar.   The legions and the allies are banding together——

DECENTIUS.   Rebelling against the Emperor's will!

SINTULA.   The soldiers are shouting that they appeal to Cæsar's promises.

JULIAN.   Hark! hark! that roar outside——!

SINTULA.   The rioters are rushing hither——

DECENTIUS.   Let no one enter!

SALLUST (*at the window*).   Too late; the whole place is filled with angry soldiers.

DECENTIUS.   Cæsar's precious life is in danger! Where is Florentius?

SINTULA.   Fled.

DECENTIUS.   The blustering coward! And Severus?

SINTULA.   Severus pretends to be ill; he has driven out to his farm.

JULIAN.   I myself will speak to the madmen.

DECENTIUS.   Not a step, noble Cæsar!

JULIAN.   What now?

DECENTIUS.   It is my duty, gracious lord; the Emperor's order—; his beloved kinsman's life—; Cæsar is my prisoner.

SALLUST.   Ah!

JULIAN.   So it has come to this!

DECENTIUS.   The household guard, Sintula!   You must conduct Cæsar in safety to Rome.

JULIAN. To Rome!

SINTULA. What do you say, my lord?

DECENTIUS. To Rome, I say!

JULIAN. Like Gallus! (*He shouts through the window.*) Help, help!

SALLUST. Fly, my Cæsar! Fly, fly!

> (*Wild cries are heard without. Soldiers of the Roman legions, Batavian auxiliaries, and other allies climb in through the window. At the same time, others swarm in by the door in the back. Among the foremost is the Standard-Bearer* MAURUS; *women, some with children in their arms, follow the intruders.*)

CRIES AMONG THE SOLDIERS. Cæsar, Cæsar!

OTHER VOICES. Cæsar, why have you betrayed us?

AGAIN OTHERS. Down with the faithless Cæsar!

JULIAN (*casts himself with outstretched arms into the midst of the soldiers, crying:*) Fellow-soldiers, brothers in arms,—save me from my enemies!

DECENTIUS. Ah, what is this——?

A WILD CRY. Down with Cæsar! Strike him down!

JULIAN. Form a circle round me; draw your swords!

MAURUS. They are drawn already!

WOMEN. Strike him, cut him down!

JULIAN. I thank you for coming! Maurus! Honest Maurus! Yes, yes; you I can trust.

A BATAVIAN SOLDIER. How dare you send us to the ends of the earth? Was *that* what you promised us?

Other Allies.   Not over the Alps! We are not bound to go!

Julian.   Not to Rome! I will not go; they want to murder me, as they murdered my brother Gallus!

Maurus.   What do you say, my lord?

Decentius.   Do not believe him!

Julian.   Lay no finger on the noble Decentius; the fault is not his.

Laipso (*a Subaltern*).   That is true; the fault is Cæsar's.

Julian.   Ah, is that you, Laipso, my gallant friend? You fought well at Argentoratum.

Laipso.   Cæsar has not forgotten that?

Varro (*a Subaltern*).   But he forgets his promises!

Julian.   Was not that the voice of the undaunted Varro? Ah, there he is! Your wound is healed, I see. Oh well-deserving soldier,—why would they not let me make you captain?

Varro.   Did you really wish to?

Julian.   Do not blame the Emperor for refusing my request. The Emperor does not know any of you, as I know you.

Decentius.   Soldiers, hear me——!

Many Voices.   We have nothing to do with the Emperor!

Others (*pressing forward menacingly*).   It is Cæsar we call to account!

Julian.   What power has your unhappy Cæsar, my friends? They want to take me to Rome. They deprive me even of the control of my private affairs.

They confiscate my share of the spoils of war. I thought to give every soldier five gold pieces and a pound of silver, but——

THE SOLDIERS. What does he say?

JULIAN. It is not the Emperor who forbids it, but bad and envious councillors. The Emperor is good, my dear friends! But oh, the Emperor is sick; he can do nothing——

MANY SOLDIERS. Five gold pieces and a pound of silver!

OTHER SOLDIERS. And that they deny us!

OTHERS AGAIN. Who dares deny Cæsar anything?

MAURUS. Is it thus they treat Cæsar, the soldiers' father?

LAIPSO. Cæsar, who has been rather our friend than our master? Has he not?

MANY VOICES. Yes, yes, he has!

VARRO. Should not Cæsar, the victorious general, have leave to choose his captains as he pleases?

MAURUS. Should he not have free control over the spoils that fall to his share?

A LOUD SHOUT. Yes, yes, yes!

JULIAN. Ah, but what use would it be to you? What need you care for worldly goods, you, who are to be led forth to the most distant lands, to meet a doubtful fate——?

SOLDIERS. We will not go!

JULIAN. Do not look at me; I am ashamed; for I can scarcely help weeping when I think that in a few months you will be a prey to pestilence, hunger, and the weapons of a bloodthirsty enemy.

Many Soldiers (*pressing round him*). Cæsar!
Kind Cæsar!

Julian. And your defenceless wives and children,
whom you must leave behind in your scattered homes!
Who shall protect them in their pitiable plight,
widowed and fatherless (for so they soon may be),
and exposed to the vengeful onslaughts of the
Alemanni?

The Women (*weeping*). Cæsar, Cæsar, protect us!

Julian (*weeping likewise*). What is Cæsar? What
can the fallen Cæsar do?

Laipso. Write to the Emperor, and let him
know——

Julian. Ah, what is the Emperor? The Emperor
is sick in mind and body; he is broken down by his
care for the empire's weal. Is he not, Decentius?

Decentius. Yes, doubtless; but——

Julian. How it cut me to the heart, when I
heard——

(*Pressing the hands of those around him.*)

Pray for his soul, you who worship the good Christ!
Offer sacrifices for his recovery, you who have remained faithful to the gods of your fathers!—— ——
Do you know that the Emperor has held a triumphal
entry into Rome?

Maurus. The Emperor!

Varro. What? Beaten, as he was on the
Danube?

Julian. As he returned from the Danube, he
held a triumph for our victories——

Decentius (*threateningly*). Noble Cæsar, reflect——!

JULIAN. Yes, the Tribune says well; reflect how our Emperor's mind must be clouded, when he can do such things! Oh my sorely afflicted kinsman! When he rode through the mighty arch of Constantine, he fancied himself so tall that he bent his back and bowed his head down to his saddle-bow.

MAURUS. Like a cock in an archway. (*Laughter among the soldiers.*)

SOME VOICES. Is *he* an Emperor?

VARRO. Shall we obey him?

LAIPSO. Away with him!

MAURUS. Cæsar, do you take the helm!

DECENTIUS. Rebellion——!

MANY VOICES. Seize the throne; seize the throne, Cæsar!

JULIAN. Madmen! Is this language for Romans? Would you imitate the barbarous Alemanni? What was it Knodomar cried at Argentoratum? Answer me, good Maurus,—what did he cry out?

MAURUS. He cried, "Long live the Emperor Julian!"

JULIAN. Ah, hush, hush! What are you saying?

MAURUS. Long live the Emperor Julian!

THOSE BEHIND. What is going on?

VARRO. They are proclaiming Julian Emperor!

LOUD CRIES. Long live the Emperor! Long live the Emperor Julian!

(*The cry spreads in wider and wider circles without; all talk together:* JULIAN *cannot make himself heard for some time.*)

JULIAN. Oh, I entreat you——! Soldiers, friends, brothers in arms,—see, I stretch out my trembling arms

to you——! Do not be alarmed, my Decentius!—Oh
that I should live to see this! I do not blame you,
my faithful friends; it is despair that has driven you
to this. You will have it? Good; I submit to the will
of the army.—Sintula, call the generals together.—
You, Tribune, can bear witness to Constantius that it
was only on compulsion that I—— (*He turns to*
Varro.) Go, captain, and make known this unex-
pected turn of affairs throughout the camp. I will
write without delay to Rome——

Sallust.   My lord, the soldiers wish to see you.

Maurus.   A circlet of gold on your head,
Emperor!

Julian.   I have never possessed such a thing.

Maurus.   This will do.

(*He takes off his gold chain, and winds it several
times round Cæsar's brow.*)

Shouts outside.   The Emperor, the Emperor!
We will see the Emperor!

Soldiers.   On the shield with him! Up, up!

(*The bystanders raise* Julian *aloft on a shield,
and show him to the multitude, amid long-
continued acclamations.*)

Julian.   The will of the army be done! I bow
before the inevitable, and renew all my promises——

Legionaries.   Five gold pieces and a pound of
silver!

Batavians.   Not over the Alps!

Julian.   We will occupy Vienna. It is the
strongest city in Gaul, and well supplied with all
sorts of provisions. There I intend to wait until
we see whether my afflicted kinsman sanctions what

we have here determined, for the good of the empire——

SALLUST. That he will never do, my lord!

JULIAN (*with upstretched hands.*) Divine wisdom enlighten his darkened soul, and guide him for the best! Be thou with me, Fortune, who hast never yet deserted me!

MYRRHA AND THE WOMEN (*lamenting outside on the right*). Dead, dead, dead!

Act Fifth.

(*At Vienna. A vaulted space in the catacombs. To the left a winding passage running upwards. In the background, a flight of steps is hewn in the hill-side, leading up to a closed door. In front, to the right, a number of steps lead down to the lower passages. The space is feebly lighted by a hanging-lamp.*)

(JULIAN CÆSAR, *unshaven, and in dirty clothes, stands bending over the opening to the right. A subdued sound of psalm-singing comes through the door from the church outside, built on to the catacomb.*)

JULIAN (*speaking downwards*).   Still no sign?

A VOICE (*far below*).   None.

JULIAN.   Neither yes nor no?   Neither for nor against?

THE VOICE.   Both.

JULIAN.   That is the same as nothing.

THE VOICE.   Wait, wait.

JULIAN.   I have waited five days; you asked for only three. I tell you——I have no mind to—— (*He listens towards the entrance, and calls down.*)   Do not speak!

SALLUST (*entering by the passage on the left*).   My lord, my lord!

JULIAN.   Is it you, Sallust?   What do you want down here?

SALLUST.   This thick darkness——; ah! now I
see you.

JULIAN.   What do you want?

SALLUST.   To serve you, if I can,—to lead you out
to the living again.

JULIAN.   What news from the world above?

SALLUST.   The soldiers are restless; there are
signs on all hands that they are losing patience.

JULIAN.   Is the sun shining up there?

SALLUST.   Yes, my lord!

JULIAN.   The vault of heaven is like a sea of
glittering light.   Perhaps it is high noon.   It is
warm; the air quivers along the walls of the houses;
the river ripples, half parched, over the white
flints.—Beautiful life!   Beautiful earth!

SALLUST.   Oh come, my lord, come!   This stay in
the catacombs is interpreted to your hurt.

JULIAN   How is it interpreted?

SALLUST.   Dare I tell you?

JULIAN.   You dare, and you must.   How is it
interpreted?

SALLUST.   Many believe that it is remorse rather
than sorrow that has driven you underground in this
strange fashion.

JULIAN.   They think I killed her?

SALLUST.   The mystery of the thing may excuse
them, if——

JULIAN.   No one killed her, Sallust!   She was
too pure for this sinful world; therefore an angel
from heaven descended every night into her secret
chamber, and called upon her.   You doubt it?   Do
you not know that this is how the priests in Lutetia

accounted for her death? And the priests ought to know. Has not the transport of her body hither been like a triumphal progress through the land? Did not all the women of Vienna stream forth beyond the gates to meet her coffin, hailing her with green boughs in their hands, spreading draperies on the road, and singing songs of praise to the bride of heaven, who was being brought home to the bridegroom's house?—Why do you laugh?

SALLUST. I, my lord?

JULIAN. Ever since, I have heard bridal songs night and day. Listen, listen; they are wafting her up to glory. Yes, she was indeed a true Christian woman. She observed the commandment strictly;—she gave to Cæsar what was Cæsar's, and to the other she gave——; but it was not that you came to talk about; you are not initiated in the secrets of the faith, Sallust!—What news, I ask?

SALLUST. The weightiest news is that on learning of the events at Lutetia, the Emperor fled hastily to Antioch.

JULIAN. That news I know. No doubt Constantius already saw us in imagination before the gates of Rome.

SALLUST. The friends who boldly cast in their lot with you in this dangerous business, saw the same thing in imagination.

JULIAN. The time is not auspicious, Sallust! Do you not know that in the martial games, before we left Lutetia, my shield broke in pieces, so that only the handle remained in my grasp? And do you not know that, when I was mounting my horse, the servant stumbled as I swung myself up from his folded hands?

SALLUST. Yet you gained the saddle, my lord!

JULIAN. But the man fell.

SALLUST. Better men will fall if Cæsar loiters.

JULIAN. The Emperor is at death's door.

SALLUST. The Emperor still lives. The letters you wrote him about your election——

JULIAN. My enforced election. They constrained me; I had no choice.

SALLUST. The Emperor does not accept that explanation. He intends, as soon as he has mustered an army in the eastern provinces, to march into Gaul.

JULIAN. How do you know——?

SALLUST. By an accident, my lord! Believe me, I entreat you——!

JULIAN. Good, good; when that happens, I will go to meet Constantius—not sword in hand——

SALLUST. Not? How do you intend to meet him?

JULIAN. I will render to the Emperor what is the Emperor's.

SALLUST. Do you mean that you will abdicate?

JULIAN. The Emperor is at death's door.

SALLUST. Oh that vain hope! (*He casts himself on his knees.*) Then take my life, my lord!

JULIAN. What now?

SALLUST. Cæsar, take my life; I would rather die by your will than by the Emperor's.

JULIAN. Rise, friend!

SALLUST. No, let me lie at my Cæsar's feet, and confess all. Oh beloved master,—to have to tell you

this !—When I came to you in the camp on the
Rhine,—when I reminded you of the old friendship of
our Athenian days,—when I begged to share the
dangers of war with you,—then, oh Cæsar, I came
as a secret spy, in the Emperor's pay——

JULIAN. You—— !

SALLUST. My mind had for some time been
inflamed against you; you remember that little
difference in Milan—yet not a little one for me, who
had hoped that Cæsar would help to restore my
waning fortunes. All this they took advantage of in
Rome; they regarded me as the very man to spy out
your doings.

JULIAN. And you could sell yourself so basely?
To so black a treachery !

SALLUST. I was ruined, my lord; and I thought
Cæsar had forsaken me. Yes, my Cæsar, I betrayed
you——, during the first few months; but not afterwards. Your friendliness, your magnanimity, all the
favour you showed me——; I became, what I had
given myself out to be, your faithful adherent, and
in my secret letters to Rome I put my employers
on false scents.

JULIAN. Those letters were from you?—Oh
Sallust !

SALLUST. They contained nothing to injure you,
my lord! What others may have written, I do not
know; I only know that I often enough groaned in
anguish under my enforced and hated silence. I
ventured as far as I by any means dared. That
letter, written to an unnamed man in your camp,
which contained an account of the Emperor's

triumphal entry into Rome, and which you found one morning on the march to Lutetia pushed under your tent-flap—— ; you did find it, my lord?

JULIAN. Yes, yes——?

SALLUST. That was directed to me, and chance favoured me in bringing it into your hands. I dared not speak. I wanted to, but I could not; I put off from day to day the confession of my shame. Oh, punish me, my lord; see, here I lie!

JULIAN. Stand up; you are dearer to me thus,— conquered without my will and against your own. Stand up, friend of my soul; no one shall touch a hair of your head.

SALLUST. Rather take the life which you will not long have power to shield. You say the Emperor is at death's door. (*He rises.*) My Cæsar, what I have sworn to conceal, I now reveal to you. The Emperor's decrepitude opens no prospects for you. The Emperor is taking a new wife.

JULIAN. Ah, what madness! How can you think——?

SALLUST. The Emperor is taking a new wife, my lord! (*He hands him some papers.*) Read, read, noble Cæsar; these letters will leave you no room for doubt.

JULIAN (*seizing the papers, and reading*). Yes, by the light and might of Helios——!

SALLUST. Oh that I had dared to speak sooner!

JULIAN (*still reading*). He take a woman to wife! Constantius,—that dwindling shadow of a man——! Faustina,—what is this?—young, scarcely nineteen, —a daughter of—— ah! a daughter of that insolent

tribe.   And of course a zealous Christian.   (*He folds
the papers together.*)   You are right, Sallust ; his ill-
health gives no room for hope.   What though he be
decrepid, dying,—what of that ?   Is not Faustina
pious ?   An annunciating angel will appear ; or even
—— ; ha-ha ! in short,—by some means or other,—a
young Cæsar will be forthcoming, and thus——

SALLUST.   Delay means ruin.

JULIAN.   This move has long been planned in all
secrecy, Sallust !   Ah, now all the riddles are solved.
Helena——, it was not, as I imagined, her heedless
tongue that destroyed her——

SALLUST.   No, my lord !

JULIAN.   ——they thought,—they believed that
—— ; oh inscrutable, even-handed retribution ! that
was why she had to die.

SALLUST.   Yes, that was the reason.   I was the
man they first pitched upon in Rome.   Oh my lord,
you do not doubt that I refused to do it ?   I alleged
that it was impossible to find an opportunity ; they
assured me that the abominable design was given up,
and then—— !

JULIAN.   They will not stop at—at the double
corpse in the sarcophagus up yonder.   Constantius
takes another wife.   That is why I was to be
disarmed in Lutetia.

SALLUST.   Only one thing can save you, my
Cæsar ; you must act before the Emperor has got his
forces together.

JULIAN.   If, of my own free will, I withdrew from
the world, devoting myself to that wisdom which I
have here been forced to neglect, would the new

rulers leave me undisturbed? Would not the very
fact of my existence be like a sword hanging over
their heads?

SALLUST. The kinsmen of the Empress that is to
be are the men who surrounded Gallus Cæsar in his
last hours.

JULIAN. The tribune Scudilo. Trust me, friend,
—I have not forgotten that. And am I to yield
and fall before this bloodthirsty Emperor! Am I to
spare him who for long years has stumbled about
among the corpses of my nearest kin!

SALLUST. If you spare him, in less than three
months he will be stumbling among the corpses of
your adherents.

JULIAN. Yes, yes; there you are right. It is
almost my imperative duty to stand up against him.
If I do, it will not be for my own sake. Do not the
weal and woe of thousands hang in the balance? Are
not thousands of lives at stake? Or could I have
averted this extremity? You are more to blame
than I, Sallust! Why did you not speak before?

SALLUST. In Rome they made me swear a solemn
oath of secrecy.

JULIAN. An oath? Indeed! By the gods of
your forefathers?

SALLUST. Yes, my lord—by Zeus and by Apollo.

JULIAN. And yet you break your oath?

SALLUST. I wish to live.

JULIAN. But the gods?

SALLUST. The gods—they are far away.

JULIAN. Yes, your gods are far away; they
hamper no one; they are a burden to no one; they

leave a man elbow-room for action. Oh that Greek happiness, that sense of freedom !—— ——

You said that the Emperor, vengeful as he is, will pour out the blood of my friends. Yes, who can doubt that? Was Knodomar spared? Did not that harmless captive pay with his life for a slip of the tongue? For—I know it, Sallust—they killed him; that tale about the barbarian's home-sickness was a lie. Then what may not we expect? In what a hateful light must not Decentius have represented matters in Rome?

SALLUST.   That you may best understand from the hasty flight of the court to Antioch.

JULIAN.   And am I not my army's father, Sallust?

SALLUST.   The soldiers' father; their wives' and children's buckler and defence.

JULIAN.   And what will be the fate of the empire if I vacillate now? A decrepid Emperor, and after him a helpless child, upon the throne; faction and revolt; every man's hand against his neighbour, in the struggle for power.— Not many nights ago I saw a vision. A figure appeared before me, with a halo round its head; it looked angrily upon me, and said: "Choose!" With that it vanished away, like a morning mist. Hitherto I had interpreted it as referring to something else; but now that I know of the Emperor's approaching marriage——

Yes, indeed, it is time to choose, ere misfortune overwhelms the empire. I am not thinking of my own interest; but should I be justified in shirking the choice, Sallust? Is it not my duty to the Emperor to defend my life? Have I a right to stand with

folded arms and await the murderers whom he, in
his insane panic, is bribing to hew me down? Have
I a right to give this unhappy Constantius an opportunity of heaping fresh blood-guiltiness upon his
sinful head? Were it not better for him—as the
Scriptures say—that he should suffer wrong rather
than do wrong? If, therefore, this that I do to my
kinsman can be called a wrong, I hold that the
wrong is wiped out by the fact that it hinders my
kinsman from inflicting a wrong on me. I think that
both Plato and Marcus Aurelius, that crowned bridegroom of wisdom, would support me in that. At
any rate, it would be no unworthy problem for the
philosophers, my dear Sallust!—Oh that I had
Libanius here!

SALLUST. My lord, you are yourself so far
advanced in philosophy, that——

JULIAN. True, true; but I should like to hear the
views of certain others. Not that I am vacillating.
Do not think that! Nor do I see any reason to
doubt a favourable issue. For those omens should
by no means discourage us. The fact that I retained
the handle, when my shield broke during the games,
may quite reasonably be taken to mean, I think, that
I shall succeed in holding what my hand has grasped.
And if, in swinging myself upon my horse, I threw
down the man who helped me to mount, may not
this betoken a sudden fall to Constantius, to whom I
owe my rise? Be this as it may, my Sallust, I intend to compose a treatise which shall most clearly
justify——

SALLUST. Very good, my gracious lord; but the

soldiers are impatient; they would fain see you, and learn their fate from your own lips.

JULIAN.   Go, go, and pacify them;—tell them that Cæsar will presently show himself.

SALLUST.   My lord, it is not Cæsar, it is the Emperor himself they want to see.

JULIAN.   The Emperor is coming.

SALLUST.   Then he comes—though empty-handed —yet with the lives of thousands in his hands.

JULIAN.   A barter, Sallust; the lives of thousands against the death of thousands.

SALLUST.   Have your enemies the right to live?

JULIAN.   Happy you, whose gods are afar off. Oh to possess this hardihood of will——!

A VOICE (*calling from deep in the galleries below*). Julian, Julian!

SALLUST.   Ah!   What is that?

JULIAN.   Leave me, dear friend; go quickly!

THE VOICE.   Deaden the psalm-singing, Julian!

SALLUST.   It calls again.   Oh, then it is true!

JULIAN.   What is true?

SALLUST.   That you live down here with a mysterious stranger, a soothsayer or a magician, who came to you by night.

JULIAN.   Ha-ha; do they say that?   Go, go!

SALLUST.   I conjure you, my lord,—have done with these noxious dreams.   Come with me; come up to the light of day!

THE VOICE (*nearer, underneath*).   All my labour is vain.

JULIAN (*speaking down the passage to the right*). No sign, my brother?

THE VOICE.   Desolation and emptiness.

JULIAN.   Oh Maximus!

SALLUST.   Maximus!

JULIAN.   Go, I tell you! If I leave this house of corruption, it will be as Emperor.

SALLUST.   I implore you——; what do you seek here, in the darkness?

JULIAN.   Light.   Go, go!

SALLUST.   If Cæsar loiters, I fear he will find the way barred against him.

> (*He goes by the passage on the left. A little while afterwards, the* MYSTIC MAXIMUS *ascends the stairs; he wears a white sacrificial band round his forehead; in his hand is a long bloody knife.*)

JULIAN.   Speak, my Maximus!

MAXIMUS.   All my labour is vain, I tell you. Why could you not deaden the psalm-singing? It strangled all the omens; they would have spoken, but could utter nothing.

JULIAN.   Silence, darkness;—and I can wait no longer! What do you counsel me to do?

MAXIMUS.   Go forward blindly, Emperor Julian! The light will seek you out.

JULIAN.   Yes, yes, yes; that I, too, believe. I need not, after all, have sent for you all this long way. Do you know what I have just heard——?

MAXIMUS.   I will not know what you have heard. Take your fate into your own hands.

JULIAN (*pacing restlessly up and down*).   What is he in reality, this Constantius—this Fury-haunted sinner, this smouldering ruin of what was once a man?

MAXIMUS.   Be that his epitaph, Emperor Julian!

JULIAN. In his whole treatment of me, has he not been like a rudderless wreck,—now drifting to the left on the current of suspicion, now hurled to the right by the storm-gust of remorse? Did he not stagger, terror-stricken, up to the imperial throne, his purple mantle dripping with my father's blood? perhaps with my mother's too?—Had not all my kin to perish, that he might sit secure? No, not all; Gallus was spared, and I;—he must have a couple of lives left, on which to buy himself a little pardon. Then he drifted into the current of suspicion again. Remorse wrung from him the title of Cæsar for Gallus; then suspicion wrung from him Cæsar's death-warrant. And I? Do I owe him thanks for the life he has hitherto vouchsafed me? One after the other; first Gallus, and then——; every night I have sweated with terror lest the next day should be my last.

MAXIMUS. Were Constantius and death your worst terrors? Think.

JULIAN. No, you are right. The priests——! My whole youth has been one continuous dread of the Emperor and of Christ. Oh, he is terrible, that mysterious—that merciless god-man! At every turn, wherever I wished to go, he met me, stark and stern, with his unconditional, inexorable commands.

MAXIMUS. And these commands—were they within you?

JULIAN. Always without. Always " Thou shalt." If my soul gathered itself up in one gnawing and consuming hate towards the murderer of my kin, what said the commandment: "Love thine enemy!" If my mind, athirst for beauty, longed for scenes and rites from the bygone world of Greece, Christianity swooped down upon me with its "Seek the one thing needful!" If I felt the sweet lusts of the flesh towards this or that, the Prince of Renunciation terrified me with his : "Kill the body, that the soul may live!"—All that is human has become unlawful since the day when the seer of Galilee became ruler of the world. With him, to live means to die. Love and hatred, both are sins. Has he, then, transformed man's flesh and blood? Has not earth-bound man remained what he ever was? Our inmost, healthy soul rebels against it all;—and yet we are to *will* in the very teeth of our own will! Thou shalt, shalt, shalt!

MAXIMUS. And you have got no further than that? Shame on you!

JULIAN. I?

MAXIMUS. Yes, you, the man of Athens and of Ephesus.

JULIAN. Ah, those times, Maximus! It was easy to choose then. What were we really working at? A philosophic system ; neither more nor less.

MAXIMUS. Is it not written somewhere in your Scriptures : "Either with us or against us"?

JULIAN. Did not Libanius remain the man he was, whether he took the affirmative in a disputation, or the negative? This lies deeper. Here it is action that must be faced. "Render unto Cæsar the things that are Cæsar's." In Athens I once made a game of that ;—but it is no game. You cannot grasp it, you, who have never been under the power of the god-man. It is more than a doctrine he has spread over the world ; it is an enchantment, that binds the

soul in chains. He who has once been under it,—I
believe he can never quite shake it off.

MAXIMUS.   Because you do not wholly *will*.

JULIAN.   How can I *will* the impossible?

MAXIMUS.   Is it worth while to *will* what is
possible?

JULIAN.   Verbiage from the lecture-halls! You
can no longer cram my mind with that.   And yet——
oh no, no, Maximus!   But you cannot understand
how it is with us.   We are like vines transplanted
into a new, strange soil; transplant us back again,
and we die; yet in the new soil we cannot thrive.

MAXIMUS.   We?   Whom do you call we?

JULIAN.   All who are under the terror of the
revelation.

MAXIMUS.   A terror of shadows!

JULIAN.   Be that as it may.   But do you not see
that this paralysing terror has curdled and heaped
itself up into a wall around the Emperor?   Ah, I see
very well why the great Constantine promoted such a
will-binding doctrine to power and honour in the
empire.   No bodyguard with spears and shields
could form such a bulwark to the throne as this
benumbing creed, which is always pointing beyond
our earthly life.   Have you looked closely at these
Christians?   Hollow-eyed, pale-cheeked, flat-breasted,
all; they are like the linen-weavers of Byssus; they
brood their lives away unspurred by ambition; the
sun shines for them, and they do not see it; the
earth offers them its fulness, and they desire it not;
—all their desire is to renounce and suffer, in order
to die.

MAXIMUS. Then use them as they are ; but you yourself must stand without. Emperor, or Galilean; —*that* is the choice. Be a thrall under the terror, or monarch in the land of sunshine and gladness ! You cannot will contradictions ; and yet that is what you would fain do. You try to unite what cannot be united,—to reconcile two irreconcilables ; therefore it is that you lie here rotting in the darkness.

JULIAN. Show me light if you can !

MAXIMUS. Are you that Achilles, whom your mother dreamed that she should give to the world? A tender heel alone makes no man an Achilles. Arise, my lord ! Confident of victory, like a knight on his fiery steed, you must trample on the Galilean, if you would reach the imperial throne——

JULIAN. Maximus !

MAXIMUS. My beloved Julian, look at the world around you ! Those death-desiring Christians you speak of are a small minority. And how is it with all the others? Are not their minds falling away from the Master, one by one? Answer me,—what has become of this strange gospel of love? Does not sect rage against sect? And the bishops, those gold-bedecked dignitaries, who call themselves the head shepherds of the church ! Do they yield even to the great men of the court in greed and ambition and sycophancy——?

JULIAN. They are not all like that ; think of the great Athanasius of Alexandria——

MAXIMUS. Athanasius stood alone. And where is Athanasius now? Did they not drive him out, because he was not to be bribed into subservience

to the Emperor's will? Was he not forced to take
refuge in the Libyan desert, where he was devoured
by lions? Can you name me *one* other like Athanasius? Think of Maris, the bishop of Chalcedon,
who has now changed sides three times in the
Arian controversy. Think of old Bishop Marcus, of
Arethusa; him you know from your boyhood. Has
he not lately, in the face of both law and justice,
taken all municipal property from the citizens, and
transferred it to the church? And remember the
feeble, vacillating Bishop of Nazianzus, who is the
laughing-stock of his own community, because he
answers yes and no in the same cause, in the hope
of ingratiating himself with both parties.

JULIAN. True, true, true!

MAXIMUS. These are your brothers in arms,
Julian; you will find none better among them. Or
perhaps you reckon upon those two great Galilean
lights that were to be, in Cappadocia? Ha-ha;
Gregory, the bishop's son, is a lawyer in his native
town, and Basilius, on his estate in the far east, is
poring over the writings of secular philosophers.

JULIAN. Yes, I know it well. Falling away on
all sides! Hekebolius, my former teacher, has grown
rich through his zeal for the faith, and his theologi-
cal writings; and since then——! Maximus—I
stand almost alone in earnestness.

MAXIMUS. You stand quite alone. Your whole
army is either in headlong flight, or lying slain around
you. Blow the battle-call,—and none will hear
you; advance,—and none will follow you! Do not
imagine that you can do anything for a cause which

has despaired of itself. You will be beaten, I tell you! And where will you turn then? Disowned by Constantius, you will be disowned by all other powers on earth,—and over the earth. Or will you flee to the Galilean's bosom? How do things stand between you and him? Have you not just said that you are under the terror? Have you his commands within you? Do you love your enemy, Constantius, even if you do not smite him? Do you hate the lusts of the flesh or the alluring joys of this world, even if you do not, like a heated swimmer, plunge over head and ears into them? Do you renounce the world, because you have not courage to make it your own? And are you so very sure that—if you die here— you shall live yonder?

JULIAN (*walking up and down*). What has he done for me, he who exacts so much? If he hold the reins of the world-chariot in his hands, it must have been within his power to——

(*The psalm-singing in the church becomes louder.*)

Listen, listen! They call that serving him. And he accepts it as a sweet-smelling sacrifice. Praise of himself,—and praise of her in the coffin! If he be omniscient, how then can he——?

THE CHAMBERLAIN EUTHERIUS (*coming hastily down through the passage on the left*). My Cæsar! My lord, my lord; where are you?

JULIAN. Here, Eutherius! What do you want with me?

EUTHERIUS. You must come up, my lord; you must see it with your own eyes;—the Princess's body is working miracles.

Julian.   You lie!

Eutherius.   I do not lie, my lord! I do not believe in this foreign doctrine; but what I have seen, I cannot doubt.

Julian.   What have you seen?

Eutherius.   The whole town is in a frenzy. They are carrying the sick and crippled to the princess's bier; the priests let them touch it, and they go away healed.

Julian.   And you have yourself seen that?

Eutherius.   Yes, my lord; I saw an epileptic woman go out of the church healed, praising the Galileans' God.

Julian.   Ah, Maximus, Maximus!

Eutherius.   Hark, how the Christians exult;— some fresh miracle must have happened.

The Physician Oribases (*calling out in the passage to the left*).   Eutherius,—have you found him? Eutherius, Eutherius, where is Cæsar?

Julian (*meeting him*).   Here, here;—is it true, Oribases?

Oribases (*coming forward*).   Incredible, inexplicable,—and yet true; they touch the bier, the priests read and pray over them, and they are healed; from time to time a voice proclaims: "Holy, holy, is the pure woman!"

Julian.   A voice proclaims——?

Oribases.   The voice of one invisible, my Cæsar; a voice high up under the vaultings of the church; no one knows whence it comes.

Julian (*stands a moment immovable, then turns suddenly to* Maximus, *and cries:*)   Life or the lie!

MAXIMUS.   Choose!

ORIBASES.   Come, come, my lord; the awe-struck soldiers threaten you——

JULIAN.   Let them threaten.

ORIBASES.   They accuse you and me of the Princess's death——

JULIAN.   I will come; I will satisfy them——

ORIBASES.   There is only one way: you must turn their thoughts in another direction, my lord;—they are wild with despair over the fate that awaits them if you delay any longer.

MAXIMUS.   Now go to heaven, oh fool; now die for your Lord and Master!

JULIAN (*grasping him by the arm*).   The Emperor's empire for me!

MAXIMUS.   Achilles!

JULIAN.   What looses the covenant?

MAXIMUS (*reaching him the sacrificial knife*).   This.

JULIAN.   What washes the water away?

MAXIMUS.   The blood of the sacrifice.

(*He tears off the fillet from his own brow, and fastens it round Cæsar's.*)

ORIBASES (*drawing nearer*).   What is your purpose, my lord?

JULIAN.   Ask not.

EUTHERIUS.   Listen to the noise! Up, up, my Cæsar!

JULIAN.   First down,—then up. (*To* MAXIMUS.) The sanctuary, my beloved brother——?

MAXIMUS.   Right underneath, in the second vault.

ORIBASES.   Cæsar, Cæsar,—where are you going?

MAXIMUS.   To freedom.

JULIAN.   Through darkness to light.   Ah——!
 (*He descends into the lower galleries.*)
MAXIMUS (*softly, looking after him*).   So it has come at last!

EUTHERIUS.   Speak, speak; what mean these hidden arts?

ORIBASES.   And now, when every instant is precious——

MAXIMUS (*whispering restlessly, as he shifts his place*).   These gliding, clammy shadows! Faugh! the slimy things crawling about his feet——!

ORIBASES (*listening*).   The noise increases, Eutherius!   I... the soldiers; listen, listen!

EUTHERIUS.   It is the song in the church——

ORIBASES.   No, it is the soldiers!—here they come!
 (*The Knight* SALLUST *appears up in the gallery,
   surrounded by a great crowd of excited soldiers.
   The Standard-Bearer* MAURUS *is amongst
   them.*)

SALLUST.   Be reasonable, I entreat you——!

THE SOLDIERS.   Cæsar has betrayed us! Cæsar shall die!

SALLUST.   And what then, madmen?

MAURUS.   What then? With Cæsar's head we will buy forgiveness——

THE SOLDIERS.   Come forth, come forth, Cæsar!

SALLUST.   Cæsar,—my Cæsar, where are you?

JULIAN (*calling out, in the vault underneath*). Helios! Helios!

MAXIMUS.   Free!

THE CHOIR IN THE CHURCH ABOVE.   Our Father which art in heaven!

SALLUST. Where is he? Eutherius, Oribases,—
what is going on here?

THE CHOIR (*in the church*). Hallowed be Thy
name!

JULIAN (*comes up the steps; he has blood on his forehead, on his breast, and on his hands*). It is finished!

THE SOLDIERS. Cæsar!

SALLUST. Blood-stained——! What have you
done?

JULIAN. Cloven the mists of terror.

MAXIMUS. All creation lies in your hand.

THE CHOIR (*in the church*). Thy will be done on
earth as it is in heaven!

(*The chant continues during what follows.*)

JULIAN. Now Constantius has no longer a body-
guard.

MAURUS. What do you say, my lord?

JULIAN. Ah! my faithful ones! Up into the
daylight; to Rome, and to Greece!

THE SOLDIERS. Long live the Emperor Julian!

JULIAN. We will not look back; all ways lie open
before us. Up into the daylight! Through the
church! The liars shall be silenced——!

(*He rushes up the steps in the background.*)

The army mine, the treasure mine, the throne
mine!

THE CHOIR (*in the church*). Lead us not into
temptation; but deliver us from evil!

> (JULIAN *throws wide the doors, revealing the
> brightly-lighted interior of the church. The
> priests stand before the high altar; crowds of wor-
> shippers kneel below, around the Princess's bier.*)

Julian.   Free, free!   Mine is the kingdom!

Sallust (*calls to him*).   And the power and the glory!

The Choir (*in the church*).   Thine is the kingdom, and the power, and the glory——

Julian (*dazzled by the light*).   Ah!

Maximus.   Victory!

The Choir (*in the church*).   ——for ever, and ever, amen!

THE EMPEROR JULIAN.

DRAMA IN FIVE ACTS.

Characters.

THE EMPEROR JULIAN.
NEVITA, *a general.*
POTAMON, *a goldsmith.*
CÆSARIUS OF NAZIANZUS, *court physician.*
THEMISTIUS, *an orator.*
MAMERTINUS, *an orator.*
URSULUS, *treasurer.*
EUNAPIUS, *a barber.*
BARBARA, *a procuress.*
HEKEBOLIUS, *a theologian.*
Courtiers and State officers.
Citizens of Constantinople.
People taking part in the procession of Dionysus, flute-players, dancers, jugglers, and women.
Envoys from eastern kings.
THE CHAMBERLAIN EUTHERIUS.
Servants of the palace.
Judges, orators, teachers, and citizens of Antioch.
MEDON, *a corn-merchant.*
MALCHUS, *a tax-gatherer.*
GREGORY OF NAZIANZUS, *Cæsarius's brother.*
PHOCION, *a dyer.*
PUBLIA, *a woman of Antioch.*
HILARION, *son of Publia.*
AGATHON OF CAPPADOCIA.
MARIS, *Bishop of Chalcedon.*

People taking part in the procession of Apollo, priests, servants of the temple, harp-players and watchmen of the city.
Agathon's younger brother.
A procession of Christian prisoners.
HERACLIUS, *a poet.*
ORIBASES, *court physician.*
LIBANIUS, *an orator, and governor of Antioch.*
APOLLINARIS, *a hymn-writer.*
CYRILLUS, *a teacher.*
An old priest of Cybele.
Psalm-singers of Antioch.
FROMENTINUS, *a captain.*
JOVIAN, *a general.*
MAXIMUS THE MYSTIC.
NUMA, *a soothsayer.*
Two other Etruscan soothsayers.
PRINCE HORMISDAS, *a Persian exile.*
ANATOLUS, *captain of the life-guard.*
PRISCUS, *a philosopher.*
KYTRON, *a philosopher.*
AMMIAN, *a captain.*
BASILIUS OF CÆSAREA.
MAKRINA, *his sister.*
A Persian deserter.
Roman and Greek soldiers.
Persian warriors.

The first act passes in Constantinople, the second and third in Antioch, the fourth in and about the eastern territories of the empire, and the fifth on the plains beyond the Tigris. The events take place in the interval between December, A.D. 361, and the end of June, A.D. 363.

THE EMPEROR JULIAN.

DRAMA IN FIVE ACTS.

———◆———

Act First.

(The port at Constantinople. In the foreground, to the right, a decorated landing-stage, overlaid with carpets. On a high terrace, a little way from the landing-stage, is seen a veiled stone, surrounded by a guard. Far out on the Bosphorus lies the imperial fleet, hung with flags of mourning.)

(A countless multitude in boats, and on the beach. At the end of the landing-stage stands the EMPEROR JULIAN, *robed in purple and decked with golden ornaments. He is surrounded by courtiers and high officers of state. Among those standing nearest to him are* NEVITA, *the commander of the forces, and the court physician,* CÆSARIUS, *together with the orators* THEMISTIUS *and* MAMERTINUS.)*

JULIAN (*looking out over the water*). What a meeting! The dead and the living Emperor.—Alas that he should have drawn his last breath in such distant regions! Alas that, in spite of all my haste, I should not have had the sweet consolation of embracing my kinsman for the last time! A bitter lot for both of us!—

Where is the ship with the body?

NEVITA.   There it comes.

JULIAN.   That long boat ?

NEVITA.   Yes, most gracious Emperor.

JULIAN.   My poor kinsman! So great in life; and now to have to content you with so low a roof. Now you will not strike your forehead against the coffin-lid, you who bowed your head in riding through the arch of Constantine.

A CITIZEN AMONG THE SPECTATORS (*to the Goldsmith* POTAMON).   How young he looks, our new Emperor!

POTAMON.   But he has filled out a bit. When I last saw him he was a lean stripling; that is now nine or ten years ago.

ANOTHER CITIZEN.   Ah, he has done great things in those years.

A WOMAN.   And all the dangers he has passed through, ever since his childhood!

A PRIEST.   Marvellously has he been shielded from them all; the hand of heaven is over him.

POTAMON.   Rumour says that in Gaul he placed himself under guardianship of another sort.

THE PRIEST.   Lies, lies; you may depend upon it.

JULIAN.   Now he comes. The Sun, whom I invoke, and the great thunder-wielding God, know that I have never desired Constantius's death. That was far indeed from being my wish. I have offered up prayers for his life.—Tell me, Cæsarius,—you must know best,—have they shown all due honour, on the journey, to the imperial corpse?

CÆSARIUS.   The funeral procession was like a

conqueror's triumph, through the whole of Asia Minor. In every town we passed, believers thronged the streets; through whole nights the churches echoed with prayers and hymns; thousands of burning tapers transformed the darkness into high noon——

JULIAN. Good, good, good!—I am seized with an unspeakable misgiving at the thought of taking the helm of state after so great and virtuous and well-beloved an Emperor. Why was it not my lot to live in peaceful retirement?

MAMERTINUS. And who could have sufficed to this high and difficult calling so completely as you, incomparable lord? I call boldly upon all the others who have aspired to the empire: Come, then, and take the helm of government; but take it as Julian does. Be on the alert night and day for the common welfare. Be masters in name, and yet servants to civic freedom. Choose the foremost places in battle, and not at the feasts. Take nothing for yourselves, but lavish gifts upon all. Let your justice be equally remote from laxity and from cruelty. Live so that no virgin on earth shall wring her hands because of you. Bid defiance both to impenetrable Gaul, and inhospitable Germany. What would they answer? Appalled by such stern conditions, they would stop their effeminate ears, and cry: "Only a Julian is equal to such a task!"

JULIAN. The Omnipotent grant that such high hopes may not be disappointed. But how great are my shortcomings! A shudder comes over me. To affront comparison with Alexander, Marcus Aurelius, and so many other illustrious men! Has not Plato said that only a god can rule over men? Oh pray with me that I may escape the snares of ambition, and the temptations of power. Athens, Athens! Thither my longings turn! I was as a man taking reasonable exercise for the sake of his health;—and now, they come and say to me, "Go forth into the arena, and conquer in the Olympian games. The eyes of all Greece are upon you!" May I not well be panic-stricken even before the contest begins?

THEMISTIUS. Panic-stricken, oh Emperor? Have you not already the applause of Greece? Are you not come to reinstate all exiled virtues in their ancient rights? Do we not find concentrated in you all the victorious genius of Herakles, of Dionysus, of Solon, of——

JULIAN. Hush! Only the praise of the dead shall be heard to-day. The boat has reached the wharf. Take my crown and my chains; I will not wear the insignia of empire at such a time as this.

(*He hands the ornaments to one of the bystanders. The funeral procession advances along the landing-stage, with great pomp. Priests with lighted tapers walk at its head; the coffin is drawn on a low-wheeled carriage; church-banners are borne before and after the carriage; choristers swing censers; crowds of Christian citizens follow after.*)

JULIAN (*laying his hand on the coffin, and sighing audibly*). Ah!

A SPECTATOR. Did he cross himself?

ANOTHER IN THE CROWD. No.

The First. You see; you see!

A Third Spectator. And he did not bow before the sacred image.

The First (*to the second*). You see! What did I tell you?

Julian. Pass onward to thy home, amid pomp and honour, soulless body of my kinsman! I make not this dust answerable for the wrongs thy spirit did me. What do I say? Was it thy spirit that dealt so hardly with my house, that I alone am left? Was it thy spirit that caused my childhood to be darkened with a thousand terrors? Was it thy spirit that called for the sacrifice of that noble Cæsar's life? Was it thou, who didst assign to me, an inexperienced youth, so difficult a post in inhospitable Gaul, and afterwards, when disaffection and mischance had failed to crush me, didst try to rob me of the honour of my victories? Oh Constantius, my kinsman,—all this did not spring from thy great heart. Wherefore didst thou writhe in remorse and anguish; why didst thou see gory shades around thee, on thy last bed of pain? Evil councillors embittered thy life and thy death. I know them, these councillors ; they were men who took hurt from living in the ceaseless sunshine of thy favour. I know them, these men, who so obsequiously clothed themselves in that garb of faith, which was most favourably regarded at court.

Heathen Citizens (*among the spectators*). Long live the Emperor Julian!

Cæsarius. Most gracious lord, the procession waits——

JULIAN (*to the priests*).   Let not your pious hymns be silent on my account.   Forward, my friends!

(*The procession passes slowly out to the left.*)

Follow whoso will, and remain whoso will.   But this you shall all know to-day, that my place is here.

(*Uneasiness and movement in the crowd.*)

What am I?   The Emperor.   But in saying that, have I said all?   Is there not one imperial office, which seems to have been shamefully wiped out of remembrance in these later years?   What was that crowned philosopher, Marcus Aurelius?   Emperor?   Only Emperor?   I could almost ask : was he not something more than Emperor?   Was he not also the Supreme Pontiff?

VOICES IN THE CROWD.   What does the Emperor say?   What was that?   What did he say?

THEMISTIUS.   Oh sire, is it really your purpose——?

JULIAN.   My uncle Constantine the Great himself dared not renounce this dignity.   Even after he had conceded to a certain new faith such very extraordinary privileges, he was still called the Chief Priest by all who held fast to the ancient divinities of the Grecian race.   I shall not here enlarge upon the melancholy disuse into which this office has fallen of late years, but shall merely say that none of my exalted predecessors, not even he to whom, with tear-stained faces, we to-day bid our last farewell, has dared to reject it.   Should I presume to take any step which so wise and just emperors did not deem right or expedient?   Far be it from me!

THEMISTIUS.   Oh great Emperor, do you mean by this——?

JULIAN. I mean by this, that there shall be perfect freedom for all citizens. Cling to the Christians' God, you who find it conduce to your souls' repose. As for me, I dare not build my hopes on a god who has hitherto been a foe to me in all my undertakings. I know by infallible signs and tokens that the victories I won on the Gallic frontier I owe to those other divinities who favoured Alexander in a somewhat similar way. Under the watch and ward of these divinities I passed unscathed through all dangers ; and, in especial, it was they who furthered my journey hither with such marvellous speed and success that, as I gathered from cries in the streets, the people have come to look upon me as a divine being,—which is a great exaggeration, my friends ! But certain it is, that I dare not show myself ungrateful for such continuous proofs of favour.

VOICES IN THE CROWD (*subdued*). What is he going to do ?

JULIAN. Therefore, I restore the venerable Gods of our forefathers to their pristine rights. But no injury shall be done to the God of the Galileans, nor to the God of the Jews. The temples, which pious rulers of old erected with such admirable art, shall rise again in rejuvenated splendour, with altars and statues, each for its especial god, so that seemly worship may once more be offered them. But I will by no means tolerate any vengeful assaults upon the churches of the Christians; neither shall their graveyards be molested, nor any other places which a strange delusion leads them to regard as sacred. We will bear with the errors of others ; I myself have

wandered in the maze ;—but over that I cast a veil.
What I have thought upon things divine, since my
one-and-twentieth year, I will not now dwell upon ;
I will only say, that I congratulate those who follow
my example,—that I smile at those who will not tread
in my footsteps,—that I will doubtless try to persuade,
but will not coerce any one.

 (*He stops a moment, expectantly; feeble applause is
  heard here and there among the crowd. He
  continues with more warmth.*)

I had reckoned, not unreasonably, on grateful
acclamations, where I now find only wondering
curiosity. Yet I ought to have known it ;—there
reigns a deplorable indifference among those who
profess to hold fast to our ancient faith. Oppression
and mockery have caused us to forget the venerable
rites of our forefathers. I have inquired high and
low, but scarcely a single person have I found who
could give me certain information as to the ceremonies
attendant on an offering to Apollo or to Fortuna. I
must take the initiative in this, as in other matters.
It has cost me many sleepless nights to search out in
the ancient records what tradition prescribed in such
cases ; but I do not complain, when I remember how
much we owe to these very divinities; nor am I
ashamed to do everything with my own hands——
Whither away, Cæsarius ?

CÆSARIUS. To the church, most gracious
Emperor; I would pray for the soul of my departed
master.

JULIAN. Go, go ! In these matters every one is
free.

(CÆSARIUS, *with several of the older courtiers
and officers of state, goes out to the left.*)

But the freedom I concede to the meanest citizen, I
claim for myself as well. Be it known, therefore, to
you all, Greeks and Romans, that I revert with my
whole heart to the beliefs and rites which our
forefathers held sacred,—that they may freely be
propagated and exercised, no less than all new and
foreign opinions;—and as I am a son of the
metropolis, and therefore hold it pre-eminently dear,
this I proclaim in the name of the divinities who
protect this city.

(JULIAN *gives a sign; some of the attendants
withdraw the veil from the stone: an altar is
seen, and, at its base, a flagon of wine, a cruse of
oil, a little heap of wood, and other appurten-
ances. Strong but speechless emotion in the
multitude, as* JULIAN *goes up to the altar, and
prepares for the offering.*)

THEMISTIUS.   Oh well may I, as a Greek, melt into
tears at the sight of so much humility and pious
zeal!

A CITIZEN.   See, he breaks the fuel himself!

ANOTHER.   Over his left thigh. Is that how it
ought to be broken?

THE FIRST CITIZEN.   I suppose it is.

MAMERTINUS.   In the light of the fire you there
kindle, oh great Emperor, shall research and learning
shine forth, ay, and rise rejuvenated, like that miraculous bird——

NEVITA.   That fire will harden the weapons of
Greece. I know little of the Galilean figments; but

I have noted that all those who believe in them are spiritless and unfit for greater things.

THEMISTIUS. In this fire, oh incomparable one, I see wisdom purged of all scandal and reproach. The wine of your libation is like purple, wherewith you deck the truth, and set her on a royal throne. Now, as you lift up your hands——

MAMERTINUS. Now, as you lift up your hands, it is as though you glorified the brow of knowledge with a golden wreath; and the tears you shed——

THEMISTIUS (*pressing nearer*). Yes, yes; the tears I see you shed are like costly pearls, wherewith eloquence shall once more be rewarded in kingly wise. Once again, then, the Greeks are suffered to raise their eyes to heaven, and follow the eternal stars in their courses! How long it is since that was vouchsafed us! Have we not been forced, for fear of spies, to tremble and bow our faces to the earth, like the brutes? Which of us dared so much as to watch the sunrise or the sunset?

(*He turns to the crowd.*)

Even you husbandmen, who have flocked here in such numbers to-day, even you did not venture to note the position of the heavenly bodies, although by them you should have regulated your work——

MAMERTINUS. And you seamen,—have either you or your fathers dared to utter the names of the constellations by which you steered? Now you may do so; now all are free to——

THEMISTIUS. Now no Greek need live on land or sea without consulting the immutable laws of heaven; he need no longer let himself be tossed

about like a ball, by chance and circumstance;
he——

MAMERTINUS. Oh, how great is this Emperor, to
whom we owe such blessings!

JULIAN (*before the altar, with uplifted arms*). Thus
have I openly and in all humility made libations of oil
and wine to you, ye beneficent divinities, who have so
long been denied these seemly observances. I have
sent up my thanksgiving to thee, oh Apollo, whom
some of the sages—especially those of the east—call
by the name of the Sun-King, because thou bringest
and renewest that light, wherein life has its source
and origin.—To thee, too, I have made offering, oh
Dionysus, god of ecstasy, who dost lift up the souls
of mortals out of abasement, and exaltest them to an
ennobling communion with higher spirits. — And,
although I name thee last, I have not been least
mindful of thee, oh Fortuna! Without thy aid,
should I have stood here? I know indeed that thou
dost no longer visibly manifest thyself, as in the golden
age, of which the peerless blind singer has told us.
But this I know, too,—and herein all other philosophers are at one with me—that it is thou who hast
the determining share in the choice of the guardian
spirit, good or evil, that is to accompany every man
on his path through life. I have no reason to chide
thee, oh Fortuna! Rather have I the greatest cause
to yield thee all thanks and praise. This duty,
precious to my heart, have I this day fulfilled. I
have not shrunk from even the humblest office. Here
I stand in open day; the eyes of all Greece are
upon me; I expect that the voice of all Greece will

unite with mine in acclaiming you, oh ye immortal gods!

> (*During the sacrificial service, most of the Christian onlookers have gradually retired; only a little knot remains behind. When* JULIAN *ceases speaking, there arise only faint sounds of approval mingled with subdued laughter, and whispers of astonishment.*)

JULIAN (*looking round*). What is this? What has become of them all? Are they sneaking away?

THEMISTIUS. Yes, red with shame at the ingratitude of so many years.

MAMERTINUS. No, it was the flush of joy. They are gone to spread the great tidings through the city.

JULIAN (*leaving the altar*). The ignorant mob is ever perplexed by what is unaccustomed. I have a difficult task before me; but no labour shall daunt me. What better befits a philosopher than to root out error? In this mission I count on your aid, enlightened friends! But our thoughts must turn elsewhere, for a little time. Follow me; I go to other duties.

> (*He departs hastily without returning the citizens' greetings; the courtiers, and his other attendants, follow him.*)

> (*A great hall in the Imperial Palace. Doors on both sides, and in the back; in front, to the left, on a daïs by the wall, stands the imperial throne.*)

(*The* EMPEROR JULIAN, *surrounded by his court and high officials, among whom is* URSULUS, *the Treasurer, with the orators* THEMISTIUS *and* MAMERTINUS.)

JULIAN.   So far have the gods aided us.   Now the work will roll onwards, like the waves of a spring flood. The sullen ill-will which I can trace in certain quarters where I least expected it, shall not disturb the balance of my mind.   Is it not precisely the distinguishing mark of true wisdom, that it begets patience?   We all know that by suitable remedies the evils of the body may be removed ;—but can fire and sword annihilate delusions as to things divine ?   And what avails it though your hands make offerings, if your souls condemn the action of your hands?

Thus will we live in concord with each other.   My court shall be open to all men of mark, whatever their opinions.   Let us show the world the rare and august spectacle of a court without hypocrisy— certainly the only one of its kind—a court in which flatterers are reckoned the most dangerous of enemies. We will oppose and censure one another, when it is needful, yet without loving one another the less.

(*To* NEVITA, *who enters by the back.*)

Your face is radiant, Nevita ;—what good tidings do you bring ?

NEVITA.   The best and happiest indeed.   A great number of envoys from princes in furthest India have come to bring you gifts, and entreat your friendship.

JULIAN.   Ah, tell me,—to what peoples do they belong ?

NEVITA.   To the Armenians, and other races

beyond the Tigris.   Indeed, some of the strangers say they come from the islands of Diu and Serandib.

JULIAN.   From the uttermost verge of the earth, my friends!

THEMISTIUS.   Even so far has rumour carried your name and your glory!

MAMERTINUS.   Even in those unknown regions is your sword a terror to princes and peoples!

THEMISTIUS.   Diu and Serandib!   Far east in the Indian sea——

MAMERTINUS.   I do not hesitate to say: beyond the circle of the earth——

JULIAN.   Bid the barber come!

(*A courtier goes out to the right.*)

I will receive the envoys in seemly guise,—yet without display or adornment.   So would the august Marcus Aurelius have received them; and I make him my pattern, rather than the Emperor whose death we have lately had to mourn.   No more parade of transitory worldly splendour.   Even the barbarians shall see that wisdom—in the person, truly, of her meanest servant—has resumed her place upon the throne.

(*The courtier returns with* EUNAPIUS, *the barber, who wears magnificent clothing.*)

JULIAN (*looks at him in astonishment, then goes to meet him, and greets him*).   What do you seek here, my lord?

EUNAPIUS.   Gracious Emperor, you have commanded me to come——

JULIAN.   You mistake, friend; I have not sent for any of my councillors.

EUNAPIUS. Most gracious Emperor——

URSULUS. Pardon me, sire; this man is the imperial barber.

JULIAN. What do I hear? Can it be? This man —oh, you are jesting—this man, in silken raiment, with gold-embroidered shoes, is——? Ah, indeed! So you are the barber! (*He bows before him.*) Never shall I presume to let myself be served by such delicate hands.

EUNAPIUS. Most gracious Emperor,—I pray you for God and my Saviour's sake——

JULIAN. Ho-ho! A Galilean! Did I not think so! Is this the self-denial you boast of? But I know you well! What divinity's temple have you plundered, or how many dips have you made into the Emperor's coffers, to attain such magnificence as this? —You can go; I have no occasion for you.

(EUNAPIUS *goes out to the right.*)

Tell me, Ursulus, what is that man's wage?

URSULUS. Gracious Emperor, by your august predecessor's command, the daily maintenance of twenty men is assigned him——

JULIAN. Aha! No more than that?

URSULUS. Yes, sire; latterly he has had free stabling in the imperial stables, together with a certain yearly allowance of money, and a gold piece for every time he——

JULIAN. And all this for a barber! What, then, must the others——? This shall not go on a day longer—— Admit the foreign envoys!

(NEVITA *goes out by the back.*)

I will receive them with uncut hair. Better so;

for although I know well that it is not the unkempt
hair, nor the tattered cloak, that makes the true
philosopher, yet I think the example given by both
Antisthenes and Diogenes may well be respected by
one who—even on the throne—desires to follow in
such great teachers' footsteps.

> (*He ascends the daïs where the throne is placed.*
> *The court ranges itself below. The Envoys,*
> *introduced by* NEVITA *and the Chamberlain*
> EUTHERIUS, *enter in magnificent procession,*
> *accompanied by slaves, who bear gifts of all*
> *sorts.*)

NEVITA. Most gracious Lord and Emperor! Not
being possessed of the noble idiom which so many
eloquent men, and you yourself not the least, have
perfected beyond all other tongues,—and therewith
fearful of letting barbarous sounds offend your ear,—
these envoys from oriental princes have deputed me
to be their spokesman.

JULIAN (*sitting on the throne*). I am ready to hear
you.

NEVITA. First, the King of Armenia lays at your
feet this suit of mail, begging you to wear it in battle
against the foes of the empire, although he knows
that you, invincible hero, stand under the protecting
eye of the gods, who will suffer no weapon of mortal
man to wound you.—Here are priceless carpets,
tents, and saddle-housings from the princes beyond
the Tigris. They thereby acknowledge that, if the
gods have granted those lands exceeding riches, it
was with the design that these riches should be at the
service of their favourite.—The King of Serandib,

and likewise the King of Diu, send you these weapons, sword, spear, and shield, with bows and arrows ; for, they say, " We esteem it wisest to stand unarmed before the victorious lord who, like a divinity, has shown himself mighty enough to crush all opposition."—In return, all pray for the supreme favour of your friendship, and especially beg that if, as report says, you purpose next spring to annihilate the audacious Persian king, you will spare their territories from hostile invasion.

JULIAN. Such an embassy cannot come quite as a surprise to me. The gifts shall be deposited in my treasury, and through you I inform your masters that it is my intention to maintain friendship with all nations who do not—whether by force or craft—stand in the way of my designs.—As to your being led, in your distant lands, to regard me as a divinity on account of my fortunate victories, I will not enter further into the matter. I reverence the gods too highly to arrogate to myself an unmerited place in their midst, although I know that frequently, and chiefly in the days of old, there have lived heroes and rulers who have been so greatly distinguished by the favour and grace of the gods, that it has been difficult to determine whether they should rightly be reckoned among mortals or immortals. But of such things it is rash to judge, even for us Greeks. How much more, then, for you ? Therefore enough of that.—Eutherius, conduct the strangers to repose, and see that they lack nothing.

> (*The Envoys and their train leave the hall, conducted by* EUTHERIUS. JULIAN *descends from*

the daïs; the courtiers and orators surround
him with admiring congratulations.)

THEMISTIUS.   So young,—and already so highly
honoured above all other Emperors!

MAMERTINUS.   I ask: will not Fame lack lungs
to proclaim your renown, if the gods, as I confidently
hope, grant you a long life?

THEMISTIUS.   The yell of fear uttered by the
flying Alemanni on the furthest shores of the Rhine
has swept eastward, until it dashed against Taurus
and Caucasus——

MAMERTINUS.   ——and now rolls, in thundering
reverberations, over the whole of Asia.

NEVITA.   What has so overawed the Indians is
the likeness between our Greek Julian and the
Macedonian Alexander——

MAMERTINUS.   Oh where is the likeness?   Had
King Alexander secret enemies in his own camp?
Had he to struggle against an envious and backbiting
imperial court?

NEVITA.   True, true; and there were no incapable
generals to clog Alexander's progress.

JULIAN.   Ursulus, it is my will that the coming of
these envoys shall be made known both in the city
and all regions of the empire.   Everything shall be
exactly set forth,—where they came from, and what
gifts they brought with them.   I will not withhold from
the citizens anything that concerns my government.
You may also mention in passing the strange idea of
the Indians, that Alexander has returned to earth.

URSULUS (*hesitatingly*).   Pardon me, most gracious
Emperor, but——

JULIAN. Well?

URSULUS. You have yourself said that in this court no flattery is to be tolerated——

JULIAN. True, my friend!

URSULUS. Then let me honestly tell you that these envoys came to seek your predecessor, not you.

JULIAN. What do you dare to tell me?

THEMISTIUS. Pooh, what preposterous nonsense!

MAMERTINUS. What a fable!

URSULUS. It is the truth. I have long known that these men were on their way,—long before the Emperor Constantius closed his eyes. Oh, my most gracious lord, let not a false vanity gain entrance into your young mind——

JULIAN. Enough, enough! Then you mean to say that—— ?

URSULUS. Think for yourself. How could your victories in Gaul, glorious as they have been, reach the ears of such distant nations with such rapidity? When the envoys spoke of the Emperor's heroic deeds, they were thinking of the war against the King of Persia——

NEVITA. I did not know that the war against King Sapor had been conducted in such a way as to spread terror to the ends of the earth.

URSULUS. True; fortune has been against our arms in those regions. But it was the rumour of the great armament which the Emperor Constantius was preparing for the spring that alarmed the Armenians and the other nations.—Oh, calculate the time, sire, count the days if you will, and say if it can possibly be otherwise. Your march hither from Gaul was marvellously rapid; but the journey of these men from the Indian isles——; it would be tenfold more marvellous if——; ask them, and you will hear——

JULIAN (*pale with anger*). Why do you say all this to me?

URSULUS. Because it is the truth, and because I cannot bear to see your fresh and fair renown darkened by borrowed trappings.

THEMISTIUS. What audacity!

MAMERTINUS. What incredible audacity!

JULIAN. You cannot bear, indeed! You cannot bear! Oh, I know you better. I know all you old courtiers. It is the gods whose glory you would disparage. For is it not to the glory of the gods, that they can make a man the instrument of great exploits? But you hate them, these gods, whose temples you have thrown down, whose statues you have broken to pieces, and whose treasures you have seized. You have scarcely even tolerated our beneficent deities. You have scarcely suffered the pious to cherish them secretly in their hearts. And now you would also break down the temple of gratitude which I have dedicated to them in my heart; you would rob me of the grateful belief that I am indebted to the immortals for a new and much to be coveted benefaction;—for may not renown be so termed?

URSULUS. The one God of heaven is my witness that——

JULIAN. The one God! There we have it again! So are you always. What intolerance! Contrast

yourselves with us. Do we say that our gods are the
only ones? Do we not esteem both the gods of the
Egyptians and the Jewish Jehovah, who has certainly
done great things among his people? But you, on
the contrary,—and a man like you, too, Ursulus—!
Are *you* a Roman, born of Grecian race? The one
God! What barbarous effrontery!

URSULUS. You have promised to hate no man on
account of his opinions.

JULIAN. I have promised that; but neither will
I suffer you to treat us too insolently. These
envoys have not come to—— ? That is to say, in
other words, that the great and divine Dionysus,
whose especial charge it is to reveal what is hidden,
—that he is not as powerful now as in bygone ages.
Ought I to suffer this? Is it not overweening
audacity? Am I not forced to call you to account?

URSULUS. Then all Christians will say that it is
their faith you are persecuting.

JULIAN. No one shall be persecuted for his faith's
sake. But have I the right to overlook whatever
faults you may commit, simply because you are
Christians? Shall your delusions shield your misdeeds? What have not your impudent crew for
long been doing, both here at court and elsewhere?
Have you not flattered all vices, and bowed before
all caprices? Ay, what have not you, Ursulus,
looked through your fingers at? I am thinking of
that shameless, bedizened barber, that salve-stinking
fool, who just now filled me with loathing. Are not
you treasurer? How could you give way to his
impudent demands?

URSULUS.   Is it a crime to have done my master's will ?

JULIAN.   I will have nothing to do with such luxurious servants.   All those insolent fops shall be hunted out of the palace ; and all cooks, and jugglers, and dancers after them.   A becoming frugality shall once more be the order of the day.

(*To* THEMISTIUS *and* MAMERTINUS.)

You, my friends, shall aid me in this.—And you, Nevita, on whom, as a mark of special distinction, I bestow the title of general,—you I depute to investigate how the offices of state have been administered under my predecessor, especially of late years.   You may call in the aid of qualified men, at your own choice, to decide with you in these affairs.

(*To the older courtiers and councillors.*)

I have no need of you.   When my lamented kinsman, on his death-bed, appointed me his successor, he also bequeathed to me that justice which his long illness had prevented him from enforcing.   Go home; and when you have given an account of yourselves, you may go whither you please.

URSULUS.   The Lord God uphold and shield you, my Emperor !

(*He bows, and goes out by the back, together with the older men.   NEVITA, THEMISTIUS, and MAMERTINUS, with all the younger men, gather round the Emperor.*)

NEVITA.   My august master, how can I sufficiently thank you for the mark of favour which you——

JULIAN.   No thanks.   In these few days I have learnt to value your fidelity and judgment.   I also

commission you to draw up the despatch concerning
the eastern envoys. Word it so that the beneficent
gods may find in it no reason to be offended with
any of us.

NEVITA. I will perform my Emperor's will in
both matters. (*He goes out to the right.*)

JULIAN. And now, my faithful friends, now let us
praise the immortal powers who have shown us the
right way.

THEMISTIUS. The immortals, and their more than
mortal favourite! What joy there will be throughout
the empire, when it is known that you have dismissed
those violent and rapacious men!

MAMERTINUS. With what anxiety and impatient
hope will the choice of their successors be awaited!

THEMISTIUS. All the Greeks will exclaim with one
voice : " Plato himself has taken the helm of state ! "

MAMERTINUS. No, no, worthy friend ; all the
Greeks will exclaim : " Plato's ideal is realised—' Only
a god can reign over men ! ' "

THEMISTIUS. I trust that the goodwill of the
beneficent powers may follow Nevita. He has received a great and difficult charge ; I do not know
very much of him ; but we must all hope that he will
prove himself to be the right——

MAMERTINUS. Undoubtedly; although there may
perhaps be other men who——

THEMISTIUS. I do not mean to say that your
choice, oh peerless Emperor——

MAMERTINUS. No, no, far from it !

THEMISTIUS. But if it be an error to burn with
zeal to serve a beloved master——

MAMERTINUS. ——then, in truth, you have more than one erring friend——

THEMISTIUS. ——even if you do not honour them, as you have honoured the thrice-fortunate Nevita——

MAMERTINUS. ——even if they have to be content without any visible token of your favour——

JULIAN. We will leave no capable man idle or unrewarded. As regards you, Themistius, I bestow upon you the governorship of this city of Constantinople ; and you, Mamertinus, prepare to betake yourself to Rome during the coming year, to enter upon one of the vacant consulships.

THEMISTIUS. My Emperor ! I am dizzy with so much honour——!

MAMERTINUS. So high a distinction ! Consul ! Was there ever a consul so honoured as I ? Lucius, or Brutus, or Publius Valerius ? What was their honour to mine ? They were chosen by the people, I by Julian !

A COURTIER. Praise be to the Emperor, who makes justice his guide !

ANOTHER COURTIER. Praise be to him, whose very name strikes terror to the barbarians !

THEMISTIUS. Praise be to all the exalted gods, who have united in casting their enamoured eyes on one single man, so that when the day comes—distant may it be !—when he shall for the first time inflict pain on us by departing hence, this one man may be said to have cast Socrates, Marcus Aurelius, and Alexander, into the shade !

JULIAN. There you touched the kernel of the matter, my Themistius ! It is to the gods that we

must uplift our hands and hearts.   I say this, not as
instructing you, but merely to remind you of what
has so long been forgotten at this court.   Far be it
from me to wish to coerce any one.   But can I be
blamed because I would fain have others share in the
sweet rapture which possesses me when I feel myself
initiated into the communion of the immortals?
Praise, praise to thee, vine-crowned Dionysus!   For it
is chiefly thou who dost bring about such great and
mysterious things.   Go now, each to his business.   I,
for my part, have ordered a festive procession through
the streets of the city.   It shall be no mere revel for
my courtiers, nor a banquet within four walls.   The
populace shall be free to join me or to hold aloof; I
will discern the pure from the impure, the pious from
the misguided.

Oh Sun-King, shed light and beauty over the day!
Oh Dionysus, let thy glory descend in floods upon our
minds; fill our souls with thy sacred storm-wind;
fill them till all trammels are burst asunder, and
liberated ecstasy draws breath in dance and song!—
Life, life, life in beauty!

(*He goes out hastily to the right.   The courtiers
break up into whispering groups, and gradually
disperse.*)

(*A narrow street in Constantinople.*)

(*A great concourse of people, all looking in one
direction down the street.   Noise, singing, and
the music of flutes and drums is heard at some
distance.*)

A SHOEMAKER (*at his house-door, calls across the street*). What is going on, dear neighbour?

A SHOPKEEPER (*in the house opposite*). They say it is some Syrian jugglers, who have come to town.

A FRUIT-SELLER (*in the street*). No, no; it is a band of Egyptians, going around with apes and dromedaries.

EUNAPIUS THE BARBER (*poorly clad, trying in vain to slip through the crowd*). Make room, you fools! How the devil can you joke and chatter on such a day of misfortune?

A WOMAN (*at a small window*). Hist, hist, Eunapius! My comely master!

EUNAPIUS. How dare you speak to me in the open street, you procuress?

THE WOMAN. Slip in by the back way, sweet friend!

EUNAPIUS. Fie upon you! Am I in the humour for folly——

THE WOMAN. You shall soon be in the humour. Come, fair Eunapius; I had a consignment of fresh doves the day before yesterday——

EUNAPIUS. Oh sinful world! (*Tries to pass.*) Make room, there, in Satan's name; let me pass!

HEKEBOLIUS (*clad for a journey, and followed by a couple of laden slaves, comes from a side street*). Has the town turned into a madhouse? Every one is trying to out-bellow his neighbour, and no one can give me any information. Aha,—Eunapius, my pious brother!

EUNAPIUS. All hail to you, reverend sir! So you have come back to town?

HEKEBOLIUS.   This very moment;—I have consecrated the warm autumn months to quiet devotion,
on my estate in Crete.   And now pray tell me what
is going on here?

EUNAPIUS.   Bad luck and confusion.   The new
Emperor——

HEKEBOLIUS.   Yes, yes, I have heard strange
rumours——

EUNAPIUS.   The truth is ten times worse.   All
faithful servants are hunted out of the palace.

HEKEBOLIUS.   Is it possible?

EUNAPIUS.   Alackaday; I myself was the first——

HEKEBOLIUS.   Terrible!   Then, perhaps, I too
——?

EUNAPIUS.   Most certainly.   All accounts are
to be examined, all gifts resumed, all irregular perquisites——

HEKEBOLIUS (*growing pale*).   God have mercy on
us!

EUNAPIUS.   The Lord be praised, I have a good
conscience!

HEKEBOLIUS.   I too, I too; but nevertheless——;
ah, then it is no doubt true that the Emperor has
sacrificed to Apollo and Fortuna?

EUNAPIUS.   Certainly; but who cares for such
trifles?

HEKEBOLIUS.   Trifles?   Do you not see, my short-
sighted friend, that it is our faith, as good Christians,
that he is persecuting?

EUNAPIUS.   What do you say?   God's cross, is it
possible?

A WOMAN (*in the crowd*).   There they come!

A MAN (*on a housetop*).   I can seen him!

OTHER VOICES.   Who is coming?   Who, who?

THE MAN ON THE HOUSETOP.   The Emperor Julian.   He has vine-leaves in his hair.

PEOPLE IN THE STREET.   The Emperor!

EUNAPIUS.   The Emperor!

HEKEBOLIUS.   Come, come, my godly brother!

EUNAPIUS.   Let me go, sir; I am not in the least godly.

HEKEBOLIUS.   Not godly——?

EUNAPIUS.   Who dares accuse me of——?   Do you want to ruin me?   Godly?   When was I godly? I once belonged to the sect of the Donatists; that was years and years ago.   Devil take the Donatists!   (*He knocks at the window.*)   Hi, Barbara, Barbara; open the door, old she-cat!   (*He slips in through the doorway.*)

THE MULTITUDE.   There he is!   There he comes!

HEKEBOLIUS.   All irregular perquisites——! Accounts examined!   Oh thunderbolt of disaster! (*He slips away, followed by his two slaves.*)

> (*The procession of Dionysus comes down the street. Flute-players go foremost; drunken men, some of them dressed as fauns and satyrs, dance to the measure.   In the middle of the procession comes the* EMPEROR JULIAN, *riding on an ass, which is covered with a panther-skin; he is dressed as the god Dionysus, with a panther-skin over his shoulders, a wreath of vine-leaves round his head, in his hands a staff, wreathed with green, and with a pine-cone fastened on its*

upper end.   Half-naked, painted women and youths, dancers and jugglers, surround him; some carry wine-cans and goblets, others play tambourines, and move forward with wild leaps and antics.)

THE DANCERS (*singing*).

Potions of fire drain from goblets o'erflowing!
            Potions of fire!
            Lips deeply sipping,
            locks unguent-dripping,
            goat-haunches tripping,
    Wine-God, we hail thee in rapturous quire!

THE WOMEN (*singing*).

Come, Bacchanalians, while noontide is glowing—
            come, do not flee us—
plunge we in love-sports night blushes at knowing!
            There rides Lyæus,
            pard-borne, delivering!
            Come, do not flee us;
know, we are passionate; feel, we are quivering!
            Leaping all, playing all,
            staggering and swaying all—
            come, do not flee us!

JULIAN. Make room! Clear the way, citizens! Stand reverently aside; not for us, but for him to whom we are doing honour!

A VOICE IN THE CROWD. The Emperor in the company of mummers and harlots!

JULIAN. The shame is yours, that I must content myself with such as these. Do you not blush to find more piety and zeal among these than among yourselves?

AN OLD MAN.   Christ enlighten you, sire!

JULIAN.   Aha, you are a Galilean!   And you want to put in your word?   Did not your great Master sit at meat with sinners?   Did he not frequent houses that were held less than reputable?   Answer me that.

EUNAPIUS (*surrounded by girls, in the doorway of* BARBARA'S *house*).   Yes, answer, answer, if you can, you fool!

JULIAN.   Aha,—are not you that barber whom——?

EUNAPIUS.   A new-made freeman, gracious Emperor!   Make way, Bacchanalians; room for a brother!

(*He and the girls dance into the ranks of the Bacchanalians.*)

JULIAN.   I like this well.   Take example by this Greek, if you have a spark of your fathers' spirit left in you.   And this is sorely needed, you citizens; for no divinity has been so much misunderstood—ay, even ridiculed—as this ecstatic Dionysus, whom the Romans call Bacchus.   Think you he is the god of sots?   Oh ignorant creatures, I pity you, if that is your idea.   Who but he inspires poets and prophets with their marvellous gifts?   I know that some attribute this function to Apollo, and certainly not without a show of reason; but in that case the whole matter must be regarded in quite another aspect,—as I could prove by many authorities.   But I will not discuss this with you in the open streets.   This is neither the place nor the time.   Yes, mock away!   Make the sign of the cross!   I see it!   You would like to whistle with your fingers; you would stone me, if you dared.—Oh, how I blush for this city, so

sunk in barbarism that it knows no better than to
cling to an ignorant Jew's deluded fantasies!—Forward! Stand aside,—do not block the way!

THE DANCERS.

> There rides Lyæus,
> pard-borne, delivering!

THE WOMEN.

> Know, we are passionate; feel, we are quivering;
> come, do not flee us!

> (*During the singing of the refrain the procession
> turns into a side street; the crowd looks on in
> dumb astonishment.*)

> (*The Emperor's library in the Palace.   Entrance
> door on the left; a lesser doorway, with a curtain
> before it, on the right.*)

> (*The Chamberlain* EUTHERIUS *enters from the
> left, followed by two servants, bearing carpets.*)

EUTHERIUS (*calling out to the right*).   Agilo, Agilo,
warm rose-water! The Emperor is going to the bath.
(*He goes out to the right, with both servants.*)

> (*The* EMPEROR JULIAN *enters hastily from the
> left.   He still wears the panther-skin and the
> vine-leaves; in his hand is the green-wreathed
> staff.   He paces the room once or twice, then
> flings the staff into a corner.*)

JULIAN.   Was there beauty in that?——

Where were the white-bearded elders? Where the
pure maidens, with the fillets on their brows, modest,
and of seemly bearing, even in the rapture of the dance?

Out upon you, harlots!

(He tears off the panther-skin, and casts it aside.)

Whither has beauty fled? When the Emperor bids her come forth again, will she not obey?

Out upon this stinking ribaldry!——

What faces! All the vices crying aloud in their distorted features. Ulcers on soul and body——

Faugh, faugh! A bath, Agilo! The stench chokes me.

THE BATH-SERVANT AGILO *(in the doorway to the right).* The bath is ready, gracious sire!

JULIAN. The bath? Why trouble about that? What is the filth of the body compared with all the rest? Go!

(AGILO goes out again. The Emperor stands some time in thought.)

The seer of Nazareth sat at meat among publicans and sinners.—

Where lies the gulf between that and this?——

(HEKEBOLIUS enters from the left, and stops apprehensively at the door.)

JULIAN. What do you want, man?

HEKEBOLIUS *(kneeling).* Sire!

JULIAN. Ah, what do I see? Hekebolius;—is it really you?

HEKEBOLIUS. The same, and yet another.

JULIAN. My old teacher. What would you have? Stand up!

HEKEBOLIUS. No, no, let me lie. And be not angry with me for presuming on my former right of entrance to your presence.

JULIAN *(coldly).* I asked you what you want?

HEKEBOLIUS. "My old teacher," you said. Oh

that I could cast the veil of oblivion over those
times!

JULIAN (*as before*). I understand. You mean
that——

HEKEBOLIUS. Oh that I could sink into the
earth, and hide the shame I feel! See, see,—here
I lie at your feet, a man whose hair is growing grey
—a man who has pored and pondered all his days,
and has to confess at last that he has gone astray, and
led his beloved pupil into error!

JULIAN. What would you have me understand
by that?

HEKEBOLIUS. You called me your old teacher.
See, here I lie in the dust before you, looking up to
you with wonder, and calling you my new teacher.

JULIAN. Rise, Hekebolius!

HEKEBOLIUS (*rising*). You shall hear everything,
sire, and judge me according to your righteousness.—
When you were gone, life at your august predecessor's
court became almost intolerable to me. I do not know
whether you have heard that I was promoted to be
the Empress's reader and almoner. Ah, could posts
of honour console me for the loss of my Julian!
I could scarcely endure to see how men of osten-
tatious outward virtue accepted gifts and bribes of all
sorts. I grew to hate this daily intercourse with
grasping money-grubbers, whose advocacy was at the
beck of any one who could pay down sounding gold
for sounding words. Oh my Emperor, you do not
know what went on here——!

JULIAN. I know, I know.

HEKEBOLIUS. A frugal life in retirement allured

me.   As often as possible, I withdrew to Crete,
to my modest Tusculum—my little country house,
—where virtue did not seem to have entirely abandoned the earth.   There I have been living this
summer also ; meditating upon human life and
heavenly truths.

JULIAN.   Happy Hekebolius!

HEKEBOLIUS.   Then the rumour of all your marvellous exploits reached Crete——

JULIAN.   Ah!

HEKEBOLIUS.   I asked myself : Is he more than
mortal, this peerless youth ?   Under whose protection
does he stand ?   Is it thus that the God of the
Christians is wont to manifest his power ?

JULIAN (*in rapt attention*).   Well, well!

HEKEBOLIUS.   I set myself to search the writings
of the ancients once more.   Light after light dawned
upon me—— ; oh, to have to confess this !

JULIAN.   Speak out—I beseech you !

HEKEBOLIUS (*falling on his knees*).   Punish me
according to your righteousness, sire ; but renounce
your youthful errors on things divine !   Yes, most
gracious Emperor, you are entangled in error ; and
I—— oh, I marvel that the shame does not kill me
—I, I have helped to lead you astray——

JULIAN (*with outstretched arms*).   Come to my
closest embrace !

HEKEBOLIUS.   Oh, I entreat you, show gratitude
to the immortal gods, whose darling you are !   And
if you cannot, then punish me because I do it in your
stead——

JULIAN.   Come, come to my open arms, I tell you !

(*He lifts him up, presses him in his arms, and kisses him.*)

My Hekebolius! What a great and unlooked-for joy!

HEKEBOLIUS. Sire, how am I to understand this?

JULIAN. Oh, then you do not know——? When did you arrive in the city?

HEKEBOLIUS. I landed an hour ago.

JULIAN. And hurried hither at once?

HEKEBOLIUS. On the wings of anxiety and remorse, sire!

JULIAN. And you have spoken to no one?

HEKEBOLIUS. No, no, I have spoken to no one; but——?

JULIAN. Oh then you cannot know——

(*He embraces him again.*)

My Hekebolius, let me tell you at once! I too, like you, have cast off the yoke of error. The immortal Sun-King, to whom we mortals owe so much, I have restored to his ancient state; Fortuna has received her offering from my humble hands; and if, at this moment, you find me weary and somewhat languid, it is because I have just been celebrating a festival in honour of the divine Dionysus.

HEKEBOLIUS. I hear, and am amazed!

JULIAN. Look,—the garland is still in my hair. Amid the joyous applause of the multitude—yes, I may call it a multitude——

HEKEBOLIUS. And I did not even dream of such great things!

JULIAN. Now we will gather around us all friends of truth, and lovers of wisdom, all seemly and reverent worshippers of the gods ;—there are already some—but not very many——

> (*The physician* CÆSARIUS, *accompanied by several officials and gentlemen of the former court, enters from the left.*)

JULIAN.   Ah, here we have the good Cæsarius,— with a great following, and a face that betokens important business.

CÆSARIUS.   Most gracious Emperor, will you permit your servant to ask a question, in his own name, and that of these anxious men?

JULIAN.   Ask, my dearest Cæsarius!   Are you not my beloved Gregory's brother?   Ask, ask!

CÆSARIUS.   Tell me then, sire—— (*He observes* HEKEBOLIUS.)   What do I see!   Hekebolius here?

JULIAN.   Newly returned——

CÆSARIUS (*trying to draw back*).   Then I beg leave to defer——

JULIAN.   No, no, my Cæsarius; this friend may hear everything.

CÆSARIUS.   Friend, do you say?   Oh my Emperor, then you have not ordered these imprisonments?

JULIAN.   What do you mean?

CÆSARIUS.   Do you not know?   Nevita—the general-in-chief, as he now calls himself—is instituting prosecutions under pretence of your authority, against all the trusted servants of your predecessor.

JULIAN.   Investigations, highly necessary investigations, my Cæsarius!

CÆSARIUS.   Oh sire, forbid him to go about it so harshly.   The book-keeper Pentadius is being hunted down by soldiers ; and likewise a certain captain of Prætorians, whose name you have forbidden us to mention; you know whom I mean, sire—that unhappy man who is already, with his whole household, in hiding for fear of you.

JULIAN. You do not know this man. In Gaul, he cherished the most audacious designs.

CÆSARIUS. That may be; but now he is harmless. And not he alone is threatened with destruction; the treasurer, Ursulus, is imprisoned——

JULIAN. Ah, Ursulus? So that has been found necessary.

CÆSARIUS. Necessary? Could that be necessary, sire? Think of Ursulus, that stainless old man—that man before whose word high and low bend in reverence——

JULIAN. A man utterly devoid of judgment, I tell you! Ursulus is a prodigal, who has without any demur gorged the rapacity of the court servants. And besides, he is useless in affairs of state. I have found that to my cost. I could never trust him to receive the emissaries of foreign princes.

CÆSARIUS. And yet we beg you, sire—all who are here present—to be magnanimous, both to Ursulus and to the others.

JULIAN. Who are the others?

CÆSARIUS. Too many, I fear. I will only name the under-treasurer, Evagrius, the late chamberlain, Saturninus, the supreme judge, Cyrenus, and——

JULIAN. Why do you stop?

CÆSARIUS (*with hesitation*). Sire—the late Empress's reader, Hekebolius, is also among the accused.

JULIAN. What!

HEKEBOLIUS. I? Impossible!

CÆSARIUS. Accused of having accepted bribes from unworthy office-seekers——

JULIAN. Hekebolius accused of that——? A man like Hekebolius——?

HEKEBOLIUS. What shameful slander! Oh Christ —I mean to say—oh heavenly divinities!

CÆSARIUS. Ah!

JULIAN. What do you mean?

CÆSARIUS (*coldly*). Nothing, most gracious Emperor!

JULIAN. Cæsarius!

CÆSARIUS. Yes, my august master?

JULIAN. Not master; call me your friend.

CÆSARIUS. Dare a Christian call you so?

JULIAN. I pray you, banish such thoughts, Cæsarius! You must not believe that of me. How can I help all these accused men being Christians? Does it not merely show that the Christians have managed to seize all the lucrative posts? And can the Emperor suffer the most important offices of the state to be badly administered?

(*To the others.*)

You surely do not think that it is your creed which has kindled my wrath against dishonest officials? I call all the gods to witness that I will permit no proceedings against you Christians that are not consonant with law and justice, nor will I suffer any one to do you wrong. You, or at any rate many of you, are pious in your way, since you too adore that Lord who is all-powerful, and rules over the whole visible world. Oh, my Cæsarius, is it not he whom I also adore, though under other names?

CÆSARIUS. Allow me, gracious Emperor——

JULIAN. In any case, it is my intention to show clemency wherever it is at all fit that I should do so. As to Hekebolius, his secret enemies must not imagine that they will be suffered to injure him by tale-bearing or any sort of paltry intrigues.

HEKEBOLIUS. My Emperor! My shield and my defence!

JULIAN. Neither will I have the minor court servants unmercifully deprived of their subsistence. I am thinking especially of that barber whom I dismissed. I am sorry for it. The man may remain. He struck me as one who understood his business thoroughly. All honour to such people! So far I can go, my Cæsarius, but no further. I cannot interfere on behalf of Ursulus. I must act so that the blind, and yet so keen-eyed, Goddess of Justice may have no reason to knit her brows over a mortal to whom she has confided so great a responsibility.

CÆSARIUS. After this, I have not a word more to say for those unfortunates. I only crave permission to leave the court and city.

JULIAN. Would you leave me?

CÆSARIUS. Yes, most gracious Emperor!

JULIAN. You are stiff-necked, like your brother.

CÆSARIUS. The new order of things gives me much to reflect upon.

JULIAN. I had great designs for you, Cæsarius! It would be a great joy to me, if you could renounce your errors. Can you not?

CÆSARIUS.   God knows what I might have done a month ago ;—now I cannot.

JULIAN.   A marriage into one of the most powerful families should stand open to you.   Will you not bethink you ?

CÆSARIUS.   No, most gracious lord !

JULIAN.   A man like you could quickly mount from step to step.   Cæsarius, is it not possible that you can give me your aid in furthering the new order of things ?

CÆSARIUS.   No, most gracious lord !

JULIAN.   I do not mean here, but in other places. It is my intention to go away from here.   Constantinople is very unpleasing to me ; you Galileans have in every way spoiled it for me.   I am going to Antioch ; there I shall find better soil to work upon. You ought to accompany me.   Will you, Cæsarius ?

CÆSARIUS.   Most gracious lord, I too am bound for the east ; but I will go alone.

JULIAN.   And what will you do there ?

CÆSARIUS.   Visit my old father ; help Gregory to strengthen him for the coming struggle.

JULIAN.   Go !

CÆSARIUS.   Farewell, my Emperor !

JULIAN.   Happy father, with such unhappy sons !
    (*He makes a gesture with his hand;* CÆSARIUS
        and those with him bow low, and go out to the
        left.)

HEKEBOLIUS.   What reckless and most unseemly obstinacy !

JULIAN.   My heart is wounded to the quick by this and many other things.   You, my Hekebolius,

shall accompany me.   The ground burns beneath my
feet in this poisoned Galilean city!   I will write to
those philosophers, Kytron and Priscus, who have
won so great fame of late years.   Maximus I expect
every day; he shall go with us.—I tell you, there are
joyful days of victory awaiting us, Hekebolius!   In
Antioch, my friend,—there we shall meet the incomparable Libanius,—and there we are nearer Helios
at his rising.—Oh this irresistible yearning towards the
Sun-King!

HEKEBOLIUS.   Yes, yes, yes——!

JULIAN (*embracing him*).   My Hekebolius!—Wisdom; light; beauty!

Act Second.

(A spacious vestibule in the Emperor's Palace, at Antioch.   An open entrance in the background; on the left is a door, leading into the inner rooms.)

(On a raised seat in the foreground, to the right, sits the EMPEROR JULIAN, *surrounded by his court. Judges, Orators, Poets, and Teachers, among them* HEKEBOLIUS, *sit on lower seats around him.   Leaning up against the wall near the entrance stands* A MAN, *dressed as a Christian Priest; he hides his face in his hands, and seems rapt in prayer. A great gathering of the citizens fills the hall. Guards at the entrance, and at the door on the left.)*

JULIAN *(speaking to the assemblage)*.   So great success have the gods vouchsafed me.   Hardly a single city have I approached on my journey, whence whole troops of Galileans have not streamed forth to meet me on the road, lamenting their errors, and placing themselves under the protection of the divine powers.   After that, why should we heed the senseless behaviour of the scoffers ?   May not the scoffers be likened to dogs, who in their ignorance yelp at the moon ?   Yet I will not deny that I have learned with indignation that some inhabitants of this city have spoken scornfully of the rule of life which I have enjoined on the priests of Cybele, the good goddess. Ought not reverence for so exalted a divinity to protect her servants from mockery? I say to those fool-hardy men : Are you barbarians, since you do not know who Cybele is? Must I solemnly remind you how, when the power of Rome was so gravely threatened by that Punic commander, whose grave I saw not long since in Libyssa, the Cumæan Sybil counselled that the statue of Cybele should be taken from the temple in Pessinus, and brought to Rome? As to the priests' way of life, some have wondered that they should be forbidden to eat roots, and everything that grows along the earth, while they arc allowed to partake of herbs and fruits which flourish in the upper air. Oh, how dense is your ignorance—I pity you if you cannot understand that! Can the spirit of man find nourishment in that which creeps along the ground? Does not the soul live by all that yearns upward, towards heaven and the sun? I will not enter more largely into these matters to-day. What remains to be said you will learn from a treatise on which I am busied during my sleepless nights, and which I hope will shortly be recited both in the lecture-halls and on the market-places.

(*He rises.*)

And with this, my friends, if no one has anything further to bring forward——

A CITIZEN (*pressing to the front*). Oh most gracious Emperor, let me not go unheard!

JULIAN (*sitting down again*). Certainly not, my friend. Who are you?

THE CITIZEN. I am Medon, the corn-merchant. Oh, if my love for you, exalted and divine Emperor——

JULIAN. Come to your case, man!

MEDON. I have a neighbour, Alites, who for many years has done me every imaginable injury; for he is also a dealer in corn, and takes the bread out of my mouth in the most shameful way——

JULIAN. Aha, my good Medon; yet you look not ill-fed.

MEDON. It is not that I complain of, most gracious Emperor! Oh, by the august gods, whom I learn to love and praise more highly day by day—his affronts to me I could overlook; but what I cannot suffer——

JULIAN. He surely does not insult the gods?

MEDON. He does what is worse,—or at least equally shameless; he—oh, I scarcely know whether my indignation will permit me to utter it,—he insults you yourself, most gracious Emperor!

JULIAN. Indeed? In what words?

MEDON. Not in words, but worse—in act.

JULIAN. Then in what act?

MEDON. He wears a purple robe——

JULIAN. A purple robe? Oho, that is bold.

MEDON. Oh, great wing-footed Mercury, when I think what that robe would have cost him in your predecessor's time! And this garment of vainglory I have daily before my eyes——

JULIAN. This garment, bought with money that might have been yours——

MEDON. Oh most gracious Emperor,—punish his audacity; let him be expelled the city; my love for our great and august ruler will not suffer me to remain a witness of such shameless arrogance.

JULIAN. Tell me, good Medon, what sort of clothes does Alites wear, besides the purple cloak?

MEDON. I really cannot remember, sire; ordinary clothes, I believe; I have only remarked the purple cloak.

JULIAN. A purple cloak, then, and untanned sandals——?

MEDON. Yes, sire; the effect is as ludicrous as it is audacious.

JULIAN. We must remedy this, Medon!

MEDON (*joyfully*). Ah, most gracious Emperor——?

JULIAN. Come early to-morrow to the palace——

MEDON (*still more delighted*). I will come the first thing in the morning, most gracious Emperor!

JULIAN. Give your name to my Chamberlain——

MEDON. Yes, yes, my most gracious Emperor!

JULIAN. You will receive from him a pair of purple shoes, embroidered with gold——

MEDON. Ah, my beneficent lord and Emperor!

JULIAN. These shoes you will take to Alites, place them on his feet, and say that henceforth he must not fail to put them on, whenever he intends to walk abroad by daylight in his purple cloak——

MEDON. Oh!

JULIAN. ——and that done, you may tell him from me, that he is a fool if he thinks himself honoured by a purple robe, apart from the power of the purple.—Go; and come for the shoes to-morrow!

(*The Corn Merchant slinks away, amid the laughter of the citizens; the Courtiers, Orators, Poets, and the rest clap their hands, with loud exclamations of approval.*)

ANOTHER CITIZEN (*stepping forward from the crowd*). Praised be the Emperor's justice! Oh how richly this envious corn-miser deserves his punishment! Oh hear me, and let your favour——

JULIAN. Aha; I think I know that face. Were not you one of those who shouted before my chariot as I drove into the city?

THE CITIZEN. I was one of the most enthusiastic, incomparable Emperor! I am Malchus, the taxgatherer. Ah, grant me your aid! I am engaged in a law-suit with an evil and grasping man——

JULIAN. And therefore you come to me? Are there not judges——?

MALCHUS. The affair is somewhat involved, noble Emperor! It concerns a field, which I leased to this bad man, having bought it seven years since, when part of the domain belonging to the Apostles' Church was sold.

JULIAN. Ah! it is church property, then?

MALCHUS. Honestly purchased; but now this man refuses either to pay me rent, or to give up the property, under pretext that this field once belonged to the temple of Apollo, and, as he declares, was unlawfully confiscated many years ago.

JULIAN. Tell me, Malchus,—you seem to be a follower of the Galilean?

MALCHUS. Most gracious Emperor, it is an old tradition in our family to acknowledge Christ.

JULIAN. And this you say openly, without fear?

MALCHUS. My adversary is bolder than I, sire! He goes in and out, as before; he did not flee from the city when he heard of your approach.

JULIAN. Did not flee? And why should he, a man who stands out for the rights of the gods?

MALCHUS. Most gracious Emperor, you have doubtless heard of the book-keeper, Thalassius?

JULIAN. What! That Thalassius who, to ingratiate himself with my predecessor, whilst I was being slandered and menaced in Gaul, proposed, here in Antioch, in the open market-place, that the citizens should petition the Emperor to send them Julian Cæsar's head!

MALCHUS. Sire, it is this deadly foe of yours who is wronging me.

JULIAN. Truly, Malchus, I have as great ground of complaint against this man as you have.

MALCHUS. Tenfold greater, my gracious Emperor?

JULIAN. What do you think? Shall we two combine our quarrels, and prefer a joint accusation against him?

MALCHUS. Oh, what exceeding grace! Oh tenfold happiness!

JULIAN. Oh tenfold foolishness! Thalassius goes in and out as before, you say? He has not fled the city at my approach. Thalassius knows me better than you. Away with you, man! When I indict Thalassius for my head, you may indict him for your field.

MALCHUS (*wringing his hands*). Oh tenfold misery!

(*He goes out by the back; the assembly again applauds the Emperor.*)

JULIAN. That is well, my friends; rejoice that I have succeeded in making a not altogether unworthy

beginning to this day, which is specially dedicated to
the feast of the radiant Apollo. For is it not worthy
of a philosopher to overlook affronts against himself,
whilst he severely punishes wrongs done to the
immortal gods? I do not remember whether that
crowned cultivator of learning, Marcus Aurelius, was
ever in like case; but if he was, we must hope that
he did not act quite unlike me, who make it my boast
to follow humbly in his footsteps.

Let this serve as a clue for your future guidance.
In the palace, in the market-place, even in the theatre
—if I did not loathe to enter such a place of folly—
it is fit that you should greet me with acclamation
and joyful applause. Such homage, I know, was well
received both by the Macedonian Alexander and by
Julius Cæsar, men who were also permitted by the
Goddess of Fortune to outshine other mortals in
glory.

But when I am entering a temple, that is another
affair. Then I desire you to be silent, or direct your
plaudits to the gods, and not to me, as you see me
advancing with bent head and down-cast eyes. And
above all, I trust you will take heed to-day, when I
am to sacrifice to so transcendent and mighty a
divinity as he whom we know by the name of the
Sun-King, and who seems even greater in our eyes
when we reflect that he is the same whom certain
oriental races call Mithra.

And with this—if no one has more to say——

THE PRIEST AT THE DOOR (*draws himself up*).
In the name of the Lord God!

JULIAN. Who speaks?

The Priest. A servant of God and of the Emperor.

Julian. Approach. What do you want?

The Priest. To speak to your heart, and to your conscience.

Julian (*springing up*). What voice was that! What do I see! In spite of beard and habit——! Gregory!

The Priest. Yes, my august master!

Julian. Gregory! Gregory of Nazianzus!

Gregory. Yes, gracious Emperor!

Julian (*has descended and grasped his hands; he now looks long at him*). A little older; browner; stouter. No; it was only at the first glance; now you are the same as ever.

Gregory. Oh that it were so with you, sire!

Julian. Athens. That night in the arcade. No man has lain so near my heart as you.

Gregory. Your heart? Ah, Emperor, you have driven a better friend than I out of your heart.

Julian. You mean Basilius?

Gregory. I mean a greater than Basilius.

Julian (*glooming*). Ah, indeed! That is what you come to tell me? And in that habit——

Gregory. I did not choose this habit, sire!

Julian. Not you? Who then?

Gregory. He who is greater than the Emperor.

Julian. I know your Galilean phrases. For the sake of our friendship, no more of them.

Gregory. Let me begin by telling you how it is that you see me here, ordained a priest of the church you are persecuting.

JULIAN (*with a sharp look*). Persecuting?
(*He ascends the daïs again and sits down.*)
Now speak on.

GREGORY. You know what I thought of things divine, during our happy comradeship in Athens. But then it was far from my thoughts to renounce the joys of life. Neither ambition nor the thirst for riches, I venture to say, has ever tempted me; yet I should scarcely tell the truth if I denied that my eye and my mind were fascinated by all the glories which the old learning and art of Greece displayed to me. The wranglings and petty schisms in our church afflicted me deeply; but I took no part in them; I served my countrymen in temporal things; nothing more.——

Then came tidings from Constantinople. It was said that Constantius had died of terror at your proceedings, and had declared you his heir. Heralded by the renown of your victories, and received as a superhuman being, you, the hero of Gaul and Germany, had ascended the throne of Constantius without striking a blow. The earth lay at your feet.

Then came further tidings. The lord of earth was girding himself up to war against the Lord of heaven——

JULIAN. Gregory, what do you presume——!

GREGORY. The lord of the body was girding himself up to war against the Lord of the soul. I stand here before you in bodily fear and trembling; but I dare not lie. Will you hear the truth, or shall I be silent?

JULIAN. Say on, Gregory!

GREGORY.   What have not my fellow-Christians already suffered during these few months?   How many sentences of death have been passed and executed in the cruellest fashion?   Gaudentius, the state-secretary; Artemius, the former governor of Egypt; the two tribunes Romanus and Vincentius——

JULIAN.   You do not know what you are talking of.   I tell you, the Goddess of Justice would have wept had those traitors escaped with their lives.

GREGORY.   That may be, my Emperor; but I tell you that one sentence of death has been passed which the God of Justice can never forgive you. Ursulus!   The man who stood your friend in times of need!   Ursulus who, at the risk of his own life, supplied you with money in Gaul!   Ursulus, whose whole crime was his Christian faith and his sincerity——

JULIAN.   Ah, this you have from your brother Cæsarius!

GREGORY.   Punish me, sire; but spare my brother.

JULIAN.   You well know that you risk nothing, Gregory!   Besides, I allow that Nevita has acted too harshly.

GREGORY.   Yes, that barbarian, who tries in vain to conceal his origin under a Greek veneer——!

JULIAN.   Nevita is zealous in his duty, and I cannot myself be everywhere.   For Ursulus I have mourned sincerely, and I deeply deplore that neither time nor circumstances allowed me to examine into his case myself.   I should certainly have spared him,

Gregory! I have thought, too, of restoring to his heirs any property he has left behind.

GREGORY. Great Emperor, you owe me no reckoning for your acts. I only wished to tell you that all these tidings fell like thunder-bolts in Cæsarea and Nazianzus, and the other Cappadocian cities. How shall I describe their effect? Our internal wranglings were silenced by the common danger. Many rotten branches of the Church fell away; but in many indifferent hearts the light of the Lord was kindled with a fervour before undreamt-of. Meanwhile oppression overtook God's people. The heathens—I mean, my Emperor, those whom *I* call heathens—began to threaten, to injure, to persecute us——

JULIAN. Retaliation,—retaliation, Gregory!

GREGORY. Far be it from me to justify all that my fellow-Christians may have done in their excessive zeal for the cause of the Church. But you, who are so enlightened, and have power over all alike, cannot permit the living to suffer for the faults of the dead. Yet this is the case in Cappadocia. The enemies of the Christians, few in number, but thirsting after gain, and burning with eagerness to ingratiate themselves with the new officials, have awakened fear and perturbation among the people both in town and country.

I am not referring chiefly to the insults we have had to suffer, nor to the infringements of our just rights of property, to which we have been constantly exposed of late. What most grieves me and all my earnest brethren, is the peril to souls. Many are not

firm in the faith, and cannot quite shake off the care
for earthly goods. The harsh treatment which has
now to be endured by all who bear the name of
Christian has already led to more than one apostasy.
Sire, this is soul-robbery from God's kingdom.

JULIAN. Oh, my wise Gregory,—how can you
talk so? I wonder at you! Should you not rather,
as a good Galilean, rejoice that your community is
rid of such men?

GREGORY. Gracious Emperor, I am not of that
opinion. I have myself been indifferent to the faith,
and I look upon all such as sick men, who are not
past cure, so long as they remain in the bosom of the
church. So, too, thought our little congregation at
Nazianzus. Brethren and sisters, in deep distress,
assembled to consult upon measures of defence.
They were joined by deputies from Cæsarea, and
other places. My father is infirm, and—as he himself confesses with sorrow—does not possess the
steadfast, immovable will which, in these troublous
times, is needful for him who sits in the bishop's
chair. The assembly decided that a younger man
should be chosen as his helper, to hold the Lord's
flock together.

The choice fell on me.

JULIAN. Ah!

GREGORY. I was then away from home. But
in my absence, and without consulting me, my
father ordained me a priest, and sent me the priestly
habit.

This news reached me in Tiberina, at my country
house, where I was passing some days with my

brother and with the friend of my youth, Basilius of Cæsarea.

Sire—had my sentence of death been read to me, it could not have appalled me more than this.

I a priest! I wished it, and I did not wish it. I felt it my duty—and yet I dared not. I wrestled with God the Lord, as the patriarch wrestled with him in the days of the old covenant. What passed in my soul during the night which followed, I cannot tell. But this I know, that before the cock crew, I talked face to face with the Crucified One.—Then I was his.

JULIAN. Folly, folly; I know those dreams.

GREGORY. On the journey home I passed through Cæsarea. Oh, what misery met me there! I found the town full of fugitive country-people, who had forsaken house and home because the drought had burnt up their crops, and laid all the vineyards and olive gardens desolate. To escape starvation they had fled to the starving. There they lay—men, women, and children—in heaps along the walls of the houses; fever shook them, famine gnawed their entrails. What had Cæsarea to offer them —that impoverished, unhappy town, as yet only half rebuilt since the great earthquake of two years ago? And in the midst of this, amid scorching heat and frequent shocks of earthquake, we had to see ungodly festivals going on day and night. The overturned altars were hastily rebuilt; the blood of sacrifices ran in streams; mummers and harlots paraded with dance and song through the streets.

Sire—can you wonder that my much-tried brethren

thought they recognised in the visitation they were undergoing a judgment of heaven because they had so long tolerated heathenism and its abominable symbols in their midst?

JULIAN.   What symbols do you mean?

GREGORY.   The cry of the terror-stricken and fevered multitude rose ever higher; they demanded that the rulers of the city should give a palpable witness for Christ, by ordering the destruction of what still remains of the former glory of heathenism in Cæsarea.

JULIAN.   You cannot mean to say that——?

GREGORY.   The magistrates of the city called a meeting, where I too was present. You know, gracious Emperor, that all temples are the property of the city; so that the citizens have the right to dispose of them, at their own free will.

JULIAN.   Well, well? What if it be so?

GREGORY.   In that terrible earthquake that ravaged Cæsarea two years ago, all the temples but one were destroyed.

JULIAN.   Yes, yes; the temple of Fortuna.

GREGORY.   At the meeting I speak of, the congregation determined to complete God's work of judgment, in testimony that they would trust wholly and solely to him, and no longer tolerate the abomination in their midst.

JULIAN (hoarsely).   Gregory,—once my friend— do you hold your life dear?

GREGORY.   This resolution I did not myself approve, but almost all voices were in favour of it.   But as we feared that the matter might be represented to you in a false light, and might perhaps incense you against the city, it was determined to send a man hither to announce to you what we have resolved, and what will presently happen.

Great ruler,—no one else was found willing to undertake the task. It fell perforce to me. Therefore it is, sire, that I stand here before you in all humility, to announce that we Christians in Cæsarea have resolved that the temple where the heathen in bygone days worshipped a false dcity, under the name of Fortuna, shall be pulled down and levelled with the ground.

JULIAN (*springing up*). And I have to listen to this with my own ears! One single man dares to tell me such unheard-of things!

COURTIERS, ORATORS, AND POETS. O pious Emperor, do not suffer it! Punish this audacious man!

HEKEBOLIUS. He is mad, sire! Let him go. See,—the frenzy glitters in his eyes.

JULIAN. Yes, it may well be called madness. But it is more than madness. To wish to pull down that excellent temple, dedicated to a no less excellent divinity! Is it not to the favour of this very goddess that I ascribe my achievements, the fame of which has reached the remotest nations? If I suffered this, how could I ever again hope for victory or prosperity?—Gregory, I command you to return to Cæsarea and give the citizens to understand that I forbid this outrage.

GREGORY. Impossible, sire! Things have come to such a pass that we have to choose between the

fear of man and obedience to God.   We cannot draw
back.

JULIAN.   Then you shall feel how far the Emperor's
arm can stretch!

GREGORY.   The Emperor's arm is mighty in earthly
things; and I, like others, tremble under it.

JULIAN.   Show it, then, in deeds!   Ah, you
Galileans, you reckon upon my long-suffering.   Do
not trust to it, for truly——

(*A noise at the entrance.   The barber*, EUNAPIUS,
followed by several citizens, rushes in.)

JULIAN.   What is this?   Eunapius, what has
happened to you?

EUNAPIUS.   Oh that my eyes should see such a
sight!

JULIAN.   What sight have you seen?

EUNAPIUS.   See, most gracious Emperor, I come
bleeding and bruised, yet happy to be the first to call
down your wrath——

JULIAN.   Speak, man;—who has beaten you?

EUNAPIUS.   Permit me, sire, to lay my complaint
before you.

I went forth from the town this morning to visit
the little temple of Venus which you have lately
restored.   When I came thither, the music of flutes
and singing greeted my ears.   Women were dancing
exquisitely in the outer court, and within I found the
whole space filled with a rapturous crowd, while at
the altar priests were offering up the sacrifices you
have ordained.

JULIAN.   Yes, yes; and then——?

EUNAPIUS.   Scarcely had I had time to turn

my thoughts in devotion towards that enchanting goddess, whom I especially revere and worship, when a great crowd of young men pressed into the temple——

JULIAN.   Not Galileans?

EUNAPIUS.   Yes, sire,—Galileans.

JULIAN.   Ah!

EUNAPIUS.   What a scene followed! Weeping under the assailants' insults and blows, the dancing-girls fled from the outer court to us within. The Galileans fell upon us all, belaboured and affronted us in the most shameful manner.

JULIAN (*descending from his throne*).   Wait, wait!

EUNAPIUS.   Alas, would that their violence had been confined to us! But the madmen went further. Yes, gracious Emperor—in one word, the altar is overthrown, the statue of the goddess dashed to pieces, the entrails of the sacrifices cast out to the dogs——

JULIAN (*pacing up and down*).   Wait, wait, wait!

GREGORY.   Sire, this one man's word is not enough——

JULIAN.   Be silent!

   (*To* EUNAPIUS.)

Did you know any of the sacrilegious crew?

EUNAPIUS.   Not I, sire; but these citizens knew several of them.

JULIAN.   Take a guard with you. Seize as many of the wretches as you can. Cast them into prison. The prisoners shall give up the names of the rest; and when I have them all in my power——

GREGORY.   What then, sire?

Julian.   Ask the executioner.   Both you and the citizens of Cæsarea shall be taught what you have to expect if your Galilean obstinacy should make you abide by your resolve.

> (*The Emperor goes out in great wrath, to the left;* Eunapius *and his witnesses retire with the watch; the others disperse.*)

> (*A market-place in Antioch.   In the foreground, on the right, a street debouches into the market; to the left, in the background, there is a view into a narrow and crooked street.*)
> (*A great concourse of people fills the market. Hucksters cry their wares.   In several places the townspeople have gathered into clusters, talking eagerly.*)

A Citizen.   Good God of heaven, when did this misfortune happen ?

Another Citizen.   This morning, I tell you; quite early.

Phocion the Dyer (*who has entered from the street on the right*).   My good man, do you think it fitting to call this a misfortune ?   I call it a crime, and an exceedingly audacious crime to boot.

The second Citizen.   Yes, yes ; that is quite true ; it was a most audacious thing to do.

Phocion.   Only think—of course it is the outrage on the temple of Venus you are talking of ?   Only think of their choosing a time when the Emperor was in the city——!   And this day, too, of all others—a day——

A THIRD CITIZEN (*drawing near*).   Tell me, good friend, what is the matter——?

PHOCION.   This day of all others, I say, when our august ruler is himself to officiate at the feast of Apollo.

THE THIRD CITIZEN.   Yes, I know that ; but why are they taking these Christians to prison ?

PHOCION.   What ?   Are they taking them to prison ?   Have they really caught them ?

(*Loud cries are heard.*)

Hush ; what is that ?   Yes, by the gods, I believe they have them !

(*An* OLD WOMAN, *much excited, and with dishevelled hair, makes her way through the crowd; she is beset by other women, who in vain seek to restrain her.*)

THE OLD WOMAN.   I will not be held back !   He is my only son, the child of my old age !   Let me go ; let me go !   Can no one tell me where I can find the Emperor ?

PHOCION.   What do you want with the Emperor, old mother ?

THE OLD WOMAN.   I want to have my son again. Help me !   My son !   Hilarion !   Oh, they have taken him from me !   They burst into our house, and took him away !

ONE OF THE CITIZENS (*to* PHOCION).   Who is this woman ?

PHOCION.   What ?   Do you not know the widow Publia,—the psalm-singer ?

CITIZEN.   Ah, yes, yes, yes !

PUBLIA.   Hilarion !   my child !   What will they do

to him ?   Ah, Phocion,—are you there ?   God be praised for sending me a Christian brother—— !

PHOCION.   Hush, hush, be quiet; do not scream so loud ; the Emperor is coming.

PUBLIA.   Oh, this ungodly Emperor !   The Lord of Wrath is visiting his sins upon us ; famine is ravaging the land ; the earth trembles beneath our feet !

(*A detachment of soldiers enters by the street on the right.*)

THE COMMANDER OF THE DETACHMENT.   Stand aside ; make room here !

PUBLIA.   Oh come, good Phocion ;—help me, for our friendship's and fellowship's sake——

PHOCION.   Are you mad, woman ?   I do not know you.

PUBLIA.   What ?   You do not know me ?   Are you not Phocion the dyer ?   Are you not the son of—— ?

PHOCION.   I am not the son of anybody.   Get you gone, woman !   You are mad !   I do not know you; I have never seen you.   (*He hastens in among the crowd.*)

A SUBALTERN (*with soldiers, from the right*). Clear the way here !

(*The soldiers force the multitude back towards the houses.   Old* PUBLIA *faints in the arms of the women on the left.   All gaze expectantly down the street.*)

PHOCION (*in a knot of people behind the guard, to the right*).   Yes, by the Sun-God, there he comes, the blessed Emperor !

A SOLDIER. Do not push so, behind there !

PHOCION. Can you see him ? The man with the white fillet round his brow, that is the Emperor.

A CITIZEN. The man all in white?

PHOCION. Yes, yes, that is he.

THE CITIZEN. Why is he dressed in white ?

PHOCION. Probably because of the heat ; or,— no, stop,—I think it is as the sacrificing priest that he——

A SECOND CITIZEN. Will the Emperor himself offer the sacrifice ?

PHOCION. Yes, the Emperor Julian does everything himself.

A THIRD CITIZEN. He does not look so powerful as the Emperor Constantius.

PHOCION. I think he does. He is not so tall as the late Emperor ; but his arms are longer. And then his glance—— oh my friends——! You cannot see it just now; his eyes are devoutly lowered as he walks. Yes, devout he is, I can tell you. He has no eye for women. I dare swear that since his wife's death he has scarcely ever—— ; you see, he writes the whole night. That is why his fingers are often as black as a dyer's ; just like mine ; for I am a dyer. I can tell you I know the Emperor better than most people. I was born here in Antioch ; but I have lived fifteen years in Constantinople, until just the other day.

A CITIZEN. Do you think there is anything in the rumour that the Emperor intends to settle here for good ?

PHOCION. I know the Emperor's barber, and he

says so.   I only hope these shameful disturbances
may not incense him too much.

A Citizen.   Yes indeed, that would be a pity!

A second Citizen.   If the Emperor lived here it
would be a good thing for all of us.

Phocion.   That was what I reckoned on when I
returned here.   So now we must do our best, friends;
when the Emperor comes past, we must shout lustily
both for him and for Apollo.

A Citizen (*to another*).   Who is this Apollo, that
people begin to talk so much about?

The other Citizen.   Why, it's the priest of
Corinth,—he who watered what the holy Paul had
planted.

The first Citizen.   Oh indeed; yes, yes, I
think I remember now.

Phocion.   No, no, no, it's not *that* Apollo; it's
a different one, entirely;—this is the Sun-King—the
great lyre-playing Apollo.

The other Citizen.   Ah indeed; *that* Apollo!
Is he better?

Phocion.   Yes, I should think so.—Look, look,
there he comes.   Oh, the most blessed Emperor!

> (*The* Emperor Julian, *robed as a high priest,
> enters, surrounded by priests and servants of
> the temple.   Courtiers and learned men, among
> whom is* Hekebolius, *have joined the proces-
> sion; likewise citizens.   Before the Emperor go
> flute-players and harpers.   Soldiers and men of
> the city guard, with long staves, clear the way
> before the procession and on either side.*)

The Multitude (*clapping their hands*).   Praise

to the Emperor!   Praise to Julian, hero and bene-
factor!

PHOCION.   All hail to Julian and the Sun-King!
Long live Apollo!

THE CITIZENS (*in the foreground, on the right*).
Emperor, Emperor, remain long among us!

(JULIAN *makes a sign for the procession to stop.*)

JULIAN.   Citizens of Antioch!   I should find it
hard to name anything that could rejoice my heart
more than these inspiriting acclamations.   And my
heart stands sorely in need of this refreshment.

It was with a downcast spirit that I started
on this procession, which should be one of joy and
exaltation.   I will not hide from you that I was this
morning on the verge of losing that equanimity which
it behoves a lover of wisdom to preserve under all
trials.

But can any one chide me for it?   I would have
you all remember what outrages are threatened elsewhere, and have already been committed here.

PUBLIA.   My lord, my lord!

PHOCION.   Oh pious and righteous Emperor,
punish these desperate men!

PUBLIA.   My lord, give me back my Hilarion!

PHOCION.   All good citizens implore your favour
towards this city.

JULIAN.   Seek to win the favour of the gods, and
you are sure of mine.   Is it not fitting that Antioch
should lead the way?   Does it not seem as though
the Sun-God's eye had dwelt with especial com-
placency on this city?   Ask of travellers, and you
shall hear to what melancholy extremes fanaticism

has elsewhere proceeded in laying waste our holy places. What is left? A remnant here and there; and nothing of the best.

But with you, citizens of Antioch! Oh, my eyes filled with tears of joy when first I saw that incomparable sanctuary, the very house of Apollo, which seems scarcely to be the work of human hands. Does not the image of the Glorious One stand within it, in unviolated beauty? Not a corner of his altar has broken or crumbled away; not a crack is to be seen in the stately columns.

Oh, when I think of this,—when I feel the fillet round my brow—when I look down upon these garments, dearer to me than the purple robe of empire, then I feel, with a sacred tremor, the presence of the god.

See, see, the sunlight quivers around us in its glory!

Feel, feel, the air is teeming with the perfume of fresh garlands!

Beautiful earth! The home of light and life, the home of pleasure, the home of happiness and beauty; —what thou wast shalt thou again become!—In the embrace of the Sun-King! Mithra, Mithra!

Forward on our victorious way!

(*The procession moves on again, amid the plaudits of the crowd; those in front come to a stop at the mouth of the narrow street, through which another procession enters the market-place.*)

JULIAN. What is detaining us?

HEKEBOLIUS. Gracious lord, there is something amiss in the other street.

SONG (*far off*).

> Blissful our pangs, be they never so cruel;
> blissful our rising, the death-struggle o'er.

PHOCION. The Galileans, sire! They have them!

PUBLIA. Hilarion!

PHOCION. They have them! I hear the chains——

JULIAN. Pass them by——!

EUNAPIUS (*hastening through the press*). We have succeeded marvellously, sire.

JULIAN. Who are they, these ruffians?

EUNAPIUS. Some of them belong to this city; but the majority are said to be peasants fleeing from Cappadocia.

JULIAN. I will not see them. Forward, as I commanded!

THE PRISONERS' SONG (*nearer*).

> Blissful our crowning with martyrdom's jewel;
> blissful our meeting with saints gone before.

JULIAN. The madmen. Not so near to me! My guard, my guard!

(*The two processions have meanwhile encountered each other in the crush. The procession of Apollo has to stand still while the other, with the prisoners—men in chains, surrounded by soldiers, and accompanied by a great concourse of people—passes on.*)

PUBLIA. My child! Hilarion!

HILARION (*among the prisoners*). Rejoice, my mother!

JULIAN. You poor deluded creatures! When I hear madness thus speaking in you, I almost doubt whether I have the right to punish you.

Another Voice (*among the prisoners*).   Stand aside ; take not from us our crown of thorns.

Julian.   Night and horror,—what voice is that !

The Leader of the Guard.   Sire, it was this one who spoke.

> (*He pushes one of the prisoners forward, a young man, who leads a half-grown lad by the hand.*)

Julian (*with a cry*).   Agathon !

> (The Prisoner *looks at him, and is silent.*)

Agathon, Agathon !   Answer me ; are you not Agathon ?

The Prisoner.   Yes.

Julian.   You among these ?   Speak to me !

Agathon.   I do not know you !

Julian.   You do not know me ?   You do not know who I am ?

Agathon.   I know you are the monarch of the earth ; therefore I do not recognise you.

Julian.   And the boy——?   Is he your young brother ?

> (*To the leader of the watch.*)

This man must be innocent.

Eunapius.   My lord, this man is the very ringleader.   He has confessed it ; he even glories in his exploit.

Julian.   So strangely can hunger, and sickness, and misfortune disorder a man's mind.

> (*To the prisoners.*)

If you will but say, in one word, that you repent, none of you shall suffer.

Publia (*shrieks*).   Do not say it, Hilarion !

AGATHON.   Be strong, dear brother!

PUBLIA.   Go, go to what awaits you, my only one!

JULIAN.   Hear and bethink you, you others——

AGATHON (*to the prisoners*).   Choose between Christ and the Emperor!

THE PRISONERS.   Glory to God in the highest!

JULIAN.   Terrible is the Galilean's power of delusion.   It must be broken.   Pass them by, the repulsive crew!   They cloud our gladness; they darken the day with their brooding death-hunger!—Flute-players—men, women—why are you silent?   A song —a song in praise of life, and light, and happiness.

THE PROCESSION OF APOLLO (*sings*).
> Gladsome with roses our locks to entwine;
> gladsome to bathe in the sunlight divine!

THE PROCESSION OF PRISONERS.
> Blissful to sink through the blood-sea to slumber;
> blissful to rise to delights without number!

THE PROCESSION OF APOLLO.
> Gladsome 'mid incense-clouds still to draw breath.

THE PROCESSION OF PRISONERS.
> Blissful in blood-streams to strangle to death.

THE PROCESSION OF APOLLO.
> Pleasures unbounded encircle and follow
> whoso adoreth thy godhead, Apollo.

THE PROCESSION OF PRISONERS.
> Bones racked and riven, flesh seared to a coal,
>> *He* shall make whole!

THE PROCESSION OF APOLLO.
> Gladsome to bask in the light-sea that laves
>> us!

THE PROCESSION OF PRISONERS.

Blissful to writhe in the blood-death that saves us!

(*The processions pass each other during the singing. The crowd in the market-place look on in dull silence.*)

(*The sacred grove around the temple of Apollo. The portico, supported by columns, and approached by a broad flight of steps, is seen among the trees in the background, on the left.*)

(*A number of people are rushing about in the grove with loud cries of terror. Far away is heard the music of the procession.*)

WOMEN. Mercy! The earth is quaking again!

A FLYING MAN. Oh horror! Thunderbolts under our feet——!

ANOTHER MAN. Was it really so? Was it the earth that shook?

A WOMAN. Did you not feel it? That tree there swayed so that the branches whistled through the air.

MANY VOICES. Hark, hark, hark!

SOME. It is chariots thundering on the pavements.

OTHERS. It is drums. Hark to the music——; the Emperor is coming!

(*The procession of Apollo advances from the right through the grove, and stations itself, amid music of flutes and harps, in a semicircle in front of the temple.*)

JULIAN (*turning towards the temple with upstretched hands*).   I accept the omen !——

Never have I felt myself in such close communion with the immortal gods.

The Bow-Wielder is among us. The earth rumbles beneath his tread, as when of old he stamped in wrath upon the Trojan shore.

But it is not at us he frowns. It is at those unhappy wretches who hate him and his sunlit realm.

Yes,—as surely as good or evil fortune affords the true measure of the gods' favour towards mortals,— so surely is the difference here made manifest between them and us.

Where are the Galileans now? Some under the executioner's hands, others flying through the narrow streets, ashy pale with terror, their eyes starting from their heads — a shriek between their half-clenched teeth—their hair stiffening with dread, or rent away in despair.

And where are we? Here in Daphne's pleasant grove, where the dryads' balmy breath cools our brows,— here, before the glorious temple of the glorious god, lapped in the melodies of flute and lyre,—here, in light, in happiness, in safety, the god himself made manifest among us.

Where is the God of the Galileans? Where is the Jew, the carpenter's crucified son? Let him manifest himself. Not he !

It is fitting, then, that we fill the sanctuary. There, with my own hands, I will perform the services which are so far from appearing to me mean and unbecoming, that I, on the contrary, esteem them above all others.

(*He goes at the head of the procession, through the multitude, towards the temple.*)

A Voice (*calling out in the throng*). Stay, blasphemer!

Julian.   A Galilean among us?

The Same Voice.   No further, apostate!

Julian.   Who is it that speaks?

Other Voices in the Crowd.   A Galilean priest.   A blind old man.   Here he stands.

Others again.   Away, away with the insolent wretch!

(*A blind* Old Man, *in priestly garments, and supported by two younger men, also dressed as priests, is pushed forward till he stands at the foot of the temple steps, facing the Emperor.*)

Julian.   Ah, what do I see?   Tell me, old man, art not you Bishop Maris, of Chalcedon?

The Old Man.   Yes, I am that unworthiest servant of the Church.

Julian.   "Unworthiest," you call yourself; and I think you are not far wrong.   If I am not mistaken, you have been one of the foremost in stirring up internal strife among the Galileans.

Bishop Maris.   I have done what weighs me still deeper down in penitence.   When you seized the empire, and rumour told of your bent of mind, my heart was wrapped in unspeakable dread.   Blind and enfeebled by age, I trembled at the thought of setting myself up against the mighty monarch of the world.   Yes,—God be gracious to me—I forsook the flock I was appointed to guard, shrank timidly from all the perils that lowered menacingly over the Lord's people, and sought shelter here, in my Syrian villa——

JULIAN.   How strange! You, with your timidity, you who formerly prized the Emperor's favour so highly, now step forth before me and fling insults in my very teeth!

BISHOP MARIS.   Now I no longer fear you ; for now Christ has fully possessed my heart. In the church's hour of need, light and glory burst in upon me.   All the blood you shed,—all the violence and wrong you do—cry out to heaven, and, re-echoing mightily, ring in my deaf ears, and show me, in my night of blindness, and the way I have to go.

JULIAN.   Go home, old man !

BISHOP MARIS.   Not till you have promised to renounce your devilish courses.   What would you do? Will dust rise up against the spirit ? Will the lord of earth cast down the Lord of heaven ? Do you not see that the day of wrath is upon us because of your sins ?   The fountains are parched like eyes that have wept themselves dry.   The clouds, which ought to pour the manna of fruitfulness upon us, sweep over our heads, and shed no moisture.   This earth, which has been cursed since the morning of time, quakes and trembles under the Emperor's blood-guiltiness.

JULIAN.   What favour do you expect of your God for such excessive zeal, foolish old man ?   Do you hope that, as of old, your Galilean master will work a miracle, and give you back your sight?

BISHOP MARIS.   I have all the sight I desire ; and I thank the Lord that he quenched my bodily vision, so that I am spared from seeing the man who walks in a darkness more terrible than mine.

JULIAN.   Let me pass!

BISHOP MARIS.   Whither?

JULIAN.   Into the Sun-King's temple.

BISHOP MARIS.   You shall not pass.   I forbid you in the name of the only God!

JULIAN.   Frantic old man!—Away with him!

BISHOP MARIS.   Yes, lay hands upon me!   But he who ventures to, his hand shall wither.   The God of Wrath shall manifest himself in his might——

JULIAN.   Your God is no mighty God.   I will show you that the Emperor is stronger than he——

BISHOP MARIS.   Lost creature!—Then I must call down the ban upon thee, thou recreant son of the church!

HEKEBOLIUS (*pale*).   My lord and Emperor, do not let this thing be!

BISHOP MARIS (*in a loud voice*).   Cursed be thou, Julianus Apostata!   Cursed be thou, Emperor Julian! God the Lord hath spat thee forth out of his mouth! Cursed be thine eyes and thy hands!   Cursed be thy head and all thy doings!

Woe, woe, woe to the apostate!   Woe, woe, woe——

> (*A hollow roll of thunder is heard.   The roof and columns of the temple tremble, and are seen to collapse with a thundering crash, while the whole building is wrapped in a cloud of dust. The multitude utter shrieks of terror; many flee, others fall to the ground.   There is breathless stillness for a while.   Little by little the cloud of dust settles, and the temple of Apollo is seen in ruins.*)

BISHOP MARIS (*whose two conductors have fled,* *stands alone, and says softly*).   God has spoken.

JULIAN (*pale, and in a low voice*).   Apollo has spoken.   His temple was polluted ; he crushed it.

BISHOP MARIS.   And I tell you it was that‧ Lord who laid the temple of Jerusalem in ruins.

JULIAN.   If it be so, then the churches of the Galilean shall be shut up, and his priests shall be driven with scourges to raise up that temple anew.

BISHOP MARIS.   Try, impotent man !   Has any one succeeded in restoring the temple of Jerusalem since the Prince of Golgotha called down destruction upon it ?

JULIAN.   I will succeed !   The Emperor shall succeed.   Your God shall be made a liar.   Stone by stone, I will rebuild the temple of Jerusalem in all its glory, as it was in the days of Solomon.

BISHOP MARIS.   Not one stone shall you add to another ; for it is accursed of the Lord.

JULIAN.   Wait, wait ; you shall see—if you *could* see—you who stand there forsaken and helpless, groping in the darkness, not knowing where you next may place your foot.

BISHOP MARIS.   I see before me the splendour of the lightning which shall one day fall upon you and yours.

(*He gropes his way out.*   JULIAN *remains behind,* *surrounded by a handful of pale and terrified* *attendants.*)

Act Third.

(In Antioch.   An open colonnade, with statues and a fountain in front of it.   To the left, under the colonnade, a staircase leads up to the Imperial Palace.)

(A company of Courtiers, Teachers, Poets, and Orators—among them the court-physician, ORIBASES, and the poet, HERACLIUS —are assembled, some in the colonnade, some around the fountain; most of them are dressed in ragged cloaks, with matted hair and beards.)

HERACLIUS.   I can endure this life no longer.   To get up with the sun, go into a cold bath, run or fence one's self weary——

ORIBASES.   It is all very wholesome.

HERACLIUS.   Is it wholesome to eat seaweed and raw fish?

A COURTIER.   Is it wholesome to have to devour meat in great lumps, quite bloody, as it comes from the butcher?

HERACLIUS.   I have seen little enough meat for the past week.   Most of it goes to the altars.   I believe we shall soon be able to say that the ever-venerable gods are the only meat-eaters in Antioch.

ORIBASES.   Still the same old mocker, Heraclius.

HERACLIUS.   Why, what are you thinking of, friend?   Far be it from me to mock at the Emperor's

wise decrees.   Blessed be the Emperor Julian!   Does
he not follow in the footsteps of the immortals?   For,
tell me, does not a certain frugality seem to be the
order of the day, even in the heavenly housekeeping?

A COURTIER.   Ha-ha-ha! you are not far wrong
there.

HERACLIUS.   Look at Cybele, formerly so boun-
teous a goddess, whose statue the Emperor lately
found in an ash-pit——

ANOTHER COURTIER.   It was in a dunghill——

HERACLIUS.   Very probably; fertilising is Cybele's
business.   But look at this goddess, I say;—in spite
of her hundred breasts, she flows neither with milk
nor honey.

> (*A circle of laughing hearers has collected round
> him.   While he is speaking, the* EMPEROR
> JULIAN *has come forward on the steps in the
> colonnade, unnoticed by those below.   He wears
> a tattered cloak, with a girdle of rope; his hair
> and beard are untidy, his fingers stained with
> ink; in both hands, under his arms, and stuck in
> his belt, he holds bundles of parchment rolls and
> papers.   He stops and listens to* HERACLIUS
> *with every sign of exasperation.*)

HERACLIUS (*continuing*).   It seems as though this
wet-nurse of the world had become barren.   We
might almost think that she had passed the age when
women——

A COURTIER (*perceiving* JULIAN).   Fie, fie,
Heraclius,—shame on you!

> (JULIAN *gives the courtier a sign to be silent.*)

HERACLIUS (*continuing*).   Well, enough of her.

But is it not much the same with Ceres? Does she not display a most melancholy—I had almost said an imperial—parsimony? Yes, believe me, if we had a little more intercourse with high Olympus nowadays, we should hear of retrenchment on all sides. I dare swear that nectar and ambrosia are measured out as sparingly as possible. Oh Zeus, how gaunt you must have grown! Oh roguish Dionysus, how much is there left of the fulness of your loins? Oh wanton, quick-flushing Venus, — oh Mars, inauspicious to married men——

JULIAN (*in great wrath*). Oh most shameless Heraclius! Oh scurvy, gall - spitting, venom-mouth——

HERACLIUS. Ah, my gracious Emperor!

JULIAN. Oh ribald scoffer at all sacred things! And I must endure this—to hear your croaking tongue the instant I leave my library to breathe the fresh morning air!

(*He comes nearer.*)

Do you know what I hold under my left arm? No, you do not know. It is a controversial treatise against you, blasphemous and foolish Heraclius!

HERACLIUS. What, my Emperor,—against me?

JULIAN. Yes, a treatise against you. A treatise with which my indignation has this very night inspired me. How could I help being indignant at your most unseemly behaviour yesterday? Think how you forgot yourself in the lecture-hall, in my hearing, and that of many other earnest men? Had we not to listen for several hours together to the shameful fables about the gods which you insisted on retailing?

How dared you trump up such fictions? Were they
not lies, from first to last?

HERACLIUS. Ah, my Emperor, if you call that
lying, then both Ovid and Lucian were liars.

JULIAN. What else? Oh, I cannot express the
indignation I felt when I understood whither your
impudent address was tending. " Man, let nothing
surprise you," I was tempted to say with the comic
poet, when I heard you, like a shaggy cur, barking
out, not expressions of gratitude, but a string of
absurd nursery-tales, and ill-written to boot. For
your verses were bad, Heraclius ;—I have proved
that in my treatise.

How I should have liked to rise and leave the hall
when I saw you, as in a theatre, making a show
both of Dionysus and of the great immortal, after
whom you are named! If I constrained myself to
keep my seat, I can assure you it was more out of
respect to the players—if I dare call them so—
than to the poet. But it was most of all for
my own sake. I feared it might look as though
I were fleeing like a frightened dove. Therefore
I made no sign, but quietly repeated to myself
that verse of Homer : " Bear it, my heart, for a
time ; heavier things hast thou suffered." Endure,
as before, to hear a mad dog yelp at the eternal
gods.

Yes, I see we must stomach this and more. We
are fallen on evil days. Show me the happy man
who has been suffered to keep his eyes and ears
uncontaminated in this iron age!

ORIBASES. I pray you, my noble master, do not

excite yourself. Let it comfort you that we all listened with displeasure to this man's folly.

JULIAN. That is the reverse of the truth! I saw on the faces of most of you something quite different from displeasure while this shameless mountebank was babbling forth his ribaldries, and then looking round the circle with a greasy smile, just as though he had done something to be proud of.

HERACLIUS. Alas, my Emperor, I am most unhappy——

JULIAN. That you may well be; for this is, indeed, no trifling matter. Do you think the legends of the gods have not a serious and important purpose? Are they not designed with the object of leading the human spirit, by an easy and pleasant path, up to the mystic abodes where reigns the highest god, —and thereby making our souls capable of union with him? How can it be otherwise? Was it not with that view that the old poets invented these legends, and that Plato and others repeated them, and even increased their number? Apart from this purpose, I tell you, these stories would be fit only for children or barbarians,—and scarcely for them. But was it children and barbarians, pray, that you had before you yesterday? Where do you find the audacity to address me as if I were a child? Do you imagine yourself a sage, and entitled to a sage's freedom of speech, because you wear a ragged cloak, and carry a beggar's staff in your hand?

A COURTIER. How true, my Emperor! No, no, it needs more than that.

JULIAN. Indeed? Does it really? And what?

To let his hair grow, perhaps, and never clean his
nails? Oh hypocritical Cleon! I know you, one
and all. Here, in this treatise, I have given you a
name which——; you shall hear——

> (*He searches through his bundles of papers. At
> that moment* LIBANIUS *enters from the right,
> richly clad, and with a haughty mien.*)

ORIBASES (*in a low tone*). Ah, you come in the
nick of time, most honoured Libanius!

JULIAN (*continuing his search*). Where can it
be——?

LIBANIUS (*to* ORIBASES). What do you mean,
friend?

ORIBASES. The Emperor is much enraged; your
coming will pacify him.

JULIAN. Ah, here I have it——

> (*Annoyed.*)

What does that man want?

ORIBASES. Sire, this is——

JULIAN. No matter, no matter! Now you shall
hear whether I know you or not. There are among
the wretched Galileans a number of madmen who call
themselves penitents. These renounce all earthly
possessions, and yet demand great gifts of the fools
who treat them as holy men and almost as objects of
worship. Behold, you are like these penitents, except
that I shall give you nothing. For I am not a fool.
Yes, yes, if I were not firm on that head, you would
soon overrun the whole court with your shamelessness.
Nay, do you not already do so? Are there not
many among you who would come again, even if I
drove them away? Oh my dear friends, what can this

lead to? Are you lovers of wisdom? Are you
followers of Diogenes, whose garb and habits you
ape? In truth, you do not haunt the schools nearly
so much as you besiege my treasurer. What a pitiful
and despicable thing has not wisdom become because
of you! Oh, hypocrites and babblers without understanding! Oh you―― ―― But what does that fat
man want there?

ORIBASES.   Sire, it is the chief magistrate of the
city――

JULIAN.   The chief magistrate must wait. The
matters we have in hand must take precedence of all
meaner affairs. How now? Why this air of impatience? Is your business so weighty―― ?

LIBANIUS.   By no means, sire; I can come another
day. (*He is going.*)

ORIBASES.   Sire, do you not recognise this distinguished man? This is the rhetorician Libanius.

JULIAN.   What? Libanius? Impossible. Libanius
here—the incomparable Libanius! I cannot believe
it.

LIBANIUS.   I thought the Emperor knew that the
citizens of Antioch had elected me for their chief
magistrate.

JULIAN.   Certainly I knew it. But when I made
my entrance into the city, and the magistrates came
forth to greet me with an oration, I looked in vain for
Libanius. Libanius was not among them.

LIBANIUS.   The Emperor had expressed no wish
to hear Libanius speak on that occasion.

JULIAN.   The orator Libanius ought to have known
what were the Emperor's wishes in that respect.

LIBANIUS. Libanius did not know what changes time and absence might have wrought. Libanius judged it more becoming therefore to place himself among the multitude. He chose, indeed, a sufficiently conspicuous position ; but the Emperor did not deign to let his eyes fall upon him.

JULIAN. I thought you received my letter the day after——

LIBANIUS. Your new friend Priscus brought it to me.

JULIAN. And none the less—perhaps all the more —you held aloof——?

LIBANIUS. Headache and weighty business——

JULIAN. Ah, Libanius, in bygone days you were not so chary of your presence.

LIBANIUS. I come where I am bidden. Ought I to be intrusive? Would you have me stand in the way of the Emperor's much-honoured Maximus?

JULIAN. Maximus never appears at court.

LIBANIUS. And for good reason. Maximus holds a court of his own. The Emperor has conceded him a whole palace.

JULIAN. Oh my Libanius, have I not conceded you my heart? How can you envy Maximus his palace?

LIBANIUS. I envy no man. I do not even envy my colleagues Themistius and Mamertinus, although you have given them such signal proofs of your favour. Nor do I envy Hekebolius, whose wealth you have increased by such princely presents. I am even glad to be the only man to whom you have given nothing. For I well know the reason of the exception. You wish the cities of your empire to abound in everything, and especially in oratory, knowing that it is that distinction which marks us off from the barbarians. Now you feared that I, like certain others, might become lukewarm in my art if you gave me riches. The Emperor has therefore preferred to let the teacher of his youth remain poor, in order to hold him the closer to his craft.   It is thus that I interpret a course of action which has astonished some whose names I forbear to mention.   It is for the honour and well-being of the state that you have given me nothing.   I am to lack riches that I may abound in eloquence.

JULIAN. And I, my Libanius, have also understood the reason why the teacher of my youth has let me pass many months here in Antioch without presenting himself. Libanius probably considered that any services his former pupil may have rendered to the gods, to the state, or to learning, were not great enough to deserve celebration by the man who is called the king of eloquence. Libanius no doubt thought that meaner orators were better fitted to deal with such trivial things. Moreover, Libanius has remained silent out of care for the balance of my mind. You feared, doubtless, to see the Emperor intoxicated with arrogance, reeling like one who in his thirst has drunk too deeply of the leaf-crowned wine-bowl, if you had lavished on him any of that art which is the marvel of Greece, and had, so to speak, raised him to the level of the gods, by pouring out before him so precious a libation.

LIBANIUS. Ah, my Emperor, if I could believe that my oratory possessed such a power——

JULIAN. And why should you not believe it, incomparable friend? Oh, leave me. I am angry with you, Libanius! But it is the lover's anger against the one he loves.

LIBANIUS. Is it indeed so? Oh my crowned brother, let me then tell you that not a day has passed since your coming hither on which I have not cursed the obstinacy that would not let me make the first advance. My friends assured me—not without some show of reason—that you had undertaken this long journey chiefly in order to see me and hear me speak. But Julian himself gave no sign. What could I do? Should I flatter as Emperor him whom I loved as a man?

JULIAN (*embracing and kissing him*). My Libanius!

LIBANIUS (*kissing the Emperor in return*). My friend and brother!

ORIBASES. How honourable to both!

COURTIERS AND TEACHERS (*clapping their hands*). How beautiful! How sublime!

JULIAN. Libanius, cruel friend,—how could you find it in your heart to deprive me so long of this happy moment? During the weeks and months I have waited for you, my countenance has been veiled in Scythian darkness.

LIBANIUS. Alas, you were better off than I; for you had those to whom you could speak about your absent friend.

JULIAN. Say not so. I had only the unhappy lover's comfort: that of sorrowfully repeating your name, and crying out: "Libanius, Libanius!"

LIBANIUS. Ah, whilst you spoke thus to empty air, I spoke to the four walls of my chamber. Most of the day I passed in bed, picturing to myself who was then with you—now this one, now that. " Once it was otherwise," I said to myself,—" then it was I who possessed Julian's ear."

JULIAN. And meanwhile you let me pine away with longing. Look at me. Have I not grown a century older?

LIBANIUS. Oh, have I not suffered as great a change? You did not recognise me.

JULIAN. This meeting has been to both of us as a bath, from which we go forth healed.

(*They embrace and kiss again.*)

And now, beloved friend, now tell me what has brought you here to-day; for I cannot doubt that you have some special errand.

LIBANIUS. To say nothing of my longing—so it is. Would that another had been sent in my stead! But the post of honour to which the confidence of the citizens has summoned me makes it my duty to perform all missions alike.

JULIAN. Speak, my Libanius, and tell me how I can serve you.

LIBANIUS. Let me begin by saying that the inhabitants of this city are sunk in sorrow because you have withdrawn your favour from them.

JULIAN. Hm——!

LIBANIUS. And this sorrow has been coupled with anxiety and uneasiness since Alexander, the new governor, assumed office.

JULIAN. Aha; indeed!

LIBANIUS.   The exaltation of such a man certainly took us by surprise.   Alexander has hitherto filled only trifling offices, and that in a manner not calculated to earn him either the respect or the affection of the citizens.

JULIAN.   I know that well, Libanius!

LIBANIUS.   Alexander is violent in all his dealings, and justice is of little moment in his eyes——

JULIAN.   I know it; I know all you tell me. Alexander is a rough man, without morals or eloquence.   Alexander has in no way deserved so great advancement.   But you may tell the citizens of Antioch that they have deserved Alexander.   Yes, they have, if possible, deserved a still worse ruler, avaricious and intractable as they are——

LIBANIUS.   It is, then, as we feared; this is a punishment——

JULIAN.   Listen, Libanius!   How did I come hither?   With full confidence in the people of this city.   Antioch, chosen by the Sun-King for his especial seat, was to help me to repair all the wrong and ingratitude which had so long been shown to the immortals.   But how have you met me?   Some with defiance, others with lukewarmness.   What have I not to endure here?   Does not that Cappadocian, Gregory of Nazianzus, still wander about the city, stirring up the ignorant Galileans by his audacious speeches?   Has not a poet arisen among them—a certain Apollinaris—who inflames their fanaticism to the point of positive madness with his wild songs?

And what do I not learn from other places?   In Cæsarea, have they not carried out their threat, and wrecked the temple of Fortuna? Oh shame and infamy! Where were the goddess's worshippers the while? Did they prevent it? No, they did not lift a finger, Libanius, though they should have sacrificed life itself to preserve the sanctuary.

But wait, wait! The Galileans of Cæsarea shall atone with their blood, and the whole city shall go up in flames as soon as I have time at my disposal.

LIBANIUS. My lord and friend,—if you would permit me——

JULIAN. Permit me, first. Say yourself whether I ought to tolerate such things? Say whether my zeal can bear with such insults to the divinities who hover over me and shield me? But what can I do? Have I not devoted long nights to disproving these unhappy delusions,—writing, Libanius, till my eyes were red, and my fingers black with ink? And what good do you think it has done? I have reaped scorn instead of thanks, not only from the fanatics themselves, but even from men who pretend to share my opinions. And now, to put the finishing touch to my annoyances, I find you acting as spokesman for the complaints of a handful of citizens against Alexander, who at least does his best to keep the Galileans in check.

LIBANIUS. Oh, my august friend,—that is just the ground of complaint.

JULIAN. Do *you* tell me this?

LIBANIUS. It is not with my own good will that I do the city's errands. I represented to the council that they ought to choose the most distinguished man in the town for this task, thereby implying that I did not wish to be chosen. In spite of this hint, the choice fell on me, who am certainly not——

JULIAN. Well, well, well! But that I must hear from your mouth, Libanius——?

LIBANIUS. I beg my crowned brother to remember that I speak in the name of the city! As to myself, I prize the immortal gods as highly as any one. Where would the art of oratory be without the legends which the poets of bygone days have left to us? May not these legends be compared to a rich vein of ore, whence an accomplished orator can forge himself both weapons and ornaments, if only he understands how to work the metal judiciously? How flat and insipid would not the maxims of wisdom seem, expressed without images or comparisons borrowed from the supernatural?

But think, oh my friend—can you expect the masses to take this view, especially in such an age as ours? I assure you that in Antioch, at any rate, it is out of the question. The citizens, both Galileans and the more enlightened, have of late years lived at peace without giving special heed to such points. There is scarcely a household in the city in which people are of one mind upon things divine. But, until lately, mutual forbearance has been the rule.

Now the case is altered. People have begun to weigh creed against creed. Discord has broken out between the nearest kinsmen. For example, a citizen, whose name I forbear to mention, has lately disinherited his son because the young man separated himself from the Galilean community. Commerce and society suffer from all this, especially now, when scarcity reigns and famine stands at the door.

JULIAN. Enough, enough,—more than enough, Libanius! You complain of scarcity. But tell me, has luxury ever been more rampant than now? Is the amphitheatre ever empty when it is reported that a new lion has arrived from Africa? Last week, when there was a talk of turning all idlers and loungers out of the city because of the dearth, did not the citizens demand loudly that the gladiators and dancing-girls should be excepted; for they felt they could not exist without them!

Ah, well may the gods desert you in wrath over your folly! There are plenty of teachers of wisdom in this city, but where is the wisdom? Why do so few tread in my footsteps? Why stop at Socrates? Why not go a few steps further, and follow Diogenes, or—if I dare say so—me, since we lead you to happiness? For is not happiness the object of all philosophy? And what is happiness but harmony with one's self? Does the eagle want golden feathers? Or the lion claws of silver? Or does the pomegranate-tree long to bear fruits of sparkling stone? I tell you no man has a right to enjoy until he has steeled himself to do without enjoyment. Ay, he ought not to touch enjoyment with his finger-tips until he has learned to trample it under foot.

Ah truly, we are far from that consummation! But I will work for it with all my might. For the sake of these things I will give up others which are also important. The Persian king—alarmed at my approach—has offered me terms of peace. I

think of accepting them, that I may have my
hands free to enlighten and improve you, intractable
generation! As to the other matter, it must remain
as it is. You shall keep Alexander. Make the best
you can of him.

Yet, my Libanius, it shall not be said that I have
sent you from me in disfavour——

LIBANIUS.   Ah, my Emperor——

JULIAN.   You mentioned with a certain bitterness
that I had given much to Themistius and Mamertinus. But did I not also take something from them?
Did I not take from them my daily companionship?
I intend to give you more than I gave them.

LIBANIUS.   Ah, what do you tell me, my august
brother?

JULIAN.   I do not intend to give you gold or silver.
I indulged in that folly only at first, until I saw how
people flocked round me, like thirsty harvesters round
a fountain, elbowing and jostling one another, and
each stretching out a hollow hand to have it filled
first, and filled to the brim. I have grown wiser
since. I think I may say in particular that the
Goddess of Wisdom has not withdrawn her countenance from me in the measures I have taken for the
good of this city.

LIBANIUS.   Doubtless, doubtless!

JULIAN.   Therefore I commission you, oh my
Libanius, to compose a panegyric on me.

LIBANIUS.   Ah, what an honour——!

JULIAN.   You must lay special stress on the
benefits for which the citizens of Antioch owe me
gratitude. I hope you will produce an oration that

shall do honour both to the orator and to his subject. This task, my Libanius, shall be my gift to you. I know of nothing more fitting to offer to a man like you.

LIBANIUS. Oh, my crowned friend, what a transcendent favour!

JULIAN. And now to the fencing-hall. Then, my friends, we will walk through the streets, to give these insolent townsfolk a profitable example of sobriety in dress, and simplicity in manners.

ORIBASES. Through the streets, sire? In this midday heat——

A COURTIER. Pray, sire, let me be excused; I feel extremely unwell——

HERACLIUS. I too, most gracious lord! All this morning I have been fighting against a feeling of nausea——

JULIAN. Then take an emetic, and try to throw up your folly at the same time.

Oh Diogenes,—how degenerate are your successors! They are ashamed to wear your cloak in the open street.

(*He goes out angrily through the colonnade.*)

———

(*A mean street in the outskirts of the city. In the row of houses to the left stands a small church.*)

(*A great multitude of lamenting Christians is collected. The sacred poet* APOLLINARIS, *and the teacher* CYRILLUS *are among them. Women with children in their arms utter loud cries.* GREGORY OF NAZIANZUS *passes along the street.*)

THE WOMEN (*rushing up to him and taking hold of his clothes*).   Ah Gregory, Gregory—speak to us! Comfort us in this anguish!

GREGORY.   Only One can give comfort here. Hold fast by Him.   Cling to the Lord our Shepherd.

A WOMAN.   Do you know, oh man of God,—the Emperor has commanded that all our sacred scriptures shall be burnt!

GREGORY.   I have heard it; but I cannot believe that his folly is so great.

APOLLINARIS.   It is true.   Alexander, the new governor, has sent out soldiers to search the houses of the brethren.   Even women and children are whipped till they bleed, if they are suspected of hiding books.

CYRILLUS.   The Emperor's decree does not apply to Antioch only, nor even to Syria; it applies to the empire and the whole world.   Every word that is written about Christ is to be wiped out of existence, and out of the memory of believers.

APOLLINARIS.   Oh ye mothers, weep for yourselves and for your children!

The time will come when ye shall dispute with those ye now carry in your arms, as to what was in truth written in the lost Word of God.   The time will come when your children's children shall mock at you, and shall not know who or what Christ was.

The time will come when no heart shall remember that the Saviour suffered and died for the world.

The last believer shall go in darkness to his grave, and from that hour shall Golgotha vanish away from the earth, like the place where the Garden of Eden lay.

Woe, woe, to the new Pilate! He is not content, like the first, with slaying the Saviour's body. He murders the word and the faith!

THE WOMEN (*tearing their hair and rending their clothes*). Woe, woe, woe!

GREGORY. And I say to you, be of good cheer! God does not die. It is not from Julian that the danger comes. The danger existed, long before his time, in the weakness and contentiousness of our hearts.

CYRILLUS. Oh, Gregory, how can you expect us to remain steadfast amid these horrors?—Brethren and sisters—do you know what has happened in Arethusa? The unbelievers have maltreated the old bishop Marcus, dragged him by the hair through the streets, cast him into the sewers, dragged him up again, bleeding and befouled, smeared him over with honey and set him in a tree, a prey to wasps and poisonous flies.

GREGORY. And has not God's power been gloriously manifested in this very Marcus? What was Marcus before? A man of doubtful faith. When the troubles broke out in Arethusa, he fled from the city. But behold—no sooner had he heard in his hiding-place that the raging mob were avenging the bishop's flight on innocent brethren, than he returned of his own free will. And how did he bear the torments which so appalled even his executioners, that in order to withdraw with some show of credit, they offered to release him if he would pay a very trifling fine? Was not his answer: No—and no, and again no? The Lord God was with him. He neither died nor yielded. His countenance showed neither terror nor impatience.   In the tree where he hung, he thanked God for being lifted a few steps nearer heaven, while the others, as he said, crawled about on the flat earth.

CYRILLUS.   A miracle must have happened to the resolute old man.   If you had heard, as I did, the shrieks from the prison, that day in the summer when Hilarion and the others were tortured——!   They were like no other shrieks—agonised, rasping, mixed with hissing sounds every time the white-hot iron buried itself in the raw flesh.

APOLLINARIS.   Oh, Cyrillus, do you forget how the shrieks passed over into song?   Did not Hilarion sing even in death?   Did not that heroic Cappadocian boy sing until he gave up the ghost under the hands of the torturers?   Did not Agathon, that boy's brother, sing until he swooned away, and then woke up in madness?

Verily I say unto you, so long as song rings out above our sorrows, Satan shall never conquer !

GREGORY.   Be of good cheer.   Love one another and suffer one for another, as Serapion in Doristora lately suffered for his brothers, for love of whom he let himself be scourged, and cast alive into the furnace !

See, see,—has not the Lord's avenging hand already been raised against the ungodly?   Have you not heard the tidings from Heliopolis under Lebanon ?

APOLLINARIS.   I know it.   In the midst of the ribald feast of Aphrodite, the heathen broke into the house of our holy sisters, violated them, murdered them amid tortures unspeakable——

THE WOMEN.   Woe, woe !

APOLLINARIS.   ——ay, some of the wretches even tore open the bodies of the martyrs, dragged forth the entrails and ate the liver raw!

THE WOMEN.   Woe, woe, woe!

GREGORY.   The God of Wrath seasoned the meal. How have they thriven on it?   Go to Heliopolis, and you shall see those men with a putrefying poison in all their veins, their eyes and teeth dropping out, deprived of speech and understanding.   The city is awe-stricken.   Many heathens have been converted since that night.

Therefore I fear not this pestilent monster who has risen up against the church; I fear not this crowned hireling of hell, who is bent upon finishing the work of the enemy of mankind.   Let him fall upon us with fire, with sword, with the wild beasts of the amphitheatre!   Should his madness even drive him further than hitherto—what does it matter? There is a remedy for everything, and the path lies open to victory.

THE WOMEN.   Christ, Christ!

OTHER VOICES.   There he is!   There he comes!

SOME.   Who?

OTHERS.   The Emperor!   The murderer!   The enemy of God!

GREGORY.   Hush!   Let him pass by in silence.

(*A detachment of the Imperial Guards comes along the street.* JULIAN *follows, accompanied by courtiers and philosophers, all surrounded by guards. Another division of the Household Guard, led by* FROMENTINUS, *closes the procession.*)

A WOMAN (*softly to the others*). See, see, he has wrapped himself in rags, like a beggar.

ANOTHER WOMAN. He must be out of his senses.

A THIRD WOMAN. God has already stricken him.

A FOURTH WOMAN. Hide your infants against your breasts. Do not let their eyes behold the monster.

JULIAN. Aha, are not these Galileans? What are you doing here in the sunshine, in the open street, you spawn of darkness?

GREGORY. You have closed our churches; therefore we stand without and praise the Lord our God.

JULIAN. Ah, is that you, Gregory? So you are still lingering here. But take care; my patience will not last for ever.

GREGORY. I do not seek a martyr's death; I do not even desire it; but if it be allotted me, I shall glory in dying for Christ.

JULIAN. Your phrases weary me. I will not have you here. Why do you not keep to your stinking dens? Go home, I tell you!

A WOMAN. Oh Emperor, where is our home?

ANOTHER WOMAN. Where are our houses? The heathen have plundered them and driven us out.

A VOICE IN THE THRONG. Your soldiers have taken all our goods from us!

OTHER VOICES. Oh Emperor, Emperor, why have you seized upon our possessions?

JULIAN. You ask that? I will tell you, ignorant creatures! If your riches are taken from you, it is out of care for your souls' weal. Has not the Galilean said that you shall own neither silver nor gold? Has not your Master promised that you shall one day ascend to heaven? Ought you not, then, to thank me for making your journey as easy as possible?

THE PHILOSOPHERS. Oh, incomparably answered!

APOLLINARIS. Sire, you have robbed us of what is more precious than gold and silver. You have robbed us of God's own word. You have robbed us of our sacred scriptures.

JULIAN. I know you, hollow-eyed psalm-singer! You are Apollinaris? I believe if I take away your senseless books, you are capable of making up others, just as senseless, in their stead. But you are a pitiful bungler, let me tell you, both in prose and verse! By Apollo! no true Greek would let a line of yours pass his lips. The pamphlet you sent me the other day, which you had the effrontery to entitle "The Truth," I have read, understood, and condemned.

APOLLINARIS. It is possible you may have read it; but you have not understood it; for if you had, you would not have condemned it.

JULIAN. Ha-ha! the rejoinder I am preparing will prove that I understood it.—But as to those books whose loss you lament and howl over, I assure you that you will presently hold them cheaper when it is proved that Jesus of Nazareth was a liar and deceiver.

THE WOMEN. Woe to us; woe to us!

CYRILLUS (stepping forward). Emperor—what do you mean by that?

JULIAN. Did not the crucified Jew prophesy that the temple of Jerusalem should lie in ruins till the end of time?

CYRILLUS. So shall it be!

JULIAN. Oh fools! At this moment my general, Jovian, with two thousand workmen, is at Jerusalem, rebuilding the temple in all its glory. Wait, wait, you stiff-necked doubters—you shall learn who is the mightier, the Emperor or the Galilean.

CYRILLUS. Sire, that you yourself shall learn to your terror. I was silent till you blasphemed the Highest, and called him a liar; but now I tell you that you have not a feather-weight of power against the Crucified One!

JULIAN (*constraining himself*). Who are you, and what is your name?

CYRILLUS (*coming forward*). I will tell you. First and foremost I am called a Christian, and that is a most honourable name; for it shall never be wiped away from the earth.

Furthermore, I bear the name of Cyrillus, and am known by that name among my brethren and sisters.

But if I keep the first name unspotted, I shall reap eternal life as a reward.

JULIAN. You are mistaken, Cyrillus! You know I am not unversed in the mysteries of your creed. Believe me—he in whom you put your trust is not the being you imagine. He died, in very truth, at the time when the Roman, Pontius Pilate, was governor in Judea.

CYRILLUS. I am not mistaken. It is you, oh Emperor, who are mistaken in this. It is you, who renounced Christ at the moment when he gave you dominion over the world.

Therefore I tell you, in his name, that he will quickly take from you both your dominion and your life; and then shall you recognise, too late, how strong he is whom in your blindness you despise.

Yea, as you have forgotten his benefits, he will not remember his loving-kindness, when he shall rise up to punish you.

You have cast down his altars; he shall cast you down from your throne. You have taken delight in trampling his law under foot, that very law which you yourself once proclaimed to believers. In like manner shall the Lord trample you under his heel. Your body shall be scattered to the wild winds, and your soul shall descend to a place of greater torments than you can devise for me and mine!

(*The women flock around* CYRILLUS, *with cries and lamentations.*)

JULIAN. I would willingly have spared you, Cyrillus! The gods are my witnesses that I do not hate you for your faith's sake. But you have mocked at my imperial power and authority, and that I must punish.

(*To the captain of the guard.*)

Fromentinus, lead this man to prison, and let the executioner Typhon give him as many strokes with the scourge as are needful to make him confess that the Emperor, and not the Galilean, has all power upon earth.

GREGORY. Be strong, Cyrillus, my brother!

CYRILLUS (*with upraised hands*). How blessed am I, to suffer for the glory of God!

(*The soldiers seize and drag him out.*)

THE WOMEN (*with tears and sobs*). Woe to us!
Woe, woe, to the apostate!

JULIAN. Disperse these maniacs! Let them be
driven out of the city as rebels. I will no longer
endure this defiance and these abominations!

(*The guard drives the lamenting crowd into the
side streets. Only the Emperor and his suite
remain behind. A man who has hitherto been
hidden is now seen lying at the church door; he
is in torn garments, and has ashes strewn on his
head.*)

A SOLDIER (*stirring him with a lance-shaft*). Up,
up; be off!

THE MAN (*looking up*). Tread under foot this salt
without savour, rejected of the Lord!

JULIAN. Oh everlasting gods!—Hekebolius——!

THE COURTIERS. Ah, so it is,—Hekebolius!

HEKEBOLIUS. That is no longer my name! I am
nameless. I have denied the baptism that gave me
my name!

JULIAN. Arise, friend! Your mind is distem-
pered——

HEKEBOLIUS. Judas's brother is pestiferous.
Away from me——

JULIAN. Oh weak-minded mortal——

HEKEBOLIUS. Avaunt, tempter! Take back your
thirty pieces of silver! Is it not written, "Thou
shalt forsake wife and children for the Lord's
sake"? And I——? For the sake of wife and
children have I betrayed the Lord my God!
Woe, woe, woe! (*He casts himself down again on
his face.*)

JULIAN.   Such flames of madness do these writings kindle over the earth!

And do I not well to burn them?

Wait!   Before a year has passed the Temple of the Jews shall stand again on Zion's hill,—the splendour of its golden dome shining over the world, and testifying : Liar, liar, liar!

(*He goes hastily away, followed by the philosophers.*)

(*A road outside the city.   To the left, by the wayside, stands a statue of Cybele, amid the stumps of hewn-down trees.   At a little distance to the right is a fountain, with a stone basin.   It is towards sunset.*)

(*On a step at the foot of the goddess's statue sits an old priest, with a covered basket in his lap. A number of men and women fetch water from the fountain.   Passers-by are seen on the road. From the left enters the dyer* PHOCION, *meanly clad, with a great bundle on his head.   He meets* EUNAPIUS *the barber, who comes from the city.*)

PHOCION.   Aha!—my friend Eunapius in full court dress!

EUNAPIUS.   Shame on you for mocking a poor man.

PHOCION.   Do you call that mockery?   I thought it was the highest distinction.

EUNAPIUS.   You may say so indeed.   It is the

height of distinction now to go in rags, especially if they have lain long enough in the gutter.

PHOCION. How do you think all this will end?

EUNAPIUS. What should I care? I know how it has ended with me, and that is enough.

PHOCION. Are you no longer in the Emperor's service?

EUNAPIUS. What does the Emperor want with a barber? Do you think *he* has his hair cut, or his beard trimmed? He does not even comb them. But how goes it with you? You do not look much better off.

PHOCION. Alas, Eunapius, purple-dyeing has had its day.

EUNAPIUS. Right, right; now we dye only the backs of the Christians. But what is that you are toiling with?

PHOCION. A bundle of willow bark. I am to dye fools' cloaks for the philosophers.

(*A detachment of soldiers enters from the right; they range themselves beside the statue of Cybele.*)

PHOCION (*to one of the men beside the stone basin*). What does this mean?

THE MAN. The statue is to be fed once more.

PHOCION. Is the Emperor going to sacrifice here this evening?

ANOTHER MAN. Does he not sacrifice both morning and evening—sometimes here, sometimes there?

A WOMAN. It is a misfortune for us poor people that the new Emperor is so devoted to the gods.

Another Woman.   Eh, Dione, do not say that. Should we not all be devoted to the gods?

The first Woman.   Perhaps, perhaps; but it is a misfortune all the same——

One of the Men (*points to the right*).   Look— there he comes.

> (*The* Emperor Julian *advances in priestly attire, with a sacrificial knife. Many philosophers, priests, and servants surround him, along with his guard. After them comes a crowd of people, some mocking, some indignant.*)

One of the New-Comers.   There stands the goddess.   Now you shall see sport!

An older Man.   Do you call that sport?   How many hungry mouths could be fed with what is wasted here?

Julian (*going towards the statue*).   Oh, this sight! It fills my heart with rapture and my eyes with tears of sorrow.

Yes, I must indeed weep, when I remember that this awe-inspiring goddess's statue, overthrown by impious and audacious hands, has lain so long as if in a sleep of oblivion—and that, moreover, in a place I loathe to mention.

> (*Suppressed laughter among the listeners.* Julian *turns angrily.*)

But I feel no less rapture when I remember that to *me* it was vouchsafed to rescue the divine mother from so unworthy a situation.

May I not well be enraptured by this thought?— Men say of me, that I have won a few victories over the barbarians, and praise me for them.   For my

part, I set more value on what I am doing for the
gods ; for to them we owe all our strength and all our
care.

(*To those by the stone basin.*)

I am pleased to find that there are some in this
stiff-necked town who are not deaf to my exhorta-
tions, but have come forth with seemly piety—and, no
doubt, have brought suitable offerings with them.

(*He goes up to the* OLD PRIEST.)

What do I see? One solitary old man! Where
are your brethren of the temple?

THE OLD PRIEST. Sire, they are all dead but I.

JULIAN. All dead! The road laid irreverently close
to the sanctuary. The venerable grove cut down——

Old man—where are the sacrificial offerings?

THE OLD PRIEST (*pointing to the basket*). Here,
sire!

JULIAN. Yes, yes; but the rest?

THE OLD PRIEST. This is all.

(*He opens the basket.*)

JULIAN. A goose! And this goose is all?

THE OLD PRIEST. Yes, sire!

JULIAN. And what pious man have we to thank
for so generous an offering?

THE OLD PRIEST. I myself have brought it
with me. Oh, sire, do not be angry; I had only
this one.

(*Laughter and mutterings among the bystanders.*)

SUPPRESSED VOICES. That is enough. A goose
is more than enough.

JULIAN. Oh Antioch—you put my patience to a
hard test!

A MAN IN THE CROWD. Bread first, offerings afterwards!

PHOCION (*nudging him in the side*). Well said; well said!

ANOTHER MAN. Give the citizens food; the gods may do as best they can.

A THIRD MAN. We were better off under Chi and Kappa!

JULIAN. Oh you shameless grumblers, with your Chi and Kappa! Do you think I do not know whom you mean by Chi and Kappa? Ho-ho, I know very well. It is a by-word among you. You mean Christ and Constantius. But their dominion is past, and I shall soon find means of subduing the frowardness and ingratitude you display both towards the gods and towards me. You are offended because I allot the gods their due offerings. You make sport of my modest attire, and my untrimmed beard. This beard is a very thorn in your eyes! You call it, irreverently, a goat's-beard. But I tell you, oh fools, it is a wise man's beard. I am not ashamed to let you know that this beard harbours vermin, as willow copses harbour game—and yet this despised beard is more honourable to me than your smooth-shaven chins to you!

EUNAPIUS (*half aloud*). What foolishness; most unreasonable!

JULIAN. Do you think I will leave your mockeries unanswered? No, no, you will find yourselves mistaken. Just wait; you shall hear from me sooner than you think. I am at this moment preparing a treatise, called "The Beard-Hater." And do you know against whom it is directed? It is directed against you, citizens of Antioch, whom I describe as " those ignorant hounds." You will find in it my reasons for many things that now seem strange to you in my behaviour.

FROMENTINUS (*entering from the right*). Great Emperor, I bring you good news. Cyrillus has already given way——

JULIAN. Ah, I thought so.

FROMENTINUS. Typhon did his work excellently. The prisoner was stripped, tied by the wrists, and slung to the roof, so that the tips of his toes just touched the floor; then Typhon scourged him from behind with a lash of ox-sinews, which circled his body round to the breast.

JULIAN. Oh these wretches, to force us to use such means!

FROMENTINUS. Lest he should die under our hands, we had to release the obstinate fool at last. He remained for a time quite still, and seemed to reflect; then suddenly he demanded to be brought before the Emperor.

JULIAN. This pleases mè. And you are having him brought hither?

FROMENTINUS. Yes, sire—here they come with him.

(*A detachment of soldiers enters, conducting* CYRILLUS.)

JULIAN. Ah, my good Cyrillus,—you are not quite so high-and-mighty as you were, I see.

CYRILLUS. Have you read in the bowels of some beast or bird what I have to say to you?

JULIAN. I think there needs no divination to foresee that you have come to reason, that you renounce your delusions concerning the Galilean's power, and that you acknowledge both the Emperor and our gods to be greater than he.

CYRILLUS. Imagine no such thing. Your gods are powerless; and if you cling to these graven images, that can neither hear nor see, you yourself will soon be as powerless as they.

JULIAN. Cyrillus—is that what you have to say?

CYRILLUS. No; I come to thank you. Formerly I dreaded you and your tortures. But in the hour of agony I won the victory of the spirit over all that is corruptible. Yes, Emperor, while your hirelings thought I was hanging in torment from the prison roof,—I lay, happy as a child, in my Saviour's arms; and when your executioner seemed to be flaying my body with stripes, the Lord passed his healing hand over the wounds, took away the crown of thorns, and placed on my brow the crown of life.

Therefore I thank you; for no mortal has ever done me so great a service as you.

And lest you should think I fear you for the future, see——

(*He throws back his cloak, tears open his wounds and casts pieces of flesh at the Emperor's feet.*)

—see—see—gorge yourself with the blood you thirst after! But as for me, know that I thirst after Jesus Christ alone.

(*Shrieks of horror are heard amongst the crowd.*)

MANY VOICES. This will bring disaster to us all!

JULIAN (*who has shrunk back*). Hold the madman, lest he lay hands on us!

> (*The soldiers surround* CYRILLUS *and drag him to the water basin; at the same moment the voices of singing women are heard to the right.*)

JULIAN. Look there, Fromentinus—what strange procession is that—— ?

FROMENTINUS. My gracious Emperor, it is the psalm-singers——

JULIAN. Ah, that band of madwomen——

FROMENTINUS. The governor Alexander has taken from them some writings which they hold sacred. They are going out of the city to weep at the graves of the Christians.

JULIAN (*with clenched hands*). Defiance; defiance —from men and women alike!

> (*Old* PUBLIA, *and many other women, come along the road.*)

PUBLIA (*sings*).

Their gods are of marble, and silver and gold.
> They shall crumble to mould.

CHORUS OF WOMEN. To mould; to mould!
PUBLIA.

For brothers, for sons, slain in fierce persecution,
> soar up, doves of song, and crave God's retribu-
> tion!

CHORUS OF WOMEN. Crave God's retribution.

PUBLIA (*catching sight of* JULIAN). There he stands! Woe to the miscreant who has burnt the word of the Lord! Do you think you can burn the word of the Lord with fire? I will tell you where it burns.

> (*She wrests a knife from one of the sacrificing priests, cuts open her breast and probes into the wound.*)

Here the word burns. You may burn our books; but the word shall burn in the hearts of men until the uttermost end of time!

> (*She casts the knife from her.*)

THE WOMEN (*sing with growing ecstasy*).

> Let writings be burnt, and let bodies be slain;
> > the word will remain—
> > the word will remain!

> (*They take PUBLIA into their midst, and go out towards the country.*)

THE PEOPLE BY THE FOUNTAIN. Woe to us; the God of the Galileans is the strongest!

OTHER VOICES. What avail all our gods against this One?

OTHERS AGAIN. No offering! No worship! It will incense the terrible One against us.

JULIAN. Oh fools! You fear to incense a man long dead,—a false prophet—you shall have proof of it. He is a liar, I say! Wait but a little longer. Every day, every hour, I expect tidings from Jerusalem——

> (*JOVIAN, much travel-stained, enters hastily, with a few followers, from the right.*)

JOVIAN. Most gracious Emperor, pardon your servant for seeking you here.

JULIAN (*with a cry of joy*). Jovian! Oh welcome tidings——!

JOVIAN. I come direct from Judea. I learned at the palace that you were here——

JULIAN. Oh ever-praiseworthy gods,—yon setting sun shall not go down upon the lie! How far have you progressed? Speak, my Jovian!

JOVIAN (*with a glance at the crowd*). Sire,—shall I tell all?

JULIAN. All, all—from first to last!

JOVIAN. I arrived at Jerusalem with the architects and soldiers, and the two thousand workmen. We went to work at once to clear the ground. Mighty remnants of the walls remained. They fell before our pickaxes and crowbars so easily that it seemed as though some unseen power were working with us——

JULIAN. You see! What did I tell you!

JOVIAN. In the meantime immense heaps of mortar were being brought together for the new building. Then, without any warning, there arose a whirlwind, which spread the lime like a cloud over the whole country.

JULIAN. Go on; go on!

JOVIAN. The same night the earth shook repeatedly.

VOICES IN THE CROWD. Hear that! The earth shook.

JULIAN. Go on, I say!

JOVIAN. We were nothing daunted by this strange mishap. But when we had dug so deep into the ground as to open the subterranean vaults, and the masons went down to work by torchlight——

JULIAN. Jovian,—what then?

JOVIAN. Sire, a terrible, appalling stream of fire

burst out of the caverns. A thundering noise shook the whole city. The vaults burst asunder; hundreds of workmen were killed in them, and the few who escaped fled with lacerated limbs.

WHISPERING VOICES. The Galileans' God!

JULIAN. Can I believe all this? Did you see it?

JOVIAN. With my own eyes. We began anew. Sire, in the presence of many thousands—awestruck, kneeling, rejoicing, praying—the same wonder was twice repeated.

JULIAN (*pale and trembling*). And then——? In one word,—what has the Emperor done in Jerusalem?

JOVIAN. The Emperor has fulfilled the Galilean's prophecy.

JULIAN. Fulfilled——?

JOVIAN. Through you the saying is accomplished: " Not one stone shall remain upon another."

MEN AND WOMEN. The Galilean has conquered the Emperor! The Galilean is greater than Julian!

JULIAN (*to the priest of Cybele*). You may go home, old man! And take your goose with you. We will have no sacrifice this evening.

(*He turns to the crowd.*)

I heard some say the Galilean had conquered. It may appear so; but I tell you it is a delusion. Oh senseless clods; oh contemptible dolts,—believe me, it will not be long before the tables are turned! I will——; I will——! Ah, only wait! I am already collecting material for a treatise against the Galilean. It is to be in seven chapters; and when his followers have read *that*,—and when the " Beard-Hater," too——

Give me your arm, Fromentinus! This opposition
has wearied me.

(*To the guard, as he passes the fountain.*)
Set Cyrillus free!
(*He returns with his retinue to the city.*)

THE CROWD AT THE FOUNTAIN (*shouting after
him with scornful laughter*). There goes the altar-
butcher!—There goes the ragged bear!—There goes
the ape with the long arms!

(*Moonlight. Among the ruins of the temple of
Apollo.*)
(*The* EMPEROR JULIAN *and the* MYSTIC
MAXIMUS, *both in long robes, appear among
the overthrown columns.*)

MAXIMUS. Whither, my brother?

JULIAN. Where it is loneliest.

MAXIMUS. But here—in this desolation? Among
these rubbish-heaps——?

JULIAN. Is not the whole earth a rubbish-heap?

MAXIMUS. Yet you have shown that what has
fallen can be restored.

JULIAN. Mocker! In Athens I saw how a
cobbler had made himself a little workshop in the
temple of Theseus. In Rome, I hear, a corner of the
Basilica Julia is used for a bullock-stable. Do you
call *that* restoration?

MAXIMUS. Why not? Does not everything
happen piecemeal? What is a whole but the sum of
all the parts?

Julian.   Foolish wisdom !
  (*He points to the overturned statue of Apollo.*)
See this noseless face.   See these splintered elbows,
—these shattered loins.   Does the sum of all these
deformities restore to us the divine perfection of bygone beauty ?

Maximus.   How do you know that that bygone
beauty was beautiful—in itself—apart from the
spectator's idea ?

Julian.   Ah Maximus, that is just the point.
What exists in itself?   After to-day I know of
nothing.
  (*He kicks the head of Apollo.*)
Have you ever been mightier, in yourself?

Strange, Maximus, that there should dwell such
strength in delusion.   Look at those Galileans.   And
look at me in the old days, when I thought it possible
to raise up the fallen world of beauty.

Maximus.   Friend—if delusion be a necessity to
you, return to the Galileans.   They will receive you
with open arms.

Julian.   You know well that that is impossible.
Emperor and Galilean !   How reconcile that con-
tradiction ?

Yes, this Jesus Christ is the greatest rebel that ever
lived.   What was Brutus—what was Cassius, compared with him ?   They murdered only the man
Julius Cæsar ; but he murders all that is called Cæsar
or Augustus.   Is peace conceivable between the
Galilean and the Emperor ?   Is there room for
them both upon the earth ?   For he lives on the
earth, Maximus,—the Galilean lives, I say, however

thoroughly both Jews and Romans imagined that
they had killed him;—he lives in the rebellious
minds of men; he lives in their scorn and defiance
of all visible authority.

"Render unto Cæsar the things that are Cæsar's,—
and to God the things that are God's!" Never has
the mouth of man uttered a more crafty saying than
that. What lies behind it? What, and how much,
belongs to the Emperor? That saying is nothing but
a bludgeon wherewith to strike the crown from off the
Emperor's head.

MAXIMUS. Yet the great Constantine knew how
to compound matters with the Galilean—and your
predecessor too.

JULIAN. Yes, if one could only be as easily
satisfied as they! But do you call *that* ruling the
empire of the world? Constantine widened the
boundaries of his dominion, but did he not fix narrow
boundaries to his spirit and his will? You rate that
man too high, when you call him "the great." My
predecessor I will not speak of; he was more slave
than Emperor, and I cannot be contented with the
name alone.

No, no, a truce is not to be thought of in this
contest. And yet—to have to give way! Oh,
Maximus, after these defeats I cannot retain the
crown—yet neither can I renounce it.

Maximus, you who can interpret omens whose
mystic meaning is hidden from all others—you who
can read the volume of the eternal stars,—can you
foretell the issue of this struggle?

MAXIMUS. Yes, my brother, I can foretell the issue.

Julian.   Can you?   Then tell me—!   Who shall conquer?   The Emperor or the Galilean?

Maximus.   Both the Emperor and the Galilean shall succumb.

Julian.   Succumb——?   Both——?

Maximus.   Both.   Whether in our times or in hundreds of years, I know not; but so it shall be when the right man comes.

Julian.   And who is the right man?

Maximus.   He who shall swallow up both Emperor and Galilean.

Julian.   You solve the riddle by a still darker riddle.

Maximus.   Hear me, brother and friend of truth! I say you shall both succumb—but not that you shall perish.

Does not the child succumb in the youth, and the youth in the man?   Yet neither child nor youth perishes.

Oh, my best-loved pupil—have you forgotten our colloquies in Ephesus about the three empires?

Julian.   Ah Maximus, years have passed since then.   Speak!

Maximus.   You know I have never approved your policy as Emperor.   You have tried to make the youth a child again.   The empire of the flesh is swallowed up in the empire of the spirit.   But the empire of the spirit is not final, any more than the youth is.   You have tried to hinder the growth of the youth,—to hinder him from becoming a man. Oh fool, who have drawn your sword against that which is to be—against the third empire, in which the twin-natured shall reign!

JULIAN.   And he———?

MAXIMUS.   The Jews have a name for him.   They call him Messiah, and they await him.

JULIAN (*slowly and thoughtfully*).   Messiah ?— Neither Emperor nor Redeemer ?

MAXIMUS.   Both in one, and one in both.

JULIAN.   Emperor-god ;—god-emperor.   Emperor in the kingdom of the spirit,—and god in that of the flesh.

MAXIMUS.   *That* is the third empire, Julian !

JULIAN.   Yes, Maximus, that is the third empire.

MAXIMUS.   In that empire the present watchword of revolt will be realised.

JULIAN.   " Render unto Cæsar the things that are Cæsar's,—and to God the things that are God's." Yes, yes,—then the Emperor is in God, and God in the Emperor.—Ah, dreams, dreams,—who shall break the power of the Galilean ?

MAXIMUS.   Wherein lies his power ?

JULIAN.   I have brooded over that question in vain.

MAXIMUS.   Is it not written somewhere : " Thou shalt have none other gods but me " ?

JULIAN.   Yes—yes—yes !

MAXIMUS.   The Seer of Nazareth did not preach this god or that ; he said : " God is I ;—I am God."

JULIAN.   Yes, beyond doubt———!   That is what makes the Emperor powerless.

The third empire ?   The Messiah ?   Not the Jews' Messiah, but the Messiah of the two empires, the spirit and the world———?

MAXIMUS.   The God-Emperor.

JULIAN.   The Emperor-God.

MAXIMUS.   Logos in Pan—Pan in Logos.

JULIAN.   Maximus,—how is he begotten?

MAXIMUS.   He is self-begotten in the man who wills.

JULIAN.   My beloved teacher,—I must leave you.

MAXIMUS.   Whither are you going?

JULIAN.   To the city.   The Persian king has made overtures of peace, which I too hastily accepted.   My envoys are already on their way.   They must be over-taken and recalled.

MAXIMUS.   You will reopen the war against King Sapor?

JULIAN.   I will do what Cyrus dreamed of, and Alexander attempted——

MAXIMUS.   Julian!

JULIAN.   I will possess the world.—Good-night, my Maximus!

(*He makes a gesture of farewell, and goes hastily away.*   MAXIMUS *looks thoughtfully after him.*)

THE CHORUS OF THE PSALM-SINGERS (*far away, beside the graves of the martyrs*).

Ye gods of the nations, of silver and gold,
    ye shall crumble to mould!

Act Fourth.

(*The eastern frontier of the empire. A wild mountain land-
scape. A deep valley separates the high foreground from the
mountains behind.*)

(*The* Emperor Julian, *in military dress, stands on the edge of
a rocky promontory, and looks into the depths. A little way
from him, to the left, stand* Nevita, *the Persian prince* Hormisdas, Jovian, *and several other generals. To the right,
beside a roughly-built stone altar, crouch the soothsayer,*
Numa, *and two other Etruscan soothsayers, examining the
entrails of the sacrifices for omens. Further forward sits the*
Mystic Maximus *on a stone, surrounded by* Priscus,
Kytron, *and other philosophers. Small detachments of
light-armed men now and then pass over the height from left
to right.*)

Julian (*pointing downwards*).   See, see — the
legions wind like a scaly serpent through the ravine.

Nevita.   Those just below us, in sheepskin doub-
lets, are the Scythians.

Julian.   What piercing howls——!

Nevita.   That is the Scythians' customary song,
sire!

Julian.   More howl than song.

Nevita.   Now come the Armenians.   Arsaces
himself is leading them.

Julian.   The Roman legions must already be out

on the plains.   All the neighbouring tribes are hastening to make their submission.

(*He turns to the officers.*)

The twelve hundred ships containing all our stores and munitions lie assembled on the Euphrates. I am fully assured that the fleet can cross over to the Tigris by the ancient canal. The whole army will pass the river by means of the ships. Then we will advance along by the eastern bank as quickly as the current will suffer the ships to follow us.

Tell me, Hormisdas, what think you of this plan?

HORMISDAS. Invincible general, I know that under your victorious protection it will be vouchsafed me to return to my fatherland.

JULIAN. What a relief to be rid of those narrow-breasted citizens! What terror was in their eyes when they pressed around my chariot as I was leaving the city! "Come again quickly," they cried, "and be more gracious to us than now." I will never revisit Antioch. I will never again set eyes on that ungrateful city! When I have conquered, I will return by way of Tharses.

(*He goes up to the soothsayers.*)

Numa,—what are the omens for our campaign this morning?

NUMA. The omens warn you not to pass the frontier of your empire this year.

JULIAN. Hm! How do you read this omen, Maximus?

MAXIMUS. I read it thus: the omen counsels you to subdue all the regions you traverse; thus you will never pass the frontier of the empire.

JULIAN. So is it. We must look closely into such supernatural signs; for there is generally a double meaning in them. It even seems at times as if mysterious powers took a delight in leading men astray, especially in great undertakings. Were there not some who held it an evil omen that the colonnade in Hierapolis fell in and buried half a hundred soldiers, just as we marched through the city? But I say that that portends twofold fortune. In the first place it foreshows the downfall of Persia, and in the second place the doom of the unhappy Galileans. For what soldiers were they who were killed? Why, Galilean convict-soldiers, who went most unwillingly to the war; and therefore fate decreed them that sudden and inglorious end.

JOVIAN. Most gracious Emperor, here comes a captain from the vanguard.

AMMIAN (*entering from the right*). Sire, you commanded me to inform you if anything unusual occurred during our advance.

JULIAN. Well? Has anything happened this morning?

AMMIAN. Yes, sire, two portents.

JULIAN. Quick, Ammian,—speak on!

AMMIAN. First, sire, it happened that when we had gone a little way beyond the village of Zaita, a lion of monstrous size burst from a thicket and rushed straight at our soldiers, who killed it with many arrows.

JULIAN. Ah!

THE PHILOSOPHERS. What a fortunate omen!

HORMISDAS. King Sapor calls himself the lion of the nations.

Numa (*busied at the altar*). Turn back ; turn back, Emperor Julian !

Maximus.   Go boldly forward, chosen son of victory !

Julian.   Turn back after this ? As the lion fell at Zaita, so shall the lion of the nations fall before our arrows. Have I not precedent to support me in interpreting this omen to our advantage ? Need I remind such learned men that when the Emperor Maximian conquered the Persian king, Narses, a lion, and a huge wild boar besides, were killed in the same way in front of the Roman ranks ?

(*To* Ammian.)

But now the other——?   You spoke of two signs.

Ammian.   The other is more doubtful, sire ! Your charger, Babylonius, was led forth, as you commanded, fully equipped, to await your descent on the other side of the mountain. But just at that time a detachment of Galilean convict-soldiers happened to pass. Heavily laden as they were, and by no means over willing, they had to be driven with scourges. Nevertheless they lifted up their arms as in rejoicing, and sent up a loud hymn to their God. Babylonius was startled by the sudden noise, reared in his fright, and fell backwards ; and as he sprawled upon the ground, all his golden trappings were soiled and bespattered with mud.

Numa (*at the altar*). Emperor Julian,—turn back, turn back !

Julian.   The Galileans have done this out of malice,—and yet, in spite of themselves, they have brought to pass a portent which I hail with delight.

Yes, as Babylonius fell so shall Babylon fall, stripped of all the splendour of its adornments.

PRISCUS.   What wisdom in interpretation!

KYTRON.   By the gods, it must be so!

THE OTHER PHILOSOPHERS.   So, and not otherwise!

JULIAN (*to* NEVITA).   The army shall continue to advance.   Nevertheless, for still greater security, I will sacrifice this afternoon and see what the omens indicate.

As for you Etruscan jugglers, whom I have brought hither at so great a cost, I will no longer suffer you in the camp, where you serve only to damp the soldiers' spirits.   You know nothing of the difficult calling you profess.   What effrontery! What measureless presumption!   Away with them! I will not set eyes on them again.

(*Some of the guards drive the soothsayers out to the left.*)

Babylonius fell.   The lion succumbed before my soldiers.   Yet these things do not tell us what invisible help we have to depend upon.   The gods, whose essence is as yet by no means duly ascertained, seem sometimes—if I may say so—to slumber, or, in brief, to concern themselves very little with human affairs.   We, my dear friends, are so unfortunate as to live in such an age.   We have even seen how certain divinities have neglected to support well-meant endeavours, tending to their own honour and glory.

Yet we must not judge rashly in this matter.   It might even be conjectured that the immortals, who guide and uphold the universe, sometimes depute

their power into mortal hands,—not thereby, assuredly,
lessening their own glory ; for is it not thanks to
them that so highly-favoured a mortal—if my conjecture be just—can appear upon earth ?

PRISCUS. Oh matchless Emperor, do not your
own achievements afford proof of this ?

JULIAN. I do not know, Priscus, whether I dare
rate my own achievements so highly. I will not
dwell upon the fact that the Galileans believe the
Jew, Jesus of Nazareth, to have been thus elected ;
for these men err—as I shall conclusively establish
in my treatise against them. But I will remind you
of Prometheus in ancient days. Did not that pre-
eminent hero procure for mankind still greater
blessings than the gods seemed to vouchsafe—
wherefore he had to suffer much, both pain and
despiteful usage, till he was at last exalted to the
communion of the gods—to which, in truth, he had
all the while belonged ?

And may not the same be said both of Herakles
and of Achilles, and, finally, of the Macedonian
Alexander, with whom some have compared me,
partly on account of my exploits in Gaul, partly,
and especially, on account of my designs in the
present campaign ?

NEVITA. My Emperor—the rear-guard is now
beneath us—it is perhaps time——

JULIAN. Presently, Nevita ! First I must tell
you of a strange dream I had last night.

I dreamed that I saw a child pursued by a rich
man who owned countless flocks, but despised the
worship of the gods.

This wicked man exterminated all the child's kindred. But Zeus took pity on the child itself, and held his hand over it.

Then I saw this child grow up to a youth, under the care of Minerva and Apollo.

Further, I dreamed that the youth fell asleep upon a stone beneath the open sky.

Then Hermes descended to him, in the likeness of a young man, and said: "Come; I will show thee the way to the abode of the highest god!" So he led the youth to the foot of a very steep mountain. There he left him.

Then the youth burst out into tears and lamentations, and called with a loud voice to Zeus. Lo, then, Minerva and the Sun-King who rules the earth descended to his side, bore him aloft to the peak of the mountain, and showed him the whole inheritance of his race.

But this inheritance was the orb of the earth from ocean to ocean, and beyond the ocean.

Then they told the youth that all this should belong to him. And therewith they gave him three warnings: he should not sleep, as his race had done; he should not hearken to the counsel of hypocrites; and, lastly, he should honour as gods those who resemble the gods. "Forget not," they said, on leaving him, "that thou hast an immortal soul, and that this thy soul is of divine origin. And if thou follow our counsel thou shalt see our father and become a god, even as we."

PRISCUS.   What are signs and omens to this!

KYTRON.   It can scarcely be rash to anticipate

that the Fates will think twice ere they suffer their counsels to clash with yours.

Julian.   We dare not build with certainty on such an exception.   But assuredly I cannot but find this dream significant, although my brother Maximus by his silence — which is not what I had reason to expect — seems to approve neither of the dream itself, nor of my relation of it.—But that we must bear with !

(*He takes out a roll of paper.*)

See, Jovian ; before I arose this morning, I noted down what I had dreamt.   Take this paper, let numerous copies of it be made, and read to the various divisions of the army.   I hold it of the utmost moment, on so hazardous an expedition, that amid all dangers and difficulties, the soldiers may leave their fate securely in their leader's hands, considering him infallible in all that concerns the issue of the war.

Jovian.   I pray you, my Emperor, let me be excused from this.

Julian.   What do you mean ?

Jovian.   That I cannot lend my aid to anything that is against the truth.—Oh, hear me, my august Emperor and master !   Is there a single one of your soldiers who doubts that he is safe in your hands ? Have you not on the Gallic frontier, in spite of overwhelming numbers and difficulties of all kinds, gained greater victories than any other living commander can boast of ?

Julian.   Well, well!   What startling news !

Jovian.   All know how marvellously fortune has hitherto followed you.   In learning you excel all other mortals, and in the glorious art of eloquence you bear the palm among the greatest.

JULIAN. And yet——? In spite of all this——?

JOVIAN. In spite of all this, my Emperor, you are but mortal. By publishing this dream through the army you would imply that you are a god,—and in that I dare not assist you.

JULIAN. What say you, my friends, to this speech?

KYTRON. It assuredly shows no less effrontery than ignorance.

JULIAN. You seem to forget, oh truth-loving Jovian, that the Emperor Antoninus, surnamed the Pious, has been worshipped in a special temple on the Roman forum as an immortal god. And not he alone, but also his wife, Faustina, and other Emperors before and after him.

JOVIAN. I know it, sire,—but it was not given to our forefathers to live in the light of truth.

JULIAN (*with a long look at him*). Ah, Jovian!——
Tell me,—last evening, when I was taking the omens for the coming night, you brought me a message just as I was laving the blood from my hands in the water of purification——

JOVIAN. Yes, my Emperor!

JULIAN. In my haste, I happened to sprinkle a few drops of the water on your cloak. You shrank sharply backwards and shook the water off, as if your cloak had been defiled.

JOVIAN. My Emperor,—so that did not escape you?

JULIAN. Did you think it would escape me?

JOVIAN.   Yes, sire ; for it was a matter between me and the one true God.

JULIAN.   A Galilean !

JOVIAN.   Sire, you yourself sent me to Jerusalem, and I saw all that happened there.   I have pondered much since then ; I have read the scriptures of the Christians, have spoken with many of them,—and now I am convinced that in their teaching lies the truth of God.

JULIAN.   Is this possible ?   Can it be possible ? Thus does this infectious frenzy spread ?   Even those nearest me—my own generals desert me——

JOVIAN.   Place me in the van against your foes, sire,—and you shall see how gladly I render to Cæsar the things that are Cæsar's.

JULIAN.   How much —— ?

JOVIAN.   My blood, my life.

JULIAN.   Blood and life are not enough.   He who is to rule must rule over the wills, over the minds, of men.   It is in this that your Jesus of Nazareth bars my way and contests my power.

Do not think that I will punish you, Jovian ! The Galileans covet punishment as a benefaction. They are called martyrs after it.   Have they not thus exalted those whom I have been obliged to chastise for their obstinacy ?

Go to the vanguard !   I will not willingly see your face again.—Oh, this treachery to me, which you veil in phrases about double duty and a double empire ! This shall be altered.   Other kings besides the Persian shall feel my foot on their necks.

To the vanguard, Jovian !

JOVIAN.   I shall do my duty, sire!   (*He goes out to the right.*)

JULIAN.   We will not have this morning darkened which rose amid so many happy omens. This, and more, will we bear with an even mind. But my dream shall none the less be published through the army. You, Kytron, and you, my Priscus, and my other friends, will see that this is done in a becoming manner.

THE PHILOSOPHERS.   With joy, with unspeakable joy, sire!

(*They take the roll and go out to the right.*)

JULIAN.   I beg you, Hormisdas, not to doubt my power, although it may seem as though stubbornness met me on every hand. Go; and you too, Nevita, and all the rest, each to his post;—I will follow when the troops are all gathered out on the plains.

(*All except the* EMPEROR *and* MAXIMUS *go out to the right.*)

MAXIMUS (*after a time, rises from the stone where he has been seated and goes up to the Emperor*).   My sick brother!

JULIAN.   More wounded than sick. The deer that is struck by the hunter's shaft seeks the thicket where its fellows cannot see it. It was intolerable to me to be seen in the streets of Antioch;—and now I shrink from showing myself to the army.

MAXIMUS.   No one sees you, friend; for they grope in blindness. But you shall be as a physician to restore their sight, and then they shall behold you in your glory.

JULIAN (*gazing down into the ravine*).   How far

beneath us! How tiny they seem as they wind their way forward, amid thicket and brushwood, along the stony stream!

When we stood at the mouth of this defile, all the leaders, like one man, made for the pass. It meant an hour's way shortened, a little trouble spared,—on the road to death.

And the legions were so eager to follow. No thought of taking the upward path, no longing for the free air up here, where the bosom expands with each deep draught of breath. There they march, and march, and march, and see not that the heaven is straitened above them,—and know not there are heights where it is wider.—Is it not as though men lived but to die, Maximus? The spirit of the Galilean is in this. If it be true, as they say, that his father made the world, then the son contemns his father's work. And it is just for this presumptuous frenzy that he is so highly revered!

Compare Socrates with him! Did not Socrates love pleasure, and happiness, and beauty? And yet he renounced them.—Is there not a bottomless abyss between not desiring, on the one hand, and, on the other, desiring, yet renouncing?

Oh, this treasure of lost wisdom I would fain have restored to men. Like Dionysus of old, I went forth to meet them, young and joyous, a garland on my brow, and the fulness of the vine in my arms. But they reject my gifts, and I am scorned, and hated, and derided by friends and foes alike.

Maximus. Why? I will tell you why.

Near a certain town where I once lived, there was a

vineyard, renowned far and wide for its grapes ; and
when the citizens wished to have the finest fruits on
their tables, they sent their servants out to this vineyard.

Many years after, I came again to that city; but
no one now knew anything of the grapes that were
once so renowned. Then I sought the owner of the
vineyard and said to him, "Tell me, friend, are your
vines dead, since no one now knows aught of your
grapes ? " " No," he answered, "but, you know, young
vines yield good grapes but poor wine ; old vines, on
the contrary, bad grapes but good wine. Therefore,
stranger," he added, " I still gladden the hearts of my
fellow-citizens with the abundance of my vineyard,
only in another form—as wine, not as grapes."

JULIAN (*thoughtfully*). Yes, yes, yes !

MAXIMUS. You have not given heed to this. The
vine of the world has grown old, and yet you think
that you can still offer the raw grapes to those who
thirst for the new wine.

JULIAN. Alas, my Maximus, who thirsts ? Name
me a single man, outside our brotherhood, who is
moved by a spiritual craving.—Unhappy I, to be born
in this iron age !

MAXIMUS. Do not reproach the age. Had the
age been greater, you would have been less. The
world-soul is like a rich man with innumerable sons.
If he share his riches equally, all are well to do, but
none rich. But if he disinherit all but one, and give
everything to him, then that one stands as a rich man
amid a circle of paupers.

JULIAN. No similitude could be less apt than

this.—Am I like your single heir? Is not that very thing divided among many which the ruler of the world should possess in fuller measure than all besides —nay, which he alone should possess? Oh how is not power divided? Has not Libanius the power of eloquence in such fulness that men call him the king of orators? Have not you, my Maximus, the power of mystic wisdom? Has not that madman Apollinaris of Antioch the power of ecstatic song in a measure I needs must envy him? And then Gregory the Cappadocian! Has he not the power of indomitable will in such excess, that many have applied to him the epithet, unbecoming for a subject, of "the Great"? And — what is stranger still — the same epithet has been applied to Gregory's friend, Basilius, the soft-natured man with girlish eyes. And yet he plays no active part in the world; he lives here, this Basilius—here in this remote region, wearing the habit of an anchorite, and holding converse with none but his disciples, his sister Makrina, and other women who are called pious and holy. What influence do not both he and his sister exert, through the epistles they send forth from time to time. Everything, even renunciation and seclusion, becomes a power to oppose my power. But the crucified Jew is still the worst of all.

MAXIMUS. Then make an end of all these piecemeal powers! But do not dream that you can crush the rebels, by attacking them as the emissary of a monarch whom they do not know. In your own name you must act, Julian! Did Jesus of Nazareth appear as the emissary of another? Did he not

proclaim himself to be one with him that sent him?
Truly in you is the time fulfilled, and you do not
see it. Do not all signs and omens point, with
unerring finger, to you? Must I remind you of your
mother's dream——?

JULIAN. She dreamt that she brought forth
Achilles.

MAXIMUS. Must I remind you how fortune has
borne you, as on mighty pinions, through an agitated
and perilous life? Who are you, sire? Are you Alexander born again, not, as before, in immaturity, but
perfectly equipped for the accomplishment of the task?

JULIAN. Maximus!

MAXIMUS. There is One who ever re-appears, at
certain intervals, in the course of human history. He
is like a rider taming a wild horse in the arena.
Again and yet again it throws him. A moment, and
he is in the saddle again, each time more secure and
more expert; but off he has had to go, in all his
varying incarnations, until this day. Off he had to
go as the god-created man in Eden's grove; off he
had to go as the founder of the world-empire;—off
he *must* go as the prince of the empire of God. Who
knows how often he has wandered among us when
none have recognised him?

How do you know, Julian, that you were not *in*
him whom you now persecute?

JULIAN (*looking far away*). Oh unfathomable
riddle——!

MAXIMUS. Must I remind you of the old prophecy
now set afloat again? It has been foretold that so
many years as the year has days should the empire

of the Galilean endure.   Two years more, and it will
be three hundred and sixty-five years since that man
was born in Bethlehem.

JULIAN.   Do you believe this prophecy?

MAXIMUS.   I believe in that which is to come.

JULIAN.   Always riddles!

MAXIMUS.   I believe in the free necessity.

JULIAN.   Still more enigmatic.

MAXIMUS.   Behold, Julian,—when Chaos seethed
in the fearful void abyss, and Jehovah was alone,—
that day when he, according to the old Jewish scriptures, stretched forth his hand and divided light from
darkness, sea from land,—that day the great creating
God stood on the summit of his power.

But with man arose will upon the earth.   And
men, and beasts, and trees, and herbs re-created themselves, each in its own image, according to eternal
laws; and by eternal laws the stars roll through the
heavenly spaces.

Did Jehovah repent?   The ancient traditions of all
races tell of a repenting Creator.

He had established the law of perpetuation in the
universe.   Too late to repent!   The created *will*
perpetuate itself—and is perpetuated.

But the two kingdoms of onesidedness war one
against the other.   Where, where is the king of peace,
the twin-sided one, who shall reconcile them?

JULIAN (*to himself*).   Two years?   All the gods
inactive.   No capricious power behind, which might
bethink itself to cross my plans—— ——

Two years?   In two years I can bring the earth
under my sway.

MAXIMUS.   You spoke, my Julian ;—what did you say ?

JULIAN.   I am young and strong and healthy. Maximus—it is my will to live long.

(*He goes out to the right.*   MAXIMUS *follows him.*)

———————————

(*A hilly wooded region with a brook among the trees.   Up on the heights a little farm.   It is towards sunset.*)

(*Detachments of the army pass from left to right at the foot of the slope.   BASILIUS OF CÆSAREA, and his sister MAKRINA, both in the dress of hermits, stand by the wayside and offer water and fruits to the weary soldiers.*)

MAKRINA.   Oh, Basilius, see—each paler and more haggard than the last !

BASILIUS.   And such multitudes of our Christian brethren among them !   Woe to the Emperor Julian ! This is a more ingeniously contrived cruelty than all the horrors of the torture chamber.   Against whom is he leading his hosts ?   Less against the Persian king than against Christ.

MAKRINA.   Do you believe this dreadful thing of him ?

BASILIUS.   Yes, Makrina, it becomes more and more clear to me that it is against *us* the blow is aimed.   All the defeats he has suffered in Antioch, all the resistance he has met with, all the disappointments and humiliations he has had to stomach on his

ungodly path, he hopes to bury in oblivion by means
of a victorious campaign. And he will succeed. A
great victory will blot out everything. Men are
fashioned so; they see right in success, and before
might most of them will bend.

MAKRINA (*pointing out to the left*). Fresh squad-
rons! Innumerable, unceasing——

> (*A detachment of soldiers passes by; a young man
> in the ranks sinks down on the road from
> weariness.*)

A SUBALTERN (*beating him with a stick*). Up
with you, lazy hound!

MAKRINA (*hastening up*). Oh, do not beat
him!

THE SOLDIER. Let them beat me;—I am so
glad to suffer.

AMMIAN (*entering*). Another stoppage!—Oh, it
is he. Can he really go no further?

THE SUBALTERN. I do not know what to say,
sir; he falls at every step.

MAKRINA. Oh, be patient! Who is this unhappy
man?—See, suck the juice of these fruits.—Who is he,
sir?

AMMIAN. A Cappadocian,—one of the fanatics
who helped to desecrate the temple of Venus at
Antioch.

MAKRINA. Oh, one of those martyrs——!

AMMIAN. Try to rise, Agathon! I am sorry for
this fellow. They chastised him more severely than
he could bear. He has been out of his mind ever
since.

AGATHON (*rising*). I can bear it very well, and I

am in my right mind, sir! Beat, beat, beat me—I am so glad to suffer.

AMMIAN (*to the Subaltern*). Forward; we have no time to waste.

THE SUBALTERN (*to the soldiers*). Forward, forward!

AGATHON. Babylonius fell;—soon shall the Babylonian whoremonger fall likewise. The lion of Zaita was slain—the crowned lion of the earth is doomed!

(*The soldiers are driven out to the right.*)

AMMIAN (*to* BASILIUS *and* MAKRINA). You strange people;—you go astray and yet do good. Thanks for your refreshment to the weary; and would that my duty to the Emperor permitted me to treat your brethren as forbearingly as I should desire.

(*He goes off to the right.*)

BASILIUS. God be with you, noble heathen!

MAKRINA. Who may that man be?

BASILIUS. I do not know him.

(*He points to the left.*)

Oh see, see—there he is himself!

MAKRINA. The Emperor? Is that the Emperor?

BASILIUS. Yes, it is he.

(*The* EMPEROR JULIAN, *with several of his principal officers, escorted by a detachment of guards, with their captain* ANATOLUS, *enters.*)

JULIAN (*to his retinue*). Oh, why talk of fatigue? Should the fall of a horse bring me to a standstill? Or is it less becoming to go on foot than to bestride an inferior animal? Fatigue! My ancestor said that it befits an Emperor to die standing. I say that

it befits an Emperor, not only in the hour of death,
but throughout his whole life, to set an example of
endurance ; I say—— —— Ah, by the great light of
heaven ! do I not see Basilius of Cæsarea before my
eyes ?

BASILIUS (*bowing deeply*).   Your meanest servant,
oh most mighty lord !

JULIAN.   Ah, I know what that means ! Truly
you serve me well, Basilius !

(*Approaching.*)

So this is the villa that has become so renowned
by reason of the epistles that emanate from it.   This
house is more talked of throughout the provinces
than all the lecture-halls together, although I have
spared neither care nor pains to restore their
glory.

Tell me—is not this woman your sister, Makrina ?

BASILIUS.   She is, sire !

JULIAN.   You are a fair woman, and still young.
And yet, as I hear, you have renounced life.

MAKRINA.   Sire, I have renounced life in order
truly to live.

JULIAN.   Ah, I know your delusions very well.
You sigh for that which lies beyond, of which you
have no certain knowledge ; you mortify your flesh ;
you repress all human desires.   And yet I tell you
this may be a vanity, like the rest.

BASILIUS.   Do not think, sire, that I am blind to
the danger that lurks in renunciation.   I know that
my friend Gregory says well when he writes that he
holds himself a hermit in heart, though not in the
body.   And I know that this coarse clothing is of

small profit to my soul if I take merit to myself for wearing it.

But that is not my case. This secluded life fills me with unspeakable happiness; that is all. The wild convulsions through which the world is passing in these days, do not here force themselves, in all their hideousness, upon my eyes. Here I feel my body lifted up in prayer, and my soul purified by a frugal life.

JULIAN. Oh my modest Basilius, I fear you are ambitious of more than this. If what I hear be true, your sister has gathered round her a band of young women whom she is training up after her own likeness. And you yourself, like your Galilean master, have chosen twelve disciples. What is your purpose with them?

BASILIUS. To send them out into all lands, that they may strengthen our brethren in the fight.

JULIAN. Indeed! Equipped with all the weapons of eloquence, you send your army against me. And whence did you obtain this eloquence, this glorious Greek art? From our schools of learning. What right have you to it? You have stolen like a spy into our camp, to find out where you can most safely strike at us. And this knowledge you are now applying to our greatest hurt!

Let me tell you, Basilius, that I am not inclined to suffer this scandal any longer. I will strike your weapons out of your hands. Keep to your Matthew and Luke, and other such unpolished babblers. But henceforth you shall not be permitted to interpret our ancient poets and philosophers; for I hold it

unreasonable to let you suck knowledge and skill
from sources in the truth of which you do not believe.
All Galilean scholars, too, shall be forbidden our
lecture-halls; for what is their business there? Simply
to steal our weapons and use them against us.

BASILIUS. Sire, I have already heard of this
strange determination. And I agree with Gregory
when he maintains that you have no exclusive right
either to Grecian learning or Grecian eloquence. I
agree with him in arguing that you use the alphabet
which was invented by the Egyptians, and that you
clothe yourself in purple, which first came into use
among the people of Tyre.

Yes, sire—and more than that. You subdue nations,
and make yourself ruler over peoples, whose tongues
are unknown and whose manners are strange to you.
And you have a right to do so. But by the same
right by which you rule the visible world, he whom
you call the Galilean rules the invisible——

JULIAN. Enough of that! I will no longer listen
to such talk. You speak as if there were two rulers
of the world, and on that plea you cry halt to me at
every turn. Oh fools! You set up a dead man against
a living one. But you shall soon be convinced of
your error. Do not suppose that amid the cares of
war I have laid aside the treatise I have long been
preparing against you. Perhaps you think I spend
my nights in sleep? You are mistaken! For "The
Beard-Hater" I reaped nothing but scorn,—and that
from the very people who had most reason to lay
certain truths to heart. But that shall in no wise
deter me. Should a man with a cudgel in his hand

shrink from a pack of yelping curs?—Why did you smile, woman? What were you laughing at?

MAKRINA. Why, sire, do you rage so furiously against one who, you say, is dead?

JULIAN. Ah, I understand! You mean to say that he is alive.

MAKRINA. I mean to say, oh mighty Emperor, that in your heart you feel of a surety that he lives.

JULIAN. I? What next! *I* feel——!

MAKRINA. What is it that you hate and persecute? Not him, but your belief in him. And does he not live in your hate and persecution, no less than in our love?

JULIAN. I know your tortuous phrases. You Galileans say one thing and mean another. And that you call rhetoric! Oh mediocre minds! What folly! *I* feel that the crucified Jew is alive! Oh what a degenerate age, to find satisfaction in such sophistries! But such is humanity nowadays. Madness passes for wisdom. How many sleepless nights have I not spent in searching out the true foundation of things? But where are my followers? Many praise my eloquence, but few, if any, are convinced by it.

But truly the end is not yet. You may look for something that will astonish you. You shall learn how all the scattered forces are converging into one. You shall see glorified that which you now despise— and out of the cross on which you hang your hopes I will fashion a ladder for One whom you know not of.

MAKRINA. And I tell you, Emperor Julian, that you are nothing but a scourge in the hand of God—

a scourge that *must* chasten us by reason of our sins. Woe to us that it must be so! Woe to us for the rancours and dissensions that have caused us to swerve from the true path!

There was no longer a king in Israel. Therefore has the Lord stricken you with madness, that you might chastise us.

What a spirit has he not darkened, that it should rage against us! What a blossoming tree has he not stripped to make rods for our sin-laden shoulders!

Portents warned you, and you did not heed them. Voices called you, and you heard them not. Hands wrote in letters of fire upon the wall, and you rubbed out the writing ere you had deciphered it.

JULIAN. Basilius,—would I had known this woman before to-day.

BASILIUS.   Come, Makrina!

MAKRINA. Woe is me that I have seen these shining eyes! Angel and serpent in one; the apostate's longing combined with the tempter's guile! Oh, how have our brethren and sisters borne their hope of victory so high, in the face of such an instrument of wrath? In him dwells a greater than he. Do you not see it, Basilius—in him will the Lord God smite us even to death.

JULIAN.   You have said it!

MAKRINA.   Not I!

JULIAN.   My first-won soul!

MAKRINA.   Avaunt from me!

BASILIUS.   Come—come!

JULIAN. Remain here!—Anatolus, set a watch about them!—It is my will that you shall follow the army—both you and **your** disciples,—youths and women.

BASILIUS.   Sire, you cannot desire this!

JULIAN.   It is not wise to leave fortresses in our rear.   See, I stretch out my hand and quench the burning shower of arrows which you have sent forth from yonder villa.

BASILIUS.   No, no, sire—this deed of violence——

MAKRINA.   Alas, Basilius—here or elsewhere—all is over!

JULIAN.   Is it not written " Render unto Cæsar the things that are Cæsar's "?   I require all aid in this campaign.   You can tend my sick and wounded.   In that you will be serving the Galilean at the same time ; and if you still think that a duty, I advise you to make good use of your time.   His end is near!

(*Some soldiers have surrounded* BASILIUS *and* MAKRINA, *others hasten through the thicket towards the house.*)

MAKRINA.   Sunset over our home ; sunset of hope and of light in the world!   Oh Basilius! that we should live to see the night!

BASILIUS.   The light *is*.

JULIAN.   The light shall be.   Turn your backs to the sunset, Galileans!   Your faces to the east, to the east, where Helios lies dreaming.   Verily I say unto you, you shall see the Sun-King of the world.

(*He goes out to the right ; all follow him.*)

(*Beyond the Euphrates and Tigris.   A wide plain, with the imperial camp.   Copses, to the left and in the background, hide the windings of the Tigris. Masts of ships rise over the thickets in long rows, stretching into the far distance. A cloudy evening.)*

(Soldiers and men-at-arms of all sorts are busy pitching their tents on the plain. All kinds of stores are being brought from the ships. Watch-fires far away. NEVITA, JOVIAN, and other officers come from the fleet.)

NEVITA.   See, now, how rightly the Emperor has chosen! Here we stand, without a stroke, on the enemy's territory; no one has opposed our passage of the river; not even a single Persian horseman is to be seen.

JOVIAN.   No, sir, the enemy certainly did not expect us by this route.

NEVITA.   You speak as if you still thought this route unwisely chosen.

JOVIAN.   Yes, sir, it is still my opinion that we ought to have taken a more northerly direction. Then our left wing would have rested on Armenia, which is friendly towards us, and all our supplies might have come from that fruitful province. But here? Hampered in our progress by the heavy freight-ships, surrounded by a barren plain, almost a desert—— Ah! the Emperor is coming. I will go; I am not in his good graces at present.

(He goes out to the right. At the same time JULIAN enters with his retinue from the ships. ORIBASES, the physician, the philosophers PRISCUS and KYTRON, with several others, appear from

among the tents on the right, and go to meet the Emperor.)

JULIAN.   Thus does the empire grow.   Every step I take towards the east shifts the frontier further back.

(*He stamps on the earth.*)

This earth is mine! I am in the empire, not beyond it.—Well, Priscus——?

PRISCUS.   Incomparable Emperor, your command has been executed.   Your marvellous dream has been read to every division of the army.

JULIAN.   Good, good.   And how did my dream seem to affect the soldiers?

KYTRON.   Some praised you with joyful voices, and hailed you as divine; others on the contrary——

PRISCUS.   These others were Galileans, Kytron!

KYTRON.   Yes, yes, most of them were Galileans; and these smote upon their breasts and uttered loud lamentations.

JULIAN.   I will not let the matter rest here.   The busts of myself, which I have provided for erection in the towns I am to conquer, shall be set up round the camp over all the pay-masters' tables.   Lamps shall be lighted beside the busts; a chafing dish, with sweet-smelling incense, shall burn before them; and every soldier as he comes forward to receive his pay shall cast some grains of incense on the fire.

ORIBASES.   Forgive me, most gracious Emperor, but—is that expedient?

JULIAN.   Why not?   I marvel at you, my Oribases!

PRISCUS.   Ah, sire, you may well marvel! Not expedient to—— ?

KYTRON.   Should not a Julian dare what less god-like men have dared ?

JULIAN.   I, too, think that the most daring thing in this case would be the attempt to hide the counsels of the mystic powers.   If it be the case that the divinities have deputed their sovereignty into earthly hands—as many signs justify us in concluding—it would indeed be most ungrateful to conceal the fact.   In such critical situations as the present, it is no trifling matter that the soldiers should pay their devotions in a quite different quarter from that in which they are due.

I tell you, Oribases, and all of you,—if, indeed, there is any other person present who wishes to set limits to the Emperor's power,—that this would be the very essence of impiety, against which I should have to take the strongest measures.

Has not Plato long ago enunciated the truth that only a god can rule over men ?   What did he mean by that saying ?   Answer me—what did he mean ? Far be it from me to assert that Plato—incomparable sage though he was—had any individual, even the greatest, in his prophetic eye.   But I think we have all seen what disorders result from the dismemberment, so to speak, of the supreme power.

Enough of that.   I have already commanded that the imperial busts shall be displayed about the camp.

Ah! what do you seek in such haste, Eutherius ?

(*The Chamberlain* EUTHERIUS *comes from the*

*ships, accompanied by a man in girt-up gar-
ments.*)

EUTHERIUS. Great Emperor,—this man of Antioch
is sent by the governor, Alexander, and brings you
a letter which, he says, is of great importance.

JULIAN. Ah, let me see! Light here!

(*A torch is brought; the Emperor opens and reads
the letter.*)

JULIAN. Can this be possible! More light! Yes,
here it is written—and here—; what next?—This
goes beyond all I could have imagined!

NEVITA. Bad news from the west, sire?

JULIAN. Nevita, tell me, how long will it take us
to reach Ctesiphon?

NEVITA. It cannot be done in less than thirty
days.

JULIAN. It *must* be done in less! Thirty days!
A whole month! And while we are creeping forward
here, I must let those madmen——

NEVITA. You know yourself, sire, that, on account
of the ships, we must follow all the windings of the
river. The current is rapid, and the bed, too, shallow
and stony. I hold it impossible to proceed more
quickly.

JULIAN. Thirty days! And then there is the city
to be taken,—the Persian army to be routed,—peace
to be concluded. What a time all this will take?
And there were some among you foolish enough to
recommend an even more roundabout route. Ha-ha;
they would compass my ruin!

NEVITA. Do not fear, sire; the expedition shall
advance with all possible speed.

Julian.   It must indeed.   Can you imagine what Alexander tells me ?   The madness of the Galileans has passed all bounds since I left.   And it increases day by day.   They understand that my victory in Persia will bring their extirpation in its train ; and with that shameless Gregory as their leader, they now stand like a hostile army in my rear ; in the Phrygian regions secret preparations are being made, no one knows to what end——

Nevita.   What does this mean, sire ?   What are they doing ?

Julian.   What are they doing ?   Praying, preaching, singing, and prophesying the end of the world. And would that that were all !—but they carry our adherents away, and entice them into their rebellious conspiracies.   In Cæsarea the congregation has chosen the judge Eusebius to be their bishop,— Eusebius, an unbaptised man—and he has been so misguided as to accept their call, which the canon of their own church declares invalid.

But that is far from being the worst ; worse, ten times worse, is the fact that Athanasius has returned to Alexandria.

Nevita.   Athanasius !

Priscus.   That mysterious bishop, who vanished into the desert six years ago ?

Julian.   A council of the church banished him on account of his unseemly zeal.   The Galileans were accommodating under my predecessor.

Yes, just think of it—this raging fanatic has returned to Alexandria.   His entrance was like a king's ; the road was strewn with carpets and green palm branches. And what happened next? What do you think? The same night a riot broke out among the Galileans. Georgius, their lawful bishop, that right-minded and well-disposed man, whom they accused of lukewarmness in the faith, was torn to pieces in the streets of the city.

NEVITA. But, sire, how were things suffered to go so far? Where was the governor, Artemius?

JULIAN. You may well ask where Artemius was. I will tell you. Artemius has joined the Galileans! Artemius himself has penetrated by force of arms into the Serapeion, that most glorious of earthly temples,—has broken the statues to pieces—has plundered the altars, and destroyed that vast treasury of books, which was of such inestimable value precisely in this age of error and ignorance. I would weep for them as for a friend bereft me by death, were not my wrath too great for tears.

KYTRON. Truly, this transcends belief!

JULIAN. And not to be within reach of these miserable beings to punish them! To be doomed to inactivity while such atrocities spread wider and wider around!—Thirty days, you say! Why are we loitering? Why are we pitching our tents? Why should we sleep? Do my generals not know what is at stake? We must hold a council of war. When I remember what the Macedonian Alexander achieved in thirty days——

(JOVIAN, *accompanied by a man in Persian garb, unarmed, enters from the camp.*)

JOVIAN. Forgive me, sire, for appearing before you: but this stranger——

JULIAN. A Persian warrior!

THE PERSIAN (*prostrating himself to the earth*). No warrior, oh mighty Emperor!

JOVIAN. He came riding over the plains, unarmed, and surrendered at the outposts——

JULIAN. Then your countrymen are at hand?

THE PERSIAN. No, no!

JULIAN. Whence do you come, then?

THE PERSIAN (*throws open his garments*). Look at these arms, oh ruler of the world,—bleeding from rusty fetters. Feel this flayed back,—sore upon sore. I come from the torture-chamber, sire!

JULIAN. Ah—a fugitive from King Sapor?

THE PERSIAN. Yes, mighty Emperor, to whom all things are known! I stood high in favour with King Sapor until, impelled by the terror of your approach, I ventured to prophesy that this war would end in his destruction. Would you know, sire, how he has rewarded me? My wife he gave as a prey to his archers from the mountains; my children he sold as slaves; all my possessions he divided among his servants; myself he tortured for nine days. Then he bade me ride forth and die like a beast in the desert.

JULIAN. And what would you with me?

THE PERSIAN. What would I after such treatment? I would help you to destroy my persecutor.

JULIAN. Ah, poor tortured wretch,—how can you help?

THE PERSIAN. I can lend wings to your soldiers' feet.

JULIAN. What do you mean by that? Rise, and explain yourself.

THE PERSIAN (*rising*). No one in Ctesiphon expected you to choose this route——

JULIAN. I know that.

THE PERSIAN. Now it is no longer a secret.

JULIAN. You lie, fellow! You Persians know nothing of my designs.

THE PERSIAN. You, sire, whose wisdom is born of the sun and of fire, know well that my countrymen are now acquainted with your designs. You have crossed the rivers by means of your ships; these ships, more than a thousand in number, and laden with all the supplies of the army, are to be towed up the Tigris, and the troops are to advance abreast of the ships.

JULIAN. Incredible——!

THE PERSIAN. When the ships have approached as near Ctesiphon as possible—that is to say, within two days' march—you will make straight for the city, beleaguer it, and compel King Sapor to surrender.

JULIAN (*looking round*). Who has betrayed us?

THE PERSIAN. This plan is now no longer practicable. My countrymen have hastily constructed stone dams in the bed of the river, on which your ships will run aground.

JULIAN. Man, do you know what it will cost you if you deceive me?

THE PERSIAN. My body is in your power, mighty Emperor! If I do not speak the truth, you are free to burn me alive.

JULIAN (*to* NEVITA). The river dammed! It will take weeks to make it navigable again.

NEVITA. If it can be done at all, sire! We have not the implements——

JULIAN. And that this should come upon us now —just when so much depends on a speedy victory!

THE PERSIAN. Oh ruler of the world, I have said that I can lend your army wings.

JULIAN. Speak! Do you know of a shorter way?

THE PERSIAN. If you will promise me that after your victory you will restore the possessions I have been robbed of, and give me a new wife of noble birth, I will——

JULIAN. I promise everything; only speak,— speak!

THE PERSIAN. Strike straight across the plains, and in four days you will be under the walls of Ctesiphon.

JULIAN. Do you forget the mountain chain on the other side of the plains?

THE PERSIAN. Sire, have you never heard of that strange defile among the mountains?

JULIAN. Yes, yes, a chasm; " Ahriman's Street," it is called. Is it true that it exists?

THE PERSIAN. I rode through " Ahriman's Street " two days ago.

JULIAN. Nevita!

NEVITA. In truth, sire, if it be so——

JULIAN. Miraculous help in the hour of need——!

THE PERSIAN. But if you would pass that way, oh mighty one, there is not a moment to be lost. The Persian army which had been collected in the northern provinces, is now recalled to block the mountain passes.

JULIAN. Do you know that for certain?

THE PERSIAN.   Delay, and you will discover it for
yourself.

JULIAN.   How many days will it take your countrymen to get there?

THE PERSIAN.   Four days, sire!

JULIAN.   Nevita, in three days we must be beyond
the defiles!

NEVITA (*to the Persian*).   Is it possible to reach
the defiles in three days?

THE PERSIAN.   Yes, great warrior, it is possible,
if you make use of this night as well.

JULIAN.   Let the camp be broken up!   No sleep,
no rest just now.   In four days—or five at the utmost
—I must stand before Ctesiphon.—What are you
thinking about?   Ah, I know!

NEVITA.   The fleet, sire!

JULIAN.   Yes, yes, yes, the fleet!

NEVITA.   If the Persian army reaches the defiles
a day later than we, they will—if they cannot injure
you in any other way—turn westward against your
ships——

JULIAN.   And seize a vast amount of booty, wherewith to continue the war——

NEVITA.   If we could leave twenty thousand men
with the ships, they would be safe——

JULIAN.   What are you thinking of!   Twenty
thousand?   Almost a third of our fighting strength.
Where would be the force with which I must strike
the great blow?   Divided, dispersed, frittered away.
Not one man will I detach for such a purpose.

No, no, Nevita; but there may be a middle
course——

NEVITA (*shrinking backwards*). My great Emperor——!

JULIAN. The fleet must neither fall into the hands of the Persians, nor yet cost us men. There is a middle course, I tell you! Why do you falter? Why not speak it out?

NEVITA (*to the Persian*). Do you know whether the citizens of Ctesiphon have stores of corn and oil?

THE PERSIAN. Ctesiphon overflows with supplies of all sorts.

JULIAN. And when we have once taken the city, the whole rich country lies open to us.

THE PERSIAN. The citizens will open their gates to you, sire! I am not the only one who hates King Sapor. They will rise against him and straightway submit to you, if you come upon them, unprepared and panic-stricken, with your whole collected force.

JULIAN. Yes; yes.

THE PERSIAN. Burn the ships, sire!

NEVITA. Ah!

JULIAN. His hate has eyes where your fidelity is blind, Nevita!

NEVITA. My fidelity saw, sire; but it shrank from what it saw.

JULIAN. Are not these ships like fetters on our feet? We have provisions for four full days in the camp. It is well that the soldiers should not be too heavily laden. Of what use, then, are the ships? We have no more rivers to pass——

NEVITA. Sire, if it is really your will——

JULIAN. My will,—my will? Oh, on an evening

like this,—so angry and tempestuous,—why cannot a flash of lightning descend and——

MAXIMUS (*entering hastily from the left*). Oh chosen son of Helios—hear me, hear me !

JULIAN.   Not now, my Maximus !

MAXIMUS.   Nothing can be more pressing than this.   You *must* hear me !

JULIAN.   Then in the name of fortune and wisdom, speak, my brother !

MAXIMUS (*draws him apart, and says in a low voice*). You know that I have spared no pains to spell out, both in books and through auguries, the issue of this campaign ?

JULIAN.   I know that you have failed to foretell anything.

MAXIMUS.   The omens spoke and the writings confirmed them.   But the answer which always came was so strange that I could not but think myself mistaken.

JULIAN.   But now—— ?

MAXIMUS.   When we left Antioch, I wrote to Rome to consult the sibylline books——

JULIAN.   Yes, yes—— !

MAXIMUS.   This very moment the answer has arrived ; a courier from the governor of Antioch brought it.

JULIAN.   Ah, Maximus,—and its purport—— ?

MAXIMUS.   The same as that of the omens and the books ; but now I dare interpret it.   Rejoice, my brother,—in this war you are invulnerable.

JULIAN.   The oracle,—the oracle ?

MAXIMUS.   The sibylline books say : " Julian must beware of the Phrygian regions."

Julian (*shrinking back*). The Phrygian——? Ah, Maximus !

Maximus. Why so pale, my brother ?

Julian. Tell me, dear teacher, how do you interpret this answer ?

Maximus. Is more than one interpretation possible? The Phrygian regions ? What have you to do in Phrygia ? In Phrygia, a remote province lying far behind you, and where you need never set your foot. *No* danger threatens you, fortunate man—*that* is the interpretation.

Julian. This enigmatic answer has a twofold meaning. No danger threatens me in this war,—but from that distant region——

Nevita, Nevita !

Nevita. Sire——!

Julian. In Phrygia ? Alexander writes of secret preparations taking place in Phrygia. It has been foretold that the Galilean is coming again——

Burn the ships, Nevita !

Nevita. Sire, is this your firm and irrevocable will——?

Julian. Burn them ! No delay ! Lurking dangers threaten us in the rear.

(*To one of the captains.*)

Give all heed to this stranger. He is to be our guide. Refresh him with food and drink, and let him have thorough rest.

Jovian. My Emperor, I implore you—do not build too securely on the reports of a deserter like this.

Julian. Aha—you seem agitated, my Galilean

councillor ! All this is not quite to your mind. Perhaps you know more than you care to tell.

Go, Nevita,—and burn the ships !

(NEVITA *bows and goes out to the left. The captain leads the Persian away among the tents.*)

JULIAN. Traitors in my own camp! Wait, wait, —I shall get to the bottom of these machinations.

The camp shall break up ! Go, Jovian, see that the vanguard is afoot within an hour. The Persian knows the way. Go !

JOVIAN. As you command, my august Emperor !

(*He goes out to the right.*)

MAXIMUS. Will you burn the fleet ? Then surely you have great things in your mind.

JULIAN. I should like to know whether the Macedonian Alexander would have ventured this ?

MAXIMUS. Did Alexander know where the danger threatened ?

JULIAN. True, true ! *I* know it. All the powers of victory are in league with me. Omens and signs yield up their mystic secrets to advance my empire.

Is it not said of the Galilean, that spirits came and ministered unto him ?—To whom do the spirits now minister ?

What would the Galilean say, if he were present unseen among us ?

MAXIMUS. He would say: the third empire is at hand.

JULIAN. The third empire is here, Maximus ! I feel that the Messiah of the earth lives in me. The spirit has become flesh and the flesh spirit. All creation lies within my will and my power.

See, see,—there are the first sparks drifting aloft. The flames are licking up the rigging and the clustered masts.

(*He shouts in the direction of the fire.*)

Spread ; spread !

MAXIMUS.   The wind anticipates your will.   It is rising to help you.

JULIAN (*commanding with clenched hand*).   Grow to a storm !   More westerly !   I command it !

FROMENTINUS (*enters from the right*).   Most gracious Emperor,—permit me to warn you.   A dangerous disturbance has broken out in the camp.

JULIAN.   I will have no more disturbances.   The army shall advance.

FROMENTINUS.   Yes, my Emperor,—but the refractory Galileans——

JULIAN.   The Galileans ?   What of them ?

FROMENTINUS.   Before the tables where the paymasters were serving out the soldiers' pay, your august image had been set up——

JULIAN.   It is always to be so for the future.

FROMENTINUS.   Every man was ordered, as he came forward, to cast some incense into the chafing dishes——

JULIAN.   Yes—well, well ?

FROMENTINUS.   Many of the Galilean soldiers did so without demur, but others refused——

JULIAN.   What ! they refused ?

FROMENTINUS.   At first, sire ; but when the paymasters represented to them that it was an old custom revived, and had no religious significance——

JULIAN.   Aha ; what then ?

FROMENTINUS. ——they yielded and did as they were bidden.

JULIAN. There you see; they yielded!

FROMENTINUS. But afterwards, sire, our own men laughed and mocked at them, and said, thoughtlessly, that now they had better obliterate the sign of the cross and the fish which they are wont to imprint upon their arms; for now they had worshipped the divine Emperor.

JULIAN. Yes, yes! And the Galileans?

FROMENTINUS. They broke out into loud lamentations——; listen, listen, sire! It is impossible to bring them to reason.

(*Wild cries are heard without, among the tents.*)

JULIAN. The madmen! Rebellious to the last. They do not know that their master's power is broken.

(*Christian soldiers come rushing in. Some beat their breasts; others tear their clothes, with loud cries and weeping.*)

A SOLDIER. Christ died for me, and I forsook him!

ANOTHER SOLDIER. Smite me, oh wrathful Lord in heaven; for I have worshipped false gods!

THE SOLDIER AGATHON. The devil on the throne has slain my soul! Woe, woe, woe!

OTHER SOLDIERS (*tearing off the leaden seals which they wear round their necks*). We will not serve idols!

OTHERS AGAIN. The Apostate is not our ruler! We will go home! home!

JULIAN. Fromentinus, seize these madmen! Hew them down!

(FROMENTINUS *and many of the bystanders are on the point of falling upon the Christian soldiers. At that moment a vivid glare spreads over the sky, and flames burst from the ships.*)

OFFICERS AND SOLDIERS (*terror-struck*).   The fleet is burning!

JULIAN.   Yes, the fleet is burning! And more than the fleet is burning. In that glowing, swirling pyre the crucified Galilean is burning to ashes; and the earthly Emperor is burning with the Galilean. But from the ashes shall arise—like that wondrous bird—the God of earth and the Emperor of the spirit in one, in one, in one!

SEVERAL VOICES.   Madness has seized him!

NEVITA (*entering from the left*).   It is done.

JOVIAN (*approaching hastily from the camp*).   Put out the fire! Put it out! Put it out!

JULIAN.   Let it burn! Let it burn!

AMMIAN (*from the camp*).   Sire, you are betrayed. That Persian refugee was a traitor——

JULIAN.   Man, you lie! Where is he?

AMMIAN.   Fled!

JOVIAN.   Vanished like a shadow——

NEVITA.   Fled!

JOVIAN.   His escort declare that he disappeared almost under their very eyes.

AMMIAN.   His horse, too, is gone from the enclosure where it stood; the Persian must have fled over the plains.

JULIAN.   Put out the fire, Nevita!

NEVITA.   Impossible, my Emperor!

JULIAN.   Put it out, I say. It *shall* be possible!

NEVITA. Nothing could be more impossible. All the cables are cut; the rest of the ships are all drifting down upon the burning wrecks.

PRINCE HORMISDAS (*coming from among the tents*). Curses upon my countryman! Oh sire, how could you listen to that deceiver?

CRIES FROM THE CAMP. The fleet on fire! Cut off from home! Death before us!

THE SOLDIER AGATHON. False god, false god, —bid the storm to cease; bid the flames die down!

JOVIAN. The storm increases. The fire is like a rolling sea——

MAXIMUS (*whispers*). Beware of the Phrygian regions.

JULIAN (*shouts to the army*). Let the fleet burn! Within seven days you shall burn Ctesiphon.

Act Fifth.

(*A barren, stony desert, without trees or grass. To the right, the Emperor's tent. Afternoon.*)

(*Exhausted soldiers lie in knots on the plain. Detachments now and again pass by from left to right. Outside the tent are the philosophers* PRISCUS *and* KYTRON, *with several others of the Emperor's retinue, waiting in restless anxiety. The captain of the body-guard,* ANATOLUS, *stands with soldiers before the opening of the tent.*)

KYTRON. I cannot understand how this council of war can last so long?

PRISCUS. Nor I. One would think there were only two courses to choose between: to advance or to retire.

KYTRON. It is utterly incomprehensible——

Tell me, good Anatolus, why, in the name of the gods, do we not advance?

PRISCUS. Yes, why alarm us by halting here in the middle of the desert?

ANATOLUS. Do you see the quivering air on the horizon, to the north, east, and south?

KYTRON. Of course, of course; that is the heat——

ANATOLUS. It is the desert burning.

PRISCUS. What do you say? The desert burning?

KYTRON.   Do not jest so unpleasantly, good
Anatolus! Tell us,—what is it?

ANATOLUS.   The desert burning, I tell you. Over
there, where the sand ceases, the Persians have set the
grass on fire. We cannot make any progress till the
ground cools.

KYTRON.   Oh is not this appalling! What barbarians! To have recourse to such means——!

PRISCUS.   Then there is no choice left us. Without provisions, without water——; why do we not
retreat?

ANATOLUS.   Over the Tigris and Euphrates?

KYTRON.   And the fleet burnt! Is this the way
to conduct the war? Oh, why does not the Emperor
think more of his friends! How shall I get home
again?

ANATOLUS.   Like the rest of us, friend!

KYTRON.   Like the rest? Like the rest! That is
a fine way to talk. With you it is quite another
matter. You are soldiers. It is your calling to
endure certain hardships to which I am not at all
accustomed. I did not join the Emperor's suite to
go through all this. Here am I tortured with gnats
and poisonous flies;—look at my hands!

PRISCUS.   Most certainly we did not come for this.
We consented to accompany the army in order to
compose panegyrics on the victories the Emperor
intended to win. What has come of these victories?
What has been achieved during the six toilsome
weeks since the fleet was burnt? We have destroyed
a few deserted towns of the paltriest kind. A few
prisoners have been exhibited in the camp, whom the

advance-guard are said to have taken—I really do not know in what battles! It seemed to me the prisoners looked more like poor kidnapped shepherds and peasants——

KYTRON. And to think of burning the fleet! Did I not say from the first that it would be a source of disaster?

ANATOLUS. I did not hear you say so.

KYTRON. What? Did I not say so? Oh Priscus, did you not hear me say it?

PRISCUS. I really do not know, friend; but I know that I myself in vain denounced that luckless measure. Indeed I may say I opposed the whole campaign at this time of year. What rash haste! Where were the Emperor's eyes? Is this the same hero who fought with such extraordinary success upon the Rhine? One would think he had been struck with blindness or some spiritual disease.

ANATOLUS. Hush, hush;—what talk is this?

KYTRON. It was certainly a somewhat unseemly remark for our Priscus to make. Yet I, too, cannot deny that I observe a deplorable lack of wisdom in many of the crowned philosopher's recent proceedings. How precipitate to set up his busts in the camp and claim worship, as if he were a god! How imprudent so openly to scoff at that strange teacher from Nazareth, who undeniably possesses a peculiar power, which might have stood us in good stead in these perilous conjunctures.

Ah! there comes Nevita himself. Now we shall hear——

(NEVITA *comes out of the tent. In the opening he turns and makes a sign to some one within. The physician* ORIBASES *immediately comes out.*)

NEVITA (*drawing him aside*). Tell me openly, Oribases,—is there anything amiss with the Emperor's mind?

ORIBASES. What makes you think of that, sir?

NEVITA. How else can I interpret his conduct?

ORIBASES. Oh my beloved Emperor——!

NEVITA. Oribases, you must hide nothing from me.

KYTRON (*drawing near*). Oh valiant general, do not think me indiscreet, but——

NEVITA. Presently, presently!

ORIBASES (*to* NEVITA). Do not fear, sir! No misfortune shall happen. Eutherius and I have promised each other to keep an eye upon him.

NEVITA. Ah, you do not mean to say that——?

ORIBASES. Last night he had almost shortened his days. Fortunately Eutherius was at hand——; oh do not speak of it to any one!

NEVITA. Do not lose sight of him.

PRISCUS (*drawing near*). It would greatly relieve our minds to hear what the council of war——?

NEVITA. Pardon me; I have important business to attend to.

(*He goes out behind the tent.* JOVIAN *enters at the same moment from the opening.*)

JOVIAN (*speaking into the tent*). It shall be done, my gracious Emperor!

KYTRON. Ah, most excellent Jovian! Well? Is the retreat decided on?

Jovian.   I would not counsel any one to call it a retreat.

(*He goes out behind the tent.*)

Kytron.   Oh, these soldiers!   A philosopher's peace of mind is nothing to them.   Ah!

(*The* Emperor Julian *comes out of the tent; he is pale and haggard.   With him come the Chamberlain* Eutherius *and several officers; the latter go off over the plain to the right.*)

Julian (*to the philosophers*).   Rejoice, my friends! All will soon be well now.

Kytron.   Ah, gracious Emperor, have you discovered an expedient?

Julian.   There are expedients enough, Kytron; the thing is to choose the best.   We will slightly alter the line of advance——

Priscus.   Oh, praise be to your wisdom!

Julian.   This eastward march—it leads to nothing.

Kytron.   No, no, that is certain!

Julian.   Now we will turn northward, Kytron!

Kytron.   What, sire,—northward?

Priscus.   Not westward?

Julian.   Not westward.   Certainly not.   We might meet with difficulties on account of the rivers. And Ctesiphon we must leave till another time. Without ships we cannot think of taking the city.   It was the Galileans who were chiefly concerned in the burning of the fleet; I have noticed one thing and another.

Who dares call this northward movement a retreat? What do you know of my plans?   The Persian army is somewhere in the north; of that we are now pretty

well assured.   When I have defeated Sapor—one
battle will finish the matter—we shall find ample
supplies in the Persian camp.

When I lead the Persian king as my captive through
Antioch and the other cities, I should like to see
whether the citizens will not fall at my feet.

CHRISTIAN SOLDIERS (*pass singing over the plain*).
    Doomed is the world's proud cedar-tree,
    the axe shall its roots dissever ;
    the palm He planted on Calvary,
    blood-watered, shall bloom for ever.

JULIAN (*following them with his eyes*).   The
Galileans are always singing. Songs about death,
and wounds, and pain. Those women whom I
brought with me to tend the sick—they have done
us more harm than good. They have taught the
soldiers strange songs, such as I have never heard
before.

But hereafter I will punish no one for such things.
It only leads them deeper into error. Do you know,
Priscus, what happened the other day with some of
those mutineers who refused to show due reverence to
the imperial busts ?

PRISCUS.   The other day, sire ?

JULIAN.   When, wishing to beget a wholesome
dread in their companions in error, I ordered some of
these men to be executed, the oldest of them stepped
forward with loud cries of joy, and begged to be
allowed to die first.—Look you, Priscus—when I
heard that yesterday——

PRISCUS.   Yesterday ? Oh, sire, you are mistaken.
That happened forty days ago.

JULIAN.   So long?   Yes, yes, yes!   The Hebrews had to wander forty years in the wilderness.   All the older generation had to die out.   A new generation had to spring up; but they—mark that!—they entered into the promised land.

EUTHERIUS.   It is late in the day, sire; will you not eat?

JULIAN.   Not yet, my Eutherius.   It is good for all men to mortify the flesh.

Yes, I tell you, we must make haste to become a new generation.   I can do nothing with you as you are.   If you would get out of the desert, you must lead a pure life.   Look at the Galileans.   We might learn much from these men.   There are none poverty-stricken and helpless among them; they live together as brethren and sisters,—and most of all now, when their obstinacy has obliged me to chastise them.   These Galileans, you must know, have something in their hearts which I should greatly desire to see you cultivate.   You call yourselves followers of Socrates, of Plato, of Diogenes.   But is there one of you who would face death with ecstasy for Plato's sake?   Would our Priscus sacrifice his left hand for Socrates?   Would Kytron let his ears be cut off for the sake of Diogenes?   No, truly!   I know you, ye whited sepulchres!   Begone from my sight;—I can do nothing with you!

> (*The philosophers slink away; the others also disperse, whispering anxiously.   Only* ORIBASES *and* EUTHERIUS *remain behind with the Emperor.* ANATOLUS, *the officer of the guard, still stands with his soldiers outside the tent.*)

JULIAN. How strange! Is it not inconceivable, unfathomable? Oribases,—can you read me this riddle?

ORIBASES. What riddle do you mean, my Emperor?

JULIAN. With twelve poor ignorant fishermen, he founded all this.

ORIBASES. Oh sire, these thoughts exhaust you.

JULIAN. And who has held it together until this day? Women and ignorant people, for the most part——

ORIBASES. Yes, yes, sire; but now the campaign will soon take a happy turn——

JULIAN. Very true, Oribases; as soon as fortune has taken a turn, all will be well. The dominion of the carpenter's son is drawing to its close; we know that. His reign is to last as many years as the year has days; and now we have——

EUTHERIUS. My beloved master, would not a bath refresh you?

JULIAN. Do you think so?—You may go, Eutherius! Go, go! I have something to say to Oribases.

(EUTHERIUS *goes off behind the tent. The Emperor draws* ORIBASES *over to the other side.*)

JULIAN. Has Eutherius told you anything this morning?

ORIBASES. No, sire!

JULIAN. Has he told you nothing about last night——?

ORIBASES. No, my Emperor—nothing whatever. Eutherius is very reticent.

Julian.   If he should tell you anything, do not believe it.   The thing did not happen at all as he pretends.   It is he who is seeking my life.

Oribases.   He,—your old and faithful servant !

Julian.   I shall keep an eye on him.

Oribases.   I too.

Julian.   We will both keep an eye on him.

Oribases.   Sire, I fear you had little sleep last night.

Julian.   Very little.

(Oribases *is on the point of saying something, but changes his mind.*)

Julian.   Do you know what kept me from sleeping ?

Oribases.   No, my Emperor.

Julian.   The victor of the Milvian Bridge was with me.

Oribases.   The great Constantine ?

Julian.   Yes.   For some nights past, his shade has given me no rest.   He comes a little after midnight, and does not go until towards morning.

Oribases.   The moon is full, sire ; that has always had a strange effect on your mind.

Julian.   According to the ancients such apparitions are wont—— —— What can have become of Maximus ?   But their opinions are by no means to be relied on.   We see how far wrong they went in many things.   Even what they tell us of the gods we cannot accept without reserve.   Nor what they report as to the shades and the other powers which control the destinies of men.   What do we know of these powers ?   Nothing, Oribases, except their

capriciousness and inconstancy, of which character-
istics we have ample evidence.

I wish Maximus would come.

(*To himself.*)

Here? It is not here that the menacing storm
is drawing up. It was to be in the Phrygian
regions——

ORIBASES. What regions, sire,—and what storm?

JULIAN. Oh nothing—nothing.

NEVITA (*enters from the plain on the right*). My
Emperor, the army is on the march——

JULIAN. Northwards?

NEVITA (*starts*). Of course, sire!

JULIAN. We ought to have waited till Maximus——

NEVITA. What do you mean, my Emperor?
There is nothing to wait for. We are without supplies; scattered bands of the enemy's horsemen
are already appearing both in the east and in the
south——

JULIAN. Yes, yes, we must advance,—northwards.
Maximus will come directly. I have sent to the rear
for the Etruscan soothsayers; they shall try once
more—— I have also discovered some Magi, who
say they are well versed in the Chaldean mysteries.
Our own priests are taking the omens in nine
different places——

NEVITA. Sire, whatever the omens may say, I tell
you we must go hence. The soldiers are no longer to
be depended on; they see clearly that our only hope
lies in reaching the Armenian mountains.

JULIAN. We will do so, Nevita,—whatever the

omens say.   But it nevertheless gives one a great sense of security to know that one is acting in concert with those unfathomable powers, who, if they will, can exercise so potent an influence over our fortunes.

NEVITA (*goes from him, and says shortly and imperiously*).   Anatolus, take down the Emperor's tent! (*He whispers some words to the Captain of the Guard, and goes out to the right.*)

JULIAN.   All auguries for these forty days have been inauspicious ; and that proves their trustworthiness ; for in all that time our affairs have made little progress.   But now, you see, my Oribases,—now that I have a fresh enterprise in view——
Ah ! Maximus !

MAXIMUS (*entering from the plain*).   The army is already on the march, sire ; get to horse !

JULIAN.   The auguries—the auguries ?

MAXIMUS.   Oh—the auguries !   Do not ask about the auguries.

JULIAN.   Speak !   I insist on knowing what they say.

MAXIMUS   All auguries are silent.

JULIAN.   Silent ?

MAXIMUS.   I went to the priests ; the entrails of the sacrifices gave no sign.   I went to the Etruscan jugglers ; the flight and cries of the birds said nothing. I went to the Magi, too ; their writings had no answer to give.   And I myself——

JULIAN.   You yourself, my Maximus ?

MAXIMUS.   Now I can tell you.   Last night I studied the aspect of the stars.   They told me nothing, Julian.

JULIAN.   Nothing.—Silence—silence, as though in

an eclipse.   Alone !   No bridge between me and the
spirits.

Where are you now, oh white-sailed fleet, that sped
to and fro in the sunlight and carried tidings between
earth and heaven ?

The fleet is burnt.   That fleet too is burnt.   Oh, all
my shining ships.

Tell me, Maximus—what do you believe as to all
this ?

MAXIMUS.   I believe in you.

JULIAN.   Yes, yes—believe !

MAXIMUS.   The world-will has deputed its power
into your hands ; therefore it is silent.

JULIAN.   So will we read it.   And we must act
accordingly,—although we might have preferred that
—— This silence !   To stand so utterly alone.

But there are others who may also be said to stand
alone.   The Galileans.   They have only one god ;
and one god is next thing to no god.

How is it that we daily see these men——?

ANATOLUS (*who has meanwhile had the tent taken
down*).   My Emperor, now you must get to horse ;
I dare not let you remain here longer.

JULIAN.   Yes, now I will mount.   Where is my
good Babylonius ?   See now; sword in hand——

Come, my dear friends !

(*All go out to the right.*)

(*A marshy, wooded country.   A dark, still lake
among the trees.   Watch-fires in the distance.
Moonlight, with driving clouds.*)

(Several soldiers are mounting guard in the fore-ground.)

MAKRINA AND THE WOMEN (*singing without, on the left*).

> Woe to us !   Woe !
> Upon us all
> God's wrath will fall !
> Death we shall know !

ONE OF THE SOLDIERS (*listening*).   Hush !   Do you hear ?   The Galilean women are singing out there.

ANOTHER SOLDIER.   They sing like owls and night ravens.

A THIRD SOLDIER.   Yet I would willingly be with them.   It is safer with the Galileans than with us.   The God of the Galileans is stronger than ours.

THE FIRST SOLDIER.   The thing is that the Emperor has offended the gods.   How could he think of setting himself up in their place ?

THE THIRD SOLDIER.   What is worse is that he has offended the Galileans' God.   Do you not know, they say positively that he and his magician ripped open a pregnant woman the other night, to read omens in her entrails ?

THE FIRST SOLDIER.   Yes, but I do not believe it. At any rate, I am sure it was not a Greek woman; it must have been a barbarian.

THE THIRD SOLDIER.   They say the Galileans' God cares for the barbarians too; and if so, it will be the worse for us.

THE SECOND SOLDIER.   Oh, pooh—the Emperor is a great soldier.

THE FIRST SOLDIER. King Sapor is said to be a great soldier too.

THE SECOND SOLDIER. Do you think we have the whole Persian army before us?

THE FIRST SOLDIER. Some say it is only the advance-guard; no one knows exactly.

THE THIRD SOLDIER. I wish I were among the Galileans.

THE FIRST SOLDIER. Are *you* going over to them, too?

THE THIRD SOLDIER. So many are going over. In the last few days——

THE FIRST SOLDIER (*calling out into the darkness*). Stand,—stand! Who goes there?

A VOICE. Friends from the outposts!

(*Several soldiers come from among the trees, with* AGATHON *the Cappadocian in their midst.*)

THE SECOND SOLDIER. Ho-ho; a deserter.

ONE OF THE NEW-COMERS. No; he has gone out of his mind.

AGATHON. I have *not* gone out of my mind. Oh, for God's great mercy's sake,—let me go!

THE SOLDIER FROM THE OUTPOSTS. He says he wants to kill a beast with seven heads.

AGATHON. Yes, yes, yes, I will, I will. Oh, let me go! Do you see this spear? Do you know what spear it is? With this spear I will slay the beast with seven heads, and then I shall get back my soul again. Christ himself has promised me that. He was with me to-night.

THE FIRST SOLDIER. Hunger and weariness have turned his brain.

ONE OF THE NEW-COMERS. To the camp with him; there he can have a thorough rest.

AGATHON. Let me go! Oh, if you only knew what spear this is!

(*The soldiers lead him off by the front, to the right.*)

THE THIRD SOLDIER. What could he mean by that beast?

THE FIRST SOLDIER. That is one of the Galilean secrets. They have many such secrets among them.

(EUTHERIUS *and* ORIBASES *enter hastily from the right, looking anxiously about.*)

EUTHERIUS. Do you not see him?

ORIBASES. No.—Ah, soldiers!—Tell me, good friends, has any one passed by here?

THE FIRST SOLDIER. Yes, a detachment of spearmen.

ORIBASES. Good, good! But nobody else? No great personage? None of the generals?

THE SOLDIERS. No, none.

ORIBASES. Not here then! Oh, Eutherius, how could you— ?

EUTHERIUS. Could I help—— ? Could I help it—— ? I have not closed my old eyes for three nights——

ORIBASES (*to the soldiers*). You must help us to search. I demand it in the name of the general-in-chief. Spread yourselves among the trees; and if you find any great personage, report it at the watch-fire yonder.

THE SOLDIERS. We will not fail, sir!

(*They all go out by different ways, to the left. Soon after, the* EMPEROR *emerges from behind*

*a tree, on the right.   He listens, looks round,
and beckons to some one behind him.)*

JULIAN.   Hush! Come forward, Maximus! They
did not see us.

MAXIMUS (*from the same side*).   Oribases was
one of them.

JULIAN.   Yes, yes ; both he and Eutherius keep
watch on me.   They imagine that—— Has neither
of them told you anything ?

MAXIMUS.   No, my Julian ! But why have you
awakened me ?   What do you want here in the darkness?

JULIAN.   I want to be alone with you for the last
time, my beloved teacher !

MAXIMUS.   Not for the last time, Julian !

JULIAN.   See that dark water. Do you think—
if I utterly vanished from the earth, and my body
was never found, and no one knew what had become
of me,—do you think the report would get about that
Hermes had come for me, and carried me away, and
that I had been exalted to the fellowship of the gods?

MAXIMUS.   The time is near when men will not
need to die, in order to live as gods on the earth.

JULIAN.   I am pining with home-sickness, Maximus,—with home-sick longing for light and sunshine
and all the stars.

MAXIMUS.   I implore you not to think of sorrowful
things.   The Persian army is before you. To-
morrow it will come to a battle.   You will conquer——

JULIAN.   I—conquer? You do not know who
was with me an hour ago.

MAXIMUS.   Who was with you?

JULIAN.   I had fallen asleep on my bed in the tent. Suddenly I was awakened by a strong red glare, that seemed to burn through my closed eye-lids. I looked up and saw a figure standing in the tent. Over its head was a long drapery, falling on both sides, so as to leave the face free.

MAXIMUS.   Did you know this figure?

JULIAN.   It was the same face I saw in the light that night at Ephesus, many years ago,—that night when we held symposium with the two others.

MAXIMUS.   The spirit of the empire.

JULIAN.   Since then it has appeared to me once in Gaul,—on an occasion I do not care to think of.

MAXIMUS.   Did it speak?

JULIAN.   No.   It seemed to wish to speak; but it did not.   It stood motionless, looking at me.   Its face was pale and distorted.   Suddenly, with both arms it drew the drapery together over its head, hid its face, and went straight out through the tent walls.

MAXIMUS.   The consummation stands on the threshold.

JULIAN.   Yes, on the threshold.

MAXIMUS.   Courage, Julian!   He who wills, conquers.

JULIAN.   And what does the conqueror win?   Is it worth while to conquer?   What has the Macedonian Alexander, what has Julius Cæsar won?   Greeks and Romans talk of their renown with cold admiration,— while the other, the Galilean, the carpenter's son, sits throned as the king of love in the warm believing hearts of men.

Where is he now?—Has he been at work elsewhere since that happened at Golgotha?

I dreamed about him lately. I dreamed that I had subdued the whole world. I ordained that the memory of the Galilean should be rooted out on earth, and it was rooted out.—Then the spirits came and ministered to me, and bound wings on my shoulders, and I soared aloft into infinite space till my feet rested on another world.

It *was* another world than mine. Its curve was vaster, its light more golden, and many moons circled around it.

Then I looked down at my own earth — the Emperor's earth, which I had made Galileanless— and I thought that all that I had done was very good.

But behold, Maximus,—there came a procession by me, on the strange earth where I stood. There were soldiers, and judges, and executioners at the head of it, and weeping women followed. And lo!—in the midst of the slow-moving array, was the Galilean, alive, and bearing a cross on his back. Then I called to him, and said, "Whither away, Galilean?" But he turned his face towards me, smiled, nodded slowly, and said: "To the place of the skull."

Where is he now? What if that at Golgotha, near Jerusalem, was but a wayside matter, a thing done, so to speak, in passing, in a leisure hour? What if he goes on and on, and suffers, and dies, and conquers, again and again, from world to world?

Oh that I could lay waste the world! Maximus,— is there no poison, no consuming fire, that could lay creation desolate, as it was on that day when the spirit moved alone over the face of the waters?

MAXIMUS. I hear a noise from the outposts. Come, Julian——

JULIAN. To think that century shall follow century, and that in them all shall live men, knowing that it was I who was vanquished, and he who conquered!

I *will* not be vanquished! I am young; I am invulnerable,—the third empire is at hand——

(*With a great cry.*)

There he stands!

MAXIMUS. Who? Where?

JULIAN. Do you see him? There, among the tree-stems—in a crown and purple robe——

MAXIMUS. It is the moon glimmering on the water. Come—come, my Julian!

JULIAN (*going threateningly towards the vision*). Avaunt! Thou art dead! Thy empire is past. Off with the wizard's cloak, carpenter's son!

What art thou doing there! What art thou hammering at?—Ah!

EUTHERIUS (*from the left*). All gods be praised! —Oribases,—here, here!

JULIAN. What has become of him?

ORIBASES (*from the left*). Is he here?

EUTHERIUS. Yes.—Oh my beloved Emperor!

JULIAN. Who was it that said, "I am hammering the Emperor's coffin"?

ORIBASES. What do you mean, sire?

JULIAN. Who spoke, I ask? Who was it that said, "I am hammering the Emperor's coffin"?

ORIBASES. Come with me to your tent, I implore you !

(*Shouts and cries are heard far away.*)

MAXIMUS. War-cries! The Persians are upon us——

EUTHERIUS. They are fighting at the outposts !

ORIBASES. The enemy is in the camp! Ah, sire, you have no weapons—— !

JULIAN. I will sacrifice to the gods.

MAXIMUS. To what gods, oh fool? Where are they—and what are they ?

JULIAN. I will sacrifice to this god and to that. ˙ will sacrifice to many. One or another must surely near me. I must call upon something without me and above me——

ORIBASES. There is not a moment to be lost—— !

JULIAN. Ah—did you see the burning torch behind the cloud ? It flashed forth and went out in the same instant. A message from the spirits! A shining ship between heaven and earth !—My shield ! My sword !

(*He rushes out to the right.* ORIBASES *and* EUTHERIUS *follow him.*)

MAXIMUS (*calling after him*). Emperor, Emperor —do not fight to-night !

(*He goes off to the right.*)

———————

(*An open plain, with a village far away. Daybreak and cloudy weather.*)

(*A noise of battle. Cries and the clashing of weapons out on the plain. In the foreground*

Roman spearmen, under AMMIAN'S *command,
fighting with Persian archers. The latter are
driven back by degrees towards the left.*)

AMMIAN. Right, right! In upon them! Thrust
them down! Give them no time to shoot!

NEVITA (*with followers from the right*). Well
fought, Ammian!

AMMIAN. Oh sir, why do not the cavalry come to
our help?

NEVITA. They cannot. The Persians have ele-
phants in their front rank. The mere smell makes
the horses unmanageable. Thrust—thrust! Upwards, men,—under their breast-plates?

KYTRON (*in night-clothes, laden with books and rolls
of paper, enters from the right*). Oh that I should
be mixed up in such horrors!

NEVITA. Have you seen the Emperor, friend?

KYTRON. Yes, but he takes no notice of me. Oh,
I humbly beg for a detachment of soldiers to protect
me!

NEVITA (*to his followers*). They are giving ground!
The shield-bearers forward!

KYTRON. You do not listen to me, sir! My safety
is of the utmost importance; my book, "On Equanimity in Affliction," is not finished——

NEVITA (*as before*). The Persians have been rein-
forced on the right. They are pressing forward
again!

KYTRON. Pressing forward again? Oh this
blood-thirsty ferocity! An arrow! It almost struck
me! How recklessly they shoot; no care for life or
limb!

(*He takes to flight by the foreground on the left.*)

NEVITA.   The forces are evenly matched.   Neither side gains the advantage.

(*To* FROMENTINUS, *who comes with a fresh troop from the right.*)

Ho, captain,—have you seen the Emperor?

FROMENTINUS.   Yes, sir; he is fighting at the head of the white horsemen.

NEVITA.   Not wounded?

FROMENTINUS.   He seems invulnerable.   Arrows and javelins swerve aside wherever he shows himself.

AMMIAN (*calling out from the thick of the fight*). Help, help; we can hold out no longer!

NEVITA.   Forward, my bold Fromentinus!

FROMENTINUS (*to the soldiers*).   Shoulder to shoulder, and at them, Greeks!

(*He hastens to the help of* AMMIAN ; *the mellay rolls backwards a little.*)

(ANATOLUS, *the Captain of the Guard, enters with followers from the right.*)

ANATOLUS.   Is not the Emperor here?

NEVITA.   The Emperor!   Is it not your business to answer for him?

ANATOLUS.   His horse was shot under him,—a terrible tumult arose; it was impossible to get near him——

NEVITA.   Do you think he has come to any harm?

ANATOLUS.   No, I think not.   There was a cry that he was unhurt, but——

MANY OF NEVITA'S FOLLOWERS.   There he is! There he is!

(*The* EMPEROR JULIAN, *without helmet or armour,*

with only a sword and shield, escorted by soldiers
of the Imperial Guard, enters from the right.)

JULIAN.   I am glad I have found you, Nevita!

NEVITA.   Ah, sire—without armour; how imprudent——!

JULIAN.   In these regions no weapon can touch me.   But go, Nevita; take the supreme command; my horse was shot under me, and——

NEVITA.   My Emperor, then you are hurt after all?

JULIAN.   No; only a blow on the head; a little dizzy.   Go, go—— What is this?   So many strange companies crowding in among us!

NEVITA (*in a low voice*).   Anatolus, you must answer for the Emperor.

ANATOLUS.   Never fear, sir!

(NEVITA *goes off with his followers to the right.*
The EMPEROR JULIAN, ANATOLUS, *and some*
of the Imperial Guard remain behind.   The
fight on the plain rolls further and further
back.)

JULIAN.   How many of our men do you think have fallen, Anatolus?

ANATOLUS.   Certainly no few, sire; but I am sure the Persians have lost more than we.

JULIAN.   Yes, yes; but many have fallen, both Greeks and Romans.   Do you not think so?

ANATOLUS.   You are not well, my Emperor, Your face is quite pale——

JULIAN.   Look at those lying there,—some on their backs, others on their faces, with outstretched arms?   They must all be dead?

ANATOLUS.   Yes, sire, undoubtedly.

JULIAN.   They are dead, yes!   They know nothing, then, either of the defeat at Jerusalem or the other defeats.—Do you not think many more Greeks will fall in this battle, Anatolus?

ANATOLUS.   Sire, let us hope the bloodiest work is over.

JULIAN.   Many, many more will fall, I tell you! But not enough.   What good is it that *many* should fall?   Posterity will come none the less——

Tell me, Anatolus, how do you think the Emperor Caligula pictured that sword to himself?

ANATOLUS.   What sword, sire?

JULIAN.   You know he wished for a sword with which he might at one blow——

ANATOLUS.   Hear the shouts, sire!   Now I am sure the Persians are retreating.

JULIAN (*listening*).   What song is that in the air?

ANATOLUS.   Sire, let me fetch Oribases; or still better,—come,—come; you are ill!

JULIAN.   There is singing in the air.   Can you not hear it?

ANATOLUS.   If it be so, it must be the Galileans——

JULIAN.   Yes, be sure it is the Galileans.   Ha-ha-ha, they fight in our ranks, and do not see who stands on the other side.   Oh fools, all of you!   Where is Nevita?   Why does he attack the Persians?   Does he not see that the Persians are not the most dangerous?—You betray me, all of you.

ANATOLUS (*softly to one of the soldiers*).   Hasten to the camp; fetch the Emperor's physician?

(*The soldier goes out to the right.*)

JULIAN. What innumerable hosts! Do you think they have caught sight of us, Anatolus?

ANATOLUS. Who, sire? Where?

JULIAN. Do you not see them—yonder—high up and far away! You lie! You see them well enough!

ANATOLUS. By the immortal gods, they are only the morning clouds,—it is the day dawning.

JULIAN. It is the hosts of the Galilean, I tell you! Look—those in the red-edged garments are the martyrs who died in blood. Singing women surround them, and weave bowstrings of the long hair torn from their heads. Children are with them, twining slings from their unravelled entrails. Burning torches——! Thousandfold—multitudinous! They are hastening hitherward! They are all looking at me; all rushing straight upon me!

ANATOLUS. It is the Persians, sire! Our ranks are giving way——

JULIAN. They *shall* not give way!—You *shall* not! Stand fast, Greeks! Stand, stand, Romans! To-day we will free the world!

(*The battle has in the meantime swept forward over the plain again. JULIAN hurls himself with drawn sword into the thickest of the fight. General confusion.*)

ANATOLUS (*calling out to the right*). Help, help! The Emperor is in deadly peril!

JULIAN (*among the combatants*). I see him; I see him! A longer sword! Who has a longer sword to lend me?

SOLDIERS (*streaming in from the right*). With Christ, for the Emperor!

AGATHON (*among the new-comers*). With Christ for Christ!

(*He throws his spear; it grazes the* EMPEROR'S *arm, and plunges into his side.*)

JULIAN. Ah!

(*He grasps the spear-head and draws it out, but gashes his hand, utters a loud cry, and falls.*)

AGATHON (*calls out in the tumult*). The Roman's spear from Golgotha!

(*He casts himself weaponless among the Persians, and is seen to be cut down.*)

CONFUSED CRIES. The Emperor! Is the Emperor wounded?

JULIAN (*attempts to rise, but falls back again, and cries :*) Thou hast conquered, Galilean!

MANY VOICES. The Emperor has fallen!

ANATOLUS. The Emperor is wounded! Shield him—shield him, in the name of the gods!

(*He casts himself despairingly against the advancing Persians. The* EMPEROR *is carried away senseless. At that moment,* JOVIAN *comes forward upon the plain with fresh troops.*)

JOVIAN. On—on, believing brethren; give Cæsar what is Cæsar's!

RETREATING SOLDIERS (*calling to him*). He has fallen! The Emperor has fallen!

JOVIAN. Fallen! Oh mighty God of vengeance! On, on; it is God's will that his people shall live! I see heaven open; I see the angels with flaming swords——

THE SOLDIERS (*rushing forward*). Christ is among us!

AMMIAN'S TROOPS.   The God of the Galileans is among us!   Close round him!   He is the strongest!

(*A wild tumult of battle.* JOVIAN *hews his way into the enemy's ranks. Sunrise. The Persians flee in all directions.*)

(*The Emperor's tent, with a curtained entrance in the background. Daylight.*)

(*The* EMPEROR JULIAN *lies unconscious on his couch. The wounds in his right side, arm, and hand are bound up. Close to him stand* ORIBASES *and* MAKRINA, *with* EUTHERIUS. *Further back,* BASILIUS OF CÆSAREA, *and* PRISCUS. *At the foot of the bed stands the* MYSTIC MAXIMUS.)

MAKRINA.   He is bleeding again.   I must bind the bandage tighter.

ORIBASES.   Thanks to you, tender woman; your delicate hands do us good service here.

EUTHERIUS.   Is he still alive?

ORIBASES.   Certainly he is alive.

EUTHERIUS.   But he does not breathe.

ORIBASES.   Yes, he breathes.

(AMMIAN *enters softly, with the* EMPEROR'S *sword and shield, which he lays down, and remains standing beside the curtain.*)

PRISCUS.   Ah, good captain, how go affairs without?

AMMIAN.   Better than here.   Is he already——?

PRISCUS.   No, no, not yet.   But is it true that we have beaten the Persians?

AMMIAN.   Completely.   It was Jovian who put

them to flight. Three noblemen have just arrived as envoys from King Sapor, to beg for a truce.

PRISCUS. And do you think Nevita will accede to it?

AMMIAN. Nevita has yielded up the command to Jovian. All flock around him. All recognise that in him lies our one hope of safety——

ORIBASES. Speak low; he moves.

AMMIAN. He moves? Perhaps he is awakening to consciousness! Oh, if he should live to see this!

EUTHERIUS. What, Ammian?

AMMIAN. Soldiers and leaders are consulting together as to the choice of the new Emperor.

PRISCUS. What do you say?

EUTHERIUS. Oh, what shameful haste!

AMMIAN. The perilous situation of the army partly excuses it; and yet——

MAKRINA. He is waking;—he opens his eyes——

(JULIAN *lies for a time quite still, looking kindly at the bystanders*)

ORIBASES. Sire, do you know me?

JULIAN. Very well, my Oribases.

ORIBASES. Only lie quiet.

JULIAN. Lie quiet? You remind me! I must be up!

ORIBASES. Impossible, sire; I implore you——

JULIAN. I must get up, I say. How can I lie quiet now? I must utterly vanquish Sapor.

EUTHERIUS. Sapor *is* vanquished, sire! He has sent envoys to the camp to beg for a truce.

JULIAN. Has he indeed? That is good news. So *him*, at least, I have conquered.

But no truce. I will crush him to the earth.—Ah, where is my shield? Have I lost my shield?

AMMIAN. No, my Emperor,—here are both your shield and your sword.

JULIAN. I am very glad of that. My good shield. I should grieve to think of it in the hands of the barbarians. Give it me, on my arm——

MAKRINA. Oh, sire, it is too heavy for you now!

JULIAN. Ah—you? You are right, pious Makrina; it is a little too heavy for me.—Lay it before me, that I may see it. What? Is that you, Ammian? Are you on guard here? Where is Anatolus?

AMMIAN. Sire, he is now in bliss.

JULIAN. Fallen? My trusty Anatolus fallen for my sake!—In bliss, you say? Hm!——

One friend the less. Ah, my Maximus!—I will not receive the Persian king's envoys to-day. They are only wanting to gain time. But I will accept no compromise. I will follow up the victory to the utmost. The army shall turn against Ctesiphon again.

ORIBASES. Impossible, sire; think of your wounds.

JULIAN. My wounds will soon be healed. Will they not, Oribases—do you not promise me——?

ORIBASES. Above all things rest, sire!

JULIAN. What a most unlucky chance! And just at this time, when so many weighty matters are pouring in upon me. I cannot leave these things in Nevita's hands. In such matters I cannot trust either him or others; I must do all myself.—It is true I feel somewhat weary. How annoying!—Tell me, Ammian, what is the name of that unlucky place?

AMMIAN. What place, my gracious Emperor?

JULIAN. The spot where the Persian spear struck me?

AMMIAN. It is called after the village of Phrygia——

MAXIMUS. Ah!

JULIAN. What is it called——? What did you say the region was called?

AMMIAN. It is called from the village over yonder, the Phrygian region.

JULIAN. Ah, Maximus—Maximus!

MAXIMUS. Betrayed!

(*He hides his face, and sinks down at the foot of the bed.*)

ORIBASES. My Emperor, what alarms you?

JULIAN. Nothing—nothing——

Phrygia? Indeed?—Nevita and the others will have to take the command after all. Go and tell them——

AMMIAN. Sire, they have already, on your behalf——

JULIAN. Have they? Yes, yes, that is well. The world-will has laid an ambush for me, Maximus!

MAKRINA. Your wounds bleed afresh, sire!

JULIAN. Oh Oribases, why did you seek to conceal it from me?

ORIBASES. What did I seek to conceal, my Emperor?

JULIAN. That I must die. Why not have told me before?

ORIBASES. Oh, my Emperor!

BASILIUS.   Julian—Julian!

(*He casts himself down, weeping, beside the bed.*)

JULIAN.   Basilius,—friend, brother,—we two have lived beautiful days together—— ——

You must not weep because I die so young.   It is not always a sign of the Fates' displeasure when they call a man away in his prime.   What is death?   It is nothing but paying one's debt to the ever changing empire of the dust.   No lamentations!   Do we not all love wisdom?   And does not wisdom teach us that the highest bliss lies in the life of the soul, not in that of the body?   So far the Galilean is right, although ——; but we will not speak of that.   Had the powers of life and death suffered me to finish a certain treatise, I think I should have succeeded in——

ORIBASES.   Oh my Emperor, does it not weary you to talk so much?

JULIAN.   No, no, no.   I feel very light and free.

BASILIUS.   Julian, my beloved brother,—have you nothing you would recall?

JULIAN.   No—I know of nothing.

BASILIUS.   Nothing to repent of, Julian?

JULIAN.   Nothing.   The power which circumstances placed in my hands, and which is an emanation of divinity, I am conscious of having used to the best of my skill.   I have never wittingly wronged any one.   I had good and sufficient reasons for this expedition; and if some should think that I have not fulfilled all expectations, they should in justice reflect that there is a mysterious power outside us, which in a great measure governs the issue of human undertakings.

MAKRINA (*softly to* ORIBASES). Oh listen—listen how heavily he breathes.

ORIBASES. His voice will fail soon.

JULIAN. As to the choice of my successor, I do not presume to give any advice—— You, Eutherius, will divide my possessions among those who have stood nearest to me. I do not leave much; for I have always held that a true philosopher—— ——

What is that? Is the sun setting already?

ORIBASES. Not so, my Emperor; it is still broad day.

JULIAN. Strange! It seemed to me to turn quite dark—— ——

Ah, wisdom—wisdom. Hold fast to wisdom, good Priscus! But be always armed against an unfathomable something without us, which——

Is Maximus gone?

MAXIMUS. No, my brother!

JULIAN. My throat is burning. Can you not cool it?

MAKRINA. A drink of water, sire?

(*She holds a cup to his lips.*)

ORIBASES (*whispers to* MAKRINA). His wound is bleeding inwardly.

JULIAN. Do not weep. Let no Greek weep for me; I am rising to the stars——

Beautiful temples—— Statues—— But so far away.

MAKRINA. What is he talking about?

ORIBASES. I do not know; I think his mind is wandering.

JULIAN (*with closed eyes*). Alexander held his

triumphal entry—— into Babylon.—I too will——
Beautiful wreath-crown'd youths—dancing maidens,
—but so far away.

Beautiful earth,—beautiful life on earth——
   (*He opens his eyes wide.*)
Oh, Helios, Helios—why didst thou betray me ?
   (*He dies.*)

ORIBASES (*after a pause*).   That was death.

THE BYSTANDERS.   Dead—dead !

ORIBASES.   Yes, now he is dead.

   (BASILIUS *and* MAKRINA *kneel in prayer.*
   EUTHERIUS *veils his head.   A sound of drums
   and trumpets is heard in the distance.*)

SHOUTS FROM THE CAMP.   Long live the Emperor
Jovian !

ORIBASES.   Oh, did you hear that shout ?

AMMIAN.   Jovian is proclaimed Emperor.

MAXIMUS (*laughing*).   The Galilean Jovian !   Yes
—yes—yes !

ORIBASES.   Shameful haste !   Before they knew
that——

PRISCUS.   Jovian,—the victorious hero who has
saved us all !   The Emperor Jovian assuredly
deserves a panegyric.   I trust that crafty Kytron has
not already——
   (*He hastens out.*)

BASILIUS.   Forgotten, before your hand is cold.   And
for this pitiful splendour you sold your immortal soul !

MAXIMUS (*rising*).   The world-will shall answer
for Julian's soul !

MAKRINA.   Do not blaspheme ; though surely you
have loved the dead——

MAXIMUS (*approaching the body*).   Loved, and misled him.—No, not I !

Misled like Cain.   Misled like Judas.   Your God is a prodigal God, Galileans!   He uses up many souls.

Wast thou not, after all, the chosen one—thou victim of necessity?

What is life worth?   All is sport and make-believe. —To *will* is to *have to will.*

Oh my beloved—all omens deceived me, all auguries spoke with a double tongue, so that I saw in thee the mediator between the two empires.

The third empire shall come !   The spirit of man shall once more enter into its heritage—and then shall the smoke of incense arise to thee, and to thy two guests in the symposium.

(*He goes out.*)

MAKRINA (*rising, pale*).   Basilius—did you understand the heathen's speech?

BASILIUS.   No,—but there dawns on me a great and radiant conviction that here lies a noble, shattered instrument of God.

MAKRINA.   Yes, truly, a dear, and dearly-bought instrument.

BASILIUS.   Christ, Christ—how could thy people fail to see thy manifest design?   The Emperor Julian was a rod of chastisement,—not unto death, but unto resurrection.

MAKRINA.   Terrible is the mystery of election. How do we know——?

BASILIUS.   Is it not written : " Some vessels are fashioned to honour, and some to dishonour " ?

MAKRINA. Oh brother, let us not seek to fathom that abyss.

(*She bends over the body and covers the face.*)

Erring soul of man—if thou wast indeed forced to err, it shall surely be accounted thee for good on that great day when the Mighty One shall descend in the clouds to judge the living dead and the dead who are yet alive—— ——!

THE END.

THE WALTER SCOTT PUBLISHING CO., LTD., NEWCASTLE-ON-TYNE.

VOL. IV.   7·02

5308

NEW BOOKS

IMPORTED BY

CHARLES SCRIBNER'S SONS,

NEW YORK CITY.

GREAT WRITERS.

A NEW SERIES OF CRITICAL BIOGRAPHIES OF FAMOUS WRITERS OF EUROPE AND AMERICA.

LIBRARY EDITION.

Printed on large paper of extra quality, in handsome binding, Demy 8vo, price $1.00 each.

ALPHABETICAL LIST.

PRESS NOTICES.

Life of Jane Austen. By Goldwin Smith.

" Mr. Goldwin Smith has added another to the not inconsiderable roll of eminent men who have found their delight in Jane Austen. Certainly a fascinating book."—*Spectator.*

Life of Balzac. By Frederick Wedmore.

" A finished study, a concentrated summary, a succinct analysis of Balzac's successes and failures, and the causes of these successes and failures, and of the scope of his genius."—*Scottish Leader.*

Life of Charlotte Brontë. By A. Birrell.

" Those who know much of Charlotte Brontë will learn more, and those who know nothing about her will find all that is best worth learning in Mr. Birrell's pleasant book."—*St. James's Gazette.*

Life of Browning. By William Sharp.

" This little volume is a model of excellent English, and in every respect it seems to us what a biography should be."—*Public Opinion.*

New York: CHARLES SCRIBNER'S SONS.

Life of Bunyan. By Canon Venables.

" A most intelligent, appreciative, and valuable memoir."—*Scotsman.*

Life of Burns. By Professor Blackie.

" The editor certainly made a hit when he persuaded Blackie to write about Burns."—*Pall Mall Gazette.*

Life of Byron. By Hon. Roden Noel.

" He [Mr. Noel] has at any rate given to the world the most credible and comprehensible portrait of the poet ever drawn with pen and ink."— *Manchester Examiner.*

Life of Thomas Carlyle. By R. Garnett, LL.D.

" This is an admirable book. Nothing could be more felicitous and fairer than the way in which he takes us through Carlyle's life and works." —*Pall Mall Gazette.*

Life of Cervantes. By H. E. Watts.

" Let us rather say that no volume of this series, nor, so far as we can recollect, of any of the other numerous similar series, presents the facts of the subject in a more workmanlike style, or with more exhaustive knowledge."—*Manchester Guardian.*

Life of Coleridge. By Hall Caine.

" Brief and vigorous, written throughout with spirit and great literary skill."—*Scotsman.*

Life of Congreve. By Edmund Gosse.

" Mr. Gosse has written an admirable and most interesting biography of a man of letters who is of particular interest to other men of letters." —*The Academy.*

Life of Crabbe. By T. E. Kebbel.

" No English poet since Shakespeare has observed certain aspects of nature and of human life more closely; and in the qualities of manliness and of sincerity he is surpassed by none. . . . Mr. Kebbel's monograph is worthy of the subject."—*Athenæum.*

Life of Darwin. By G. T. Bettany.

" Mr. G. T. Bettany's *Life of Darwin* is a sound and conscientious work."—*Saturday Review.*

Life of Dickens. By Frank T. Marzials.

" Notwithstanding the mass of matter that has been printed relating to Dickens and his works, . . . we should, until we came across this volume, have been at a loss to recommend any popular life of England's most popular novelist as being really satisfactory. The difficulty is removed by Mr. Marzials' little book."—*Athenæum.*

Life of George Eliot. By Oscar Browning.

" We are thankful for this interesting addition to our knowledge of the great novelist."—*Literary World.*

New York: CHARLES SCRIBNER'S SONS.

Life of Emerson. By Richard Garnett, LL.D.

"As to the larger section of the public, to whom the series of Great Writers is addressed, no record of Emerson's life and work could be more desirable, both in breadth of treatment and lucidity of style, than Dr. Garnett's."—*Saturday Review.*

Life of Goethe. By James Sime.

"Mr. James Sime's competence as a biographer of Goethe, both in respect of knowledge of his special subject, and of German literature generally, is beyond question."—*Manchester Guardian.*

Life of Goldsmith. By Austin Dobson.

"The story of his literary and social life in London, with all its humorous and pathetic vicissitudes, is here retold as none could tell it better."—*Daily News.*

Life of Nathaniel Hawthorne. By Moncure Conway.

"Easy and conversational as the tone is throughout, no important fact is omitted, no useless fact is recalled."—*Speaker.*

Life of Heine. By William Sharp.

"This is an admirable monograph, . . . more fully written up to the level of recent knowledge and criticism of its theme than any other English work."—*Scotsman.*

Life of Victor Hugo. By Frank T. Marzials.

"Mr. Marzials' volume presents to us, in a more handy form than any English, or even French, handbook gives, the summary of what, up to the moment in which we write, is known or conjectured about the life of the great poet."—*Saturday Review.*

Life of Hunt. By Cosmo Monkhouse.

"Mr. Monkhouse has brought together and skilfully set in order much widely scattered material."—*Athenæum.*

Life of Samuel Johnson. By Colonel F. Grant.

"Colonel Grant has performed his task with diligence, sound judgment good taste, and accuracy."—*Illustrated London News.*

Life of Keats. By W. M. Rossetti.

"Valuable for the ample information which it contains."—*Cambridge Independent.*

Life of Lessing. By T. W. Rolleston.

"A picture of Lessing which is vivid and truthful, and has enough of detail for all ordinary purposes."—*Nation* (New York).

New York : Charles Scribner's Sons.

Life of Longfellow. By Prof. Eric S. Robertson.

"A most readable little book."—*Liverpool Mercury.*

Life of Marryat. By David Hannay.

"What Mr. Hannay had to do—give a craftsman-like account of a great craftsman who has been almost incomprehensibly undervalued—could hardly have been done better than in this little volume."—*Manchester Guardian.*

Life of Mill. By W. L. Courtney.

"A most sympathetic and discriminating memoir."—*Glasgow Herald.*

Life of Milton. By Richard Garnett, LL.D.

"Within equal compass the life-story of the great poet of Puritanism has never been more charmingly or adequately told."—*Scottish Leader.*

Life of Renan. By Francis Espinasse.

"Sufficiently full in details to give us a living picture of the great scholar, . . . and never tiresome or dull."—*Westminster Review.*

Life of Dante Gabriel Rossetti. By J. Knight.

"Mr. Knight's picture of the great poet and painter is the fullest and best yet presented to the public."—*The Graphic.*

Life of Schiller. By Henry W. Nevinson.

"This is a well-written little volume, which presents the leading facts of the poet's life in a neatly rounded picture."—*Scotsman.*

"Mr. Nevinson has added much to the charm of his book by his spirited translations, which give excellently both the ring and sense of the original."—*Manchester Guardian.*

Life of Arthur Schopenhauer. By William Wallace.

"The series of Great Writers has hardly had a contribution of more marked and peculiar excellence than the book which the Whyte Professor of Moral Philosophy at Oxford has written for it on the attractive and still (in England) little-known subject of Schopenhauer."—*Manchester Guardian.*

Life of Scott. By Professor Yonge.

"For readers and lovers of the poems and novels of Sir Walter Scott this is a most enjoyable book."—*Aberdeen Free Press.*

Life of Shelley. By William Sharp.

"The criticisms . . . entitle this capital monograph to be ranked with the best biographies of Shelley."—*Westminster Review.*

New York: CHARLES SCRIBNER'S SONS.

Life of Sheridan. By Lloyd Sanders.

" To say that Mr. Lloyd Sanders, in this volume, has produced the best existing memoir of Sheridan is really to award much fainter praise than the book deserves."—*Manchester Guardian.*

" Rapid and workmanlike in style, the author has evidently a good practical knowledge of the stage of Sheridan's day."—*Saturday Review.*

Life of Adam Smith. By R. B. Haldane, M.P.

" Written with a perspicuity seldom exemplified when dealing with economic science."—*Scotsman.*

" Mr. Haldane's handling of his subject impresses us as that of a man who well understands his theme, and who knows how to elucidate it."—*Scottish Leader.*

" A beginner in political economy might easily do worse than take Mr. Haldane's book as his first text-book."—*Graphic.*

Life of Smollett. By David Hannay.

" A capital record of a writer who still remains one of the great masters of the English novel."—*Saturday Review.*

" Mr. Hannay is excellently equipped for writing the life of Smollett. As a specialist on the history of the eighteenth century navy, he is at a great advantage in handling works so full of the sea and sailors as Smollett's three principal novels. Moreover, he has a complete acquaintance with the Spanish romancers, from whom Smollet drew so much of his inspiration. His criticism is generally acute and discriminating; and his narrative is well arranged, compact, and accurate."—*St. James's Gazette.*

Life of Thackeray. By Herman Merivale and Frank T. Marzials.

" The book, with its excellent bibliography, is one which neither the student nor the general reader can well afford to miss."—*Pall Mall Gazette.*

" The last book published by Messrs. Merivale and Marzials is full of very real and true things."—Mrs. ANNE THACKERAY RITCHIE on " Thackeray and his Biographers," in *Illustrated London News.*

Life of Thoreau. By H. S. Salt.

" Mr. Salt's volume ought to do much towards widening the knowledge and appreciation in England of one of the most original men ever produced by the United States."—*Illustrated London News.*

Life of Voltaire. By Francis Espinasse.

" Up to date, accurate, impartial, and bright without any trace of affectation."—*Academy.*

Life of Whittier. By W. J. Linton.

" Mr. Linton is a sympathetic and yet judicious critic of Whittier."—*World.*

Complete Bibliography to each volume, by J. P. ANDERSON, British Museum, London.

New York : CHARLES SCRIBNER'S SONS.

Library of Humour.

Cloth Elegant, Large 12mo, Price $1.25 per vol.

VOLUMES ALREADY ISSUED.

The Humour of France. Translated, with an Introduction
and Notes, by ELIZABETH LEE. With numerous Illustrations by PAUL
FRÉNZENY.

The Humour of Germany. Translated, with an Introduction and Notes, by HANS MÜLLER-CASENOV. With numerous Illustrations by C. E. BROCK.

The Humour of Italy. Translated, with an Introduction and
Notes, by A. WERNER. With 50 Illustrations and a Frontispiece by
ARTURO FIELDI.

The Humour of America. Selected, with a copious Bio-
graphical Index of American Humorists, by JAMES BARR.

The Humour of Holland. Translated, with an Introduction
and Notes, by A. WERNER. With numerous Illustrations by DUDLEY
HARDY.

The Humour of Ireland. Selected by D. J. O'DONOGHUE.
With numerous Illustrations by OLIVER PAQUE.

The Humour of Spain. Translated, with an Introduction
and Notes, by SUSETTE M. TAYLOR. With numerous Illustrations by
H. R. MILLAR.

The Humour of Russia. Translated, with Notes, by
E. L. BOOLE, and an Introduction by STEPNIAK. With 50 Illustrations by PAUL FRÉNZENY.

New York: CHARLES SCRIBNER'S SONS.

The Music Story Series.

A SERIES OF LITERARY-MUSICAL MONOGRAPHS.

Edited by FREDERICK J. CROWEST,

Author of "The Great Tone Poets."

Illustrated with Photogravure and Collotype Portraits, Half-tone and Line
Pictures, Facsimiles, etc.

Square Crown 8vo, Cloth, $1.25 net.

VOLUMES NOW READY.

THE STORY OF ORATORIO. By ANNIE W. PATTER-
SON, B.A., Mus. Doc.

THE STORY OF NOTATION. By C. F. ABDY WILLIAMS,
M.A., Mus. Bac.

THE STORY OF THE ORGAN. By C. F. ABDY
WILLIAMS, M.A., Author of "Bach" and "Handel" ("Master
Musicians' Series").

THE STORY OF CHAMBER MUSIC. By N. KILBURN,
Mus. Bac. (Cantab.), Conductor of the Middlesbrough, Sunderland,
and Bishop Auckland Musical Societies.

THE STORY OF THE VIOLIN. By PAUL STOEVING,
Professor of the Violin, Guildhall School of Music, London.

THE STORY OF THE HARP. By WILLIAM H. GRATTAN
FLOOD, Author of "History of Irish Music."

NEXT VOLUME.

THE STORY OF ORGAN MUSIC. By C. F. ABDY
WILLIAMS, M.A., Mus. Bac.

IN PREPARATION.

THE STORY OF THE PIANOFORTE. By ALGERNON S.
ROSE, Author of "Talks with Bandsmen."

THE STORY OF HARMONY. By EUSTACE J. BREAK-
SPEARE, Author of "Mozart," "Musical Æsthetics," etc.

THE STORY OF THE ORCHESTRA. By STEWART
MACPHERSON, Fellow and Professor, Royal Academy of Music.

THE STORY OF BIBLE MUSIC. By ELEONORE
D'ESTERRE-KEELING, Author of "The Musicians' Birthday
Book."

THE STORY OF CHURCH MUSIC. By THE EDITOR.
ETC., ETC., ETC.

New York: CHARLES SCRIBNER'S SONS.

The Music Story Series.

A SERIES OF LITERARY-MUSICAL MONOGRAPHS.

Edited by FREDERICK J. CROWEST,

Author of "The Great Tone Poets."

Illustrated with Photogravure and Collotype Portraits, Half-tone and Line Pictures, Facsimiles, etc.

Square Crown 8vo, Cloth, $1.25 net.

VOLUMES NOW READY.

THE STORY OF ORATORIO. By ANNIE W. PATTER-SON, B.A., Mus. Doc.

THE STORY OF NOTATION. By C. F. ABDY WILLIAMS, M.A., Mus. Bac.

THE STORY OF THE ORGAN. By C. F. ABDY WILLIAMS, M.A., Author of "Bach" and "Handel" ("Master Musicians' Series").

THE STORY OF CHAMBER MUSIC. By N. KILBURN, Mus. Bac. (Cantab.), Conductor of the Middlesbrough, Sunderland, and Bishop Auckland Musical Societies.

THE STORY OF THE VIOLIN. By PAUL STOEVING, Professor of the Violin, Guildhall School of Music, London.

THE STORY OF THE HARP. By WILLIAM H. GRATTAN FLOOD, Author of "History of Irish Music."

NEXT VOLUME.

THE STORY OF ORGAN MUSIC. By C. F. ABDY WILLIAMS, M.A., Mus. Bac.

IN PREPARATION.

THE STORY OF THE PIANOFORTE. By ALGERNON S. ROSE, Author of "Talks with Bandsmen."

THE STORY OF HARMONY. By EUSTACE J. BREAK-SPEARE, Author of "Mozart," "Musical Æsthetics," etc.

THE STORY OF THE ORCHESTRA. By STEWART MACPHERSON, Fellow and Professor, Royal Academy of Music.

THE STORY OF BIBLE MUSIC. By ELEONORE D'ESTERRE-KEELING, Author of "The Musicians' Birthday Book."

THE STORY OF CHURCH MUSIC. By THE EDITOR.

ETC., ETC., ETC.

New York: CHARLES SCRIBNER'S SONS.

The Makers of British Art.

A Series of Illustrated Monographs

Edited by

James A. Manson.

Illustrated with Photogravure Portraits ; Half-tone and Line Reproductions of the Best Pictures.

Square Crown 8vo, Cloth, $1.25 net.

LANDSEER, SIR EDWIN. By the EDITOR.

" This little volume may rank as the most complete account of Landseer that the world is likely to possess."—*Times.*

REYNOLDS, SIR JOSHUA. By ELSA D'ESTERRE-KEELING.

" An admirable little volume . . . Miss Keeling writes very justly and sympathetically."—*Daily Telegraph.*
" Useful as a handy work of reference."—*Athenæum.*

TURNER, J. W. M. By ROBERT CHIGNELL, Author of "The Life and Paintings of Vicat Cole, R.A."

" This book is thoroughly competent, and at the same time it is in the best sense popular in style and treatment."—*Literary World.*

ROMNEY, GEORGE. By SIR HERBERT MAXWELL, BART., F.R.S., M.P.

" Sir Herbert Maxwell's brightly-written and accurate monograph will not disappoint even exacting students, whilst its charming reproductions are certain to render it an attractive gift-book."—*Standard.*
" It is a pleasure to read such a biography as this, so well considered, and written with such insight and literary skill."—*Daily News.*

WILKIE, SIR DAVID. By PROFESSOR BAYNE.

CONSTABLE, JOHN. By the RIGHT HONOURABLE LORD WINDSOR.

RAEBURN, SIR HENRY. By EDWARD PINNINGTON.

GAINSBOROUGH, THOMAS. By A. E. FLETCHER.

HOGARTH, WILLIAM. By PROF. G. BALDWIN BROWN.

IN PREPARATION.

MILLAIS—LEIGHTON—HENRY MOORE.

New York: CHARLES SCRIBNER'S SONS.

The Contemporary Science Series.

Edited by Havelock Ellis.

12mo. Cloth. Price $1.50 per Volume.

I. THE EVOLUTION OF SEX. By Prof. PATRICK GEDDES and J. A. THOMSON. With 90 Illustrations. Second Edition.

" The authors have brought to the task—as indeed their names guarantee —a wealth of knowledge, a lucid and attractive method of treatment, and a rich vein of picturesque language."—*Nature.*

II. ELECTRICITY IN MODERN LIFE. By G. W. DE TUNZELMANN. With 88 Illustrations.

" A clearly written and connected sketch of what is known about electricity and magnetism, the more prominent modern applications, and the principles on which they are based."—*Saturday Review.*

III. THE ORIGIN OF THE ARYANS. By Dr. ISAAC TAYLOR. Illustrated. Second Edition.

" Canon Taylor is probably the most encyclopædic all-round scholar now living. His new volume on the *Origin of the Aryans* is a first-rate example of the excellent account to which he can turn his exceptionally wide and varied information. . . . Masterly and exhaustive."—*Pall Mall Gazette.*

IV. PHYSIOGNOMY AND EXPRESSION. By P. MANTE-GAZZA. Illustrated.

" Brings this highly interesting subject even with the latest researches. . . . Professor Mantegazza is a writer full of life and spirit, and the natural attractiveness of his subject is not destroyed by his scientific handling of it." —*Literary World* (Boston).

V. EVOLUTION AND DISEASE. By J. B. SUTTON, F.R.C.S. With 135 Illustrations.

" The book is as interesting as a novel, without sacrifice of accuracy or system, and is calculated to give an appreciation of the fundamentals of pathology to the lay reader, while forming a useful collection of illustrations of disease for medical reference."—*Journal of Mental Science.*

VI. THE VILLAGE COMMUNITY. By G. L. GOMME. Illustrated.

" His book will probably remain for some time the best work of reference for facts bearing on those traces of the village community which have not been effaced by conquest, encroachment, and the heavy hand of Roman law."—*Scottish Leader.*

New York : CHARLES SCRIBNER'S SONS.

VII. THE CRIMINAL. By HAVELOCK ELLIS. Illustrated. Second Edition.

"The sociologist, the philosopher, the philanthropist, the novelist—all, indeed, for whom the study of human nature has any attraction—will find Mr. Ellis full of interest and suggestiveness."—*Academy.*

VIII. SANITY AND INSANITY. By Dr. CHARLES MERCIER. Illustrated.

"Taken as a whole, it is the brightest book on the physical side of mental science published in our time."—*Pall Mall Gazette.*

IX. HYPNOTISM. By Dr. ALBERT MOLL. Fourth Edition.

"Marks a step of some importance in the study of some difficult physiological and psychological problems which have not yet received much attention in the scientific world of England."—*Nature.*

X. MANUAL TRAINING. By Dr. C. M. WOODWARD, Director of the Manual Training School, St. Louis. Illustrated.

"There is no greater authority on the subject than Professor Woodward."—*Manchester Guardian.*

XI. THE SCIENCE OF FAIRY TALES. By E. SIDNEY HARTLAND.

"Mr. Hartland's book will win the sympathy of all earnest students, both by the knowledge it displays, and by a thorough love and appreciation of his subject, which is evident throughout."—*Spectator.*

XII. PRIMITIVE FOLK. By ELIE RECLUS.

"An attractive and useful introduction to the study of some aspects of ethnography."—*Nature.*

XIII. THE EVOLUTION OF MARRIAGE. By Professor LETOURNEAU.

"Among the distinguished French students of sociology, Professor Letourneau has long stood in the first rank. He approaches the great study of man free from bias and shy of generalisations. To collect, scrutinise, and appraise facts is his chief business. In the volume before us he shows these qualities in an admirable degree."—*Science.*

XIV. BACTERIA AND THEIR PRODUCTS. By Dr. G. SIMS WOODHEAD. Illustrated. Second Edition.

"An excellent summary of the present state of knowledge of the subject."—*Lancet.*

XV. EDUCATION AND HEREDITY. By J. M. GUYAU.

"It is at once a treatise on sociology, ethics, and pedagogics. It is doubtful whether, among all the ardent evolutionists who have had their say on the moral and the educational question, any one has carried forward the new doctrine so boldly to its extreme logical consequence."—Professor SULLY in *Mind.*

New York : CHARLES SCRIBNER'S SONS.

XVI. THE MAN OF GENIUS. By Prof. LOMBROSO. Illustrated.

"By far the most comprehensive and fascinating collection of facts and generalisations concerning genius which has yet been brought together."—*Journal of Mental Science.*

XVII. THE HISTORY OF THE EUROPEAN FAUNA. By R. F. SCHARFF, B.Sc., Ph.D., F.Z.S. Illustrated.

XVIII. PROPERTY: ITS ORIGIN AND DEVELOPMENT. By CH. LETOURNEAU, General Secretary to the Anthropological Society, Paris, and Professor in the School of Anthropology, Paris.

"M. Letourneau has read a great deal, and he seems to us to have selected and interpreted his facts with considerable judgment and learning." —*Westminster Review.*

XIX. VOLCANOES, PAST AND PRESENT. By Prof. EDWARD HULL, LL.D., F.R.S.

"A very readable account of the phenomena of volcanoes and earthquakes."—*Nature.*

XX. PUBLIC HEALTH. By Dr. J. F. J. SYKES. With numerous Illustrations.

"Not by any means a mere compilation or a dry record of details and statistics, but it takes up essential points in evolution, environment, prophylaxis, and sanitation bearing upon the preservation of public health."—*Lancet.*

XXI. MODERN METEOROLOGY. AN ACCOUNT OF THE GROWTH AND PRESENT CONDITION OF SOME BRANCHES OF METEOROLOGICAL SCIENCE. By FRANK WALDO, Ph.D., Member of the German and Austrian Meteorological Societies, etc. ; late Junior Professor, Signal Service, U.S.A. With 112 Illustrations.

"The present volume is the best on the subject for general use that we have seen."—*Daily Telegraph* (London).

XXII. THE GERM-PLASM: A THEORY OF HEREDITY. By AUGUST WEISMANN, Professor in the University of Freiburg-in-Breisgau. With 24 Illustrations. $2.50.

"There has been no work published since Darwin's own books which has so thoroughly handled the matter treated by him, or has done so much to place in order and clearness the immense complexity of the factors of heredity, or, lastly, has brought to light so many new facts and considerations bearing on the subject."—*British Medical Journal.*

New York : CHARLES SCRIBNER'S SONS.

XXIII. INDUSTRIES OF ANIMALS. By E. F. Houssay. With numerous Illustrations.

"His accuracy is undoubted, yet his facts out-marvel all romance. These facts are here made use of as materials wherewith to form the mighty fabric of evolution."—*Manchester Guardian*.

XXIV. MAN AND WOMAN. By Havelock Ellis. Illustrated. Fourth and Revised Edition.

"Mr. Havelock Ellis belongs, in some measure, to the continental school of anthropologists; but while equally methodical in the collection of facts, he is far more cautious in the invention of theories, and he has the further distinction of being not only able to think, but able to write. His book is a sane and impartial consideration, from a psychological and anthropological point of view, of a subject which is certainly of primary interest."—*Athenæum*.

XXV. THE EVOLUTION OF MODERN CAPITALISM. By John A. Hobson, M.A.

"Every page affords evidence of wide and minute study, a weighing of facts as conscientious as it is acute, a keen sense of the importance of certain points as to which economists of all schools have hitherto been confused and careless, and an impartiality generally so great as to give no indication of his [Mr. Hobson's] personal sympathies."—*Pall Mall Gazette*.

XXVI. APPARITIONS AND THOUGHT-TRANSFERENCE. By Frank Podmore, M.A.

"A very sober and interesting little book. . . . That thought-transference is a real thing, though not perhaps a very common thing, he certainly shows."—*Spectator*.

XXVII. AN INTRODUCTION TO COMPARATIVE PSYCHOLOGY. By Professor C. Lloyd Morgan. With Diagrams.

"A strong and complete exposition of Psychology, as it takes shape in a mind previously informed with biological science. . . . Well written, extremely entertaining, and intrinsically valuable." *Saturday Review*.

XXVIII. THE ORIGINS OF INVENTION: A Study of Industry among Primitive Peoples. By Otis T. Mason, Curator of the Department of Ethnology in the United States National Museum.

"A valuable history of the development of the inventive faculty."—*Nature*.

XXIX. THE GROWTH OF THE BRAIN: A Study of the Nervous System in relation to Education. By Henry Herbert Donaldson, Professor of Neurology in the University of Chicago.

"We can say with confidence that Professor Donaldson has executed his work with much care, judgment, and discrimination."—*The Lancet*.

New York : Charles Scribner's Sons.

XXX. EVOLUTION IN ART: As Illustrated by the Life-Histories of Designs. By Professor ALFRED C. HADDON. With 130 Illustrations.

"It is impossible to speak too highly of this most unassuming and invaluable book."—*Journal of Anthropological Institute.*

XXXI. THE PSYCHOLOGY OF THE EMOTIONS. By TH. RIBOT, Professor at the College of France, Editor of the *Revue Philosophique.*

"Professor Ribot's treatment is careful, modern, and adequate."—*Academy.*

XXXII. HALLUCINATIONS AND ILLUSIONS: A Study of the Fallacies of Perception. By EDMUND PARISH.

"This remarkable little volume."—*Daily News.*

XXXIII. THE NEW PSYCHOLOGY. By E. W. SCRIPTURE, Ph.D. (Leipzig). With 124 Illustrations.

XXXIV. SLEEP: Its Physiology, Pathology, Hygiene, and Psychology. By MARIE DE MANACÉÏNE (St. Petersburg). Illustrated.

XXXV. THE NATURAL HISTORY OF DIGESTION. By A. LOCKHART GILLESPIE, M.D., F.R.C.P. ED., F.R.S. ED. With a large number of Illustrations and Diagrams.

"Dr. Gillespie's work is one that has been greatly needed. No comprehensive collation of this kind exists in recent English Literature."—*American Journal of the Medical Sciences.*

XXXVI. DEGENERACY: Its Causes, Signs, and Results. By Professor EUGENE S. TALBOT, M.D., Chicago. With Illustrations.

"The author is bold, original, and suggestive, and his work is a contribution of real and indeed great value, more so on the whole than anything that has yet appeared in this country."—*American Journal of Psychology.*

XXXVII. THE RACES OF MAN: A Sketch of Ethnography and Anthropology. By J. DENIKER. With 178 Illustrations.

"Dr. Deniker has achieved a success which is well-nigh phenomenal."—*British Medical Journal.*

XXXVIII. THE PSYCHOLOGY OF RELIGION. An Empirical Study of the Growth of Religious Consciousness. By EDWIN DILLER STARBUCK Ph.D., Assistant Professor of Education, Leland Stanford Junior University.

"No one interested in the study of religious life and experience can afford to neglect this volume."—*Morning Herald.*

New York : CHARLES SCRIBNER'S SONS.

New York: CHARLES SCRIBNER'S SONS.